The Revolt
of the Primitive

The Revolt of the Primitive

An Inquiry into the Roots of Political Correctness

Howard S. Schwartz

Westport, Connecticut
London

Library of Congress Cataloging-in-Publication Data

Schwartz, Howard S., 1942–
    The revolt of the primitive : an inquiry into the roots of political correctness
/ Howard S. Schwartz.
        p.   cm.
    Includes bibliographical references and index.
    ISBN 0–275–96577–5 (alk. paper)
        1. Political correctness.   2. Feminism.   I. Title.
    BD175.5.P65S39   2001
    305.42—dc21   00–049178

British Library Cataloguing in Publication Data is available.

Library of Congress Catalog Card Number: 00–049178
ISBN: 0–275–96577–5

First published in 2001

Praeger Publishers, 88 Post Road West, Westport, CT 06881
An imprint of Greenwood Publishing Group, Inc.
www.praeger.com

Printed in the United States of America

The paper used in this book complies with the
Permanent Paper Standard issued by the National
Information Standards Organization (Z39.48–1984).

10 9 8 7 6 5 4 3 2

Copyright Acknowledgments

The author and publisher gratefully acknowledge permission for use of the following material:

Excerpts from "Knocked for Six: The Myth of a Nation of Wife-Batterers" by Neil Lyndon and Paul Ashton, from the *Sunday Times of London*, January 29, 1995. Reprinted with permission of Neil Lyndon.

Excerpts from "Women Emerge as Aggressors in Alberta Survey: 67% of Women Questioned Say They Started Severe Conflicts" by Brad Evenson and Carol Milstone, from *The National Post*, July 10, 1999. Reprinted with permission of *The National Post* and Carol Milstone.

Excerpts from "Sorting Out the Reasons Couples Turn Violent: Data on Violence between Men and Women Tell Only Part of the Story" by Scott Sleek, from the *APA Monitor*, Vol. 29, No. 4, April 1998. Copyright © 1998 by the American Psychological Association. Reprinted with permission.

Excerpts reprinted with the permission of Simon & Schuster, from *Who Stole Feminism?* by Christina Hoff Sommers. Copyright © 1994 by Christina Sommers.

Excerpts from *When Work Doesn't Work Anymore: Women, Work, and Identity* by Elizabeth Perle McKenna, copyright © 1997 by Elizabeth Perle McKenna. Used by permission of Dell Publishing, a division of Random House, Inc.

Excerpts from *When Work Doesn't Work Anymore: Women, Work, and Identity* by Elizabeth Perle McKenna, copyright © 1997 by Elizabeth Perle McKenna. United Kingdom rights for this work granted by Simon & Schuster.

Excerpts from *Divorced Dads* by Sanford L. Braver and Diane O'Connell, copyright © 1998 by Sanford L. Braver and Diane O'Connell. Used by permission of Jeremy P. Tarcher, a division of Penguin Putnam Inc.

Excerpts reprinted with the permission of Simon & Schuster, from *The Man in the Gray Flannel Suit* by Sloan Wilson. Copyright © 1955 by Sloan Wilson, Copyright © renewed 1983 by Sloan Wilson.

Excerpts from *The Feminine Mystique* by Betty Friedan. Copyright © 1983, 1974, 1973, 1963 by Betty Friedan. Used by permission of W. W. Norton & Company, Inc.

For Ann.

For Robin and Cassie.

And in memory of my parents, Bob and Hattie Schwartz.

And then this large, unimpeded social critic in a caftan could not help herself . . . with her face in her hands, she began to laugh at their obtuseness to the flimsiness of the whole contraption, to laugh and laugh and laugh at them all, pillars of a society that, much to her delight, was rapidly going under—to laugh and to relish, as some people, historically, always seem to do, how far the rampant disorder had spread, enjoying enormously the assailability, the frailty, the enfeeblement of supposedly robust things.

Yes, the breach had been pounded in their fortification . . . and now that it was opened it would not be closed again. They'll never recover. Everything is against them, everyone and everything that does not like their life. All the voices from without, condemning and rejecting their life!

And what is wrong with their life? What on earth is less reprehensible than the life of the Levovs?

—Philip Roth, *American Pastoral*

Contents

Acknowledgments

No book is the product of a solitary mind. In fact, there are no solitary minds. Many people have had an impact on this work, and I cannot mention them all. Some people have contributed more than others, in the sense of having helped determine the shape of the work. Of these, my wife, Ann Penner Winston, was certainly most important. Her insight into what I meant could always be trusted and often saved me from what I had merely said. Her intelligence and sense are responsible for much of what is best about this work. Others who have made substantial contributions have been Donald Carveth, Penny Simpson, Larry Hirschhorn, Patti Hausman, David Levine, Kenneth Kron, Antonia Feitz, and Mark Rowley. Elaine Donnelly deserves special recognition for pointing me to material that was very helpful. I'd also like to express my gratitude to my dean, John Gardner, and my department chairman, Ravi Parameswaran, for providing me with funds to purchase publication rights for some of the material quoted here. Ravi deserves an additional vote of thanks for getting me my sabbatical when I needed it. I can't say he moved heaven and earth to do it, but he did move earth, and that's quite a lot. I'd like to express my appreciation to Nita Romer, my editor at Praeger, for seeing value in this project and for making me the beneficiary of her good judgment. Finally, I'd like to thank my daughters, Robin and Cassie, for help with the index and, generally, for being pretty good kids.

Introduction

Not merely the validity of experience, but the very existence of external reality was tacitly denied by their philosophy. The heresy of heresies was
common sense.

—George Orwell, *1984*

Every day brings its quantum of strange news. On this day, my friend K., a graduate student at the University of Michigan, called my attention to a letter to the editor in the September 9, 1999, *Michigan Daily* (Pahl and Shires, 1999). In this letter, two women, writing for the Ann Arbor Coalition Against Rape, apologized for violence that had occurred at the previous spring's "Take Back the Night March."

They said:

A survivor who did not identify as male or female was forced to leave the march by other participants, who perceived this individual to be a man. In order to make the march welcome to transgendered individuals, it was stated that the march was for women as well as those who identify as women. However, this attempt failed, as it excluded individuals like this person who do not fit within male/female gender categories. It was not our intent to overlook violence against transgendered individuals.

Evidently there was quite a story behind this act of contrition. The person in question, a man who "identified as" a woman, attempted to participate in this annual march to combat violence against women. But apparently he did not manage to make his "identification" sufficiently clear, so he was attacked and beaten by a mob of women who thought he was a man. Word of this eventually leaked out and the organizers of the march felt they had to make a statement.

K. considered the possibility of writing to the newspaper. He would have pointed out that, under existing law, a "hate crime" had been committed, because the man was attacked for being a man. He might also have pointed out that, tortured as the apology is, it acknowledges only a failure in recognizing that the person attacked was a female, however that femaleness was contrived, not the attack itself. But, as he wrote to me: "to be un-PC in academia is a career-killer, so I won't."

What held my attention was the signature on the letter. Not concerned about saying anything un-PC, as my friend was, they gave their names and identified themselves as "social work students." *Social work students?*

In the end you have to trust your own perception, your own good sense. There has to be a criterion, a touchstone, by which to discern the difference between what is sensible and what is crazy. What makes our times strange is that no such touchstone is permitted. One is no longer allowed to take anything for granted.

Now, if all that were being attacked was a false sense of reality, if what were being undermined were the myths and fabrications that have often passed for established truth, it might be salutary. But that would require an even firmer reliance on perception, an even firmer grip on reality. That is not what is happening. Rather, our sense of reality is itself the focus of attack. The strange is being replaced by the even more strange, and good sense is no defense.

Where does this stuff come from? Where is it going? Why is this madness so powerful? Why are people going around solemnly saying things that no sane person could believe? These are the questions that will be of interest in our inquiry.

Much of our concern is with phenomena associated with the term "political correctness," and especially with what I take to be its central element, what I call the "sexual holy war." My main point is that what appears to be a war between the sexes is something far more dangerous. It is nothing less than a revolt of the primitive against the mature, driven by the most powerful forces within the psyche. Its potential danger is immense. We get some sense of the scope of that danger as this work unfolds.

Before doing that, however, there are a couple of preliminary points that must be made. The first is terminological. Much of our criticism is directed against feminism. The use of that term in a critical way often encounters the opposition that feminism is not just one thing, but rather that there are a wide variety of feminisms. I do not wish to get into dealing with the usual distinctions among types of feminism. That such matters typically arise from what Freud called the "narcissism of small differences" is not my point. My point is rather that there is an unconscious element in much of feminism that underlies the conscious views of many who think of themselves as feminists, independent of the conscious content of their feminism. It is this unconscious element that concerns me.

Looking at that unconscious element, what I try to show is that it is more fundamental than any of the forms of feminism that give it expression. Properly speaking, it should be called "primitivism," because it represents the expression of the deepest and most primitive elements of the psyche. Primitivism can, and generally has, been represented by other images than that of the female. It has been represented by the race, by the nation, by the idolatrized self, even by the corporation. Feminism simply demonstrates that women are no exception.

One might distinguish among forms of feminism based on whether they have this primitivism at their core. Sommers (1995), I believe, was getting at this when she distinguished between "equity" and "gender" feminism. Along those lines I would use the terms *mature feminism* and *primitive feminism* or, more precisely, *feminist primitivism*. However, we have come to the point at which feminist primitivism so far dominates public language that its defining tenets—the image of man as perfectly bad, woman as perfectly good, and of society as a stage for a war between them—have come to be accepted even by individuals who are otherwise quite mature. Many of the women I know are quite conflicted about their feminism, but it has been my observation that most are not sufficiently conflicted for the matter to be an acceptable topic of discussion. Yet it is rational discussion that makes it possible for us to get beyond primitivism, and its absence not only permits, but also *means* the domination of primitivism.

Accordingly, and sadly, it becomes possible to use the term "feminism" to refer to "primitive feminism" or "feminist primitivism" without great inaccuracy. This is the way I use the term. When feminism can be discussed rationally and critically, it will be time to reevaluate that usage.

The second point concerns method. My approach here is psychoanalytic phenomenology. I look at stories, myths, and fictions as if they are products of the mind itself, and I try to understand the mental processes that could lead to them. Psychoanalysis has, of course, come under considerable criticism in recent times. Much of this criticism has been directed against its unscientific character, against the abuses to which it may be put, and against the person of Freud himself (for a useful compilation see Crews,

1998). These criticisms have occasioned responses in their own right (e.g., Lear, 1998), but in any case they do not apply to what I am doing.

The subject matter of this book is irrationality. Trying to understand it as if it makes overt sense is not going to avail us much. Whatever its deficiencies, psychoanalytic theory provides us with our best way to understand irrational mental processes. If they are going to be understood, something like psychoanalytic theory will have to be used in that understanding; if we are not going to understand them now, I believe that some time in the future we will have compelling reasons to wish we had.

My concern here is with the meaning of our thoughts and with grounding that meaning in our basic human nature. I find psychoanalytic theory useful in this connection, but my subject matter is my own mind, and indeed its deepest and most irrational elements, as I can best and most honestly understand it.

I call upon readers to try to understand their own motivations and especially those that they do not want to understand. They may anticipate that engaging this work will arouse difficult and unpleasant feelings. The natural tendency will be, in one way or another, to avoid them. This is part of the structure of the emotions themselves. More than that, though, it is the core of our subject matter. Making the most of this book therefore requires something rather difficult on the part of the reader. It calls for maintaining ambivalence—both entertaining these feelings, and stepping away from them to look at them analytically. If readers find this daunting to do while reading, they should be assured that I found it no less daunting to do while writing. At the age of fifty-eight, I am still a nice Jewish boy from New York, and just as sensitive as anyone else.

The emotions we will engage and consider are not simply excitations of our individual minds; they are the basis of powerful social and political forces. To leave them unexamined is to acquiesce while irrational dynamics increasingly gain control of society. Such considerations will, I hope, recommend the self-analytic course of action to us despite its inherent difficulties. In all of this, it will be useful to remind ourselves of something Goethe said: "There is no crime I could not commit." This is not the sort of slogan one hears with great frequency in our politically correct times. Yet we must recall that Goethe did not commit crimes. Rather he was a poet who made good use of his understanding of human depth. We all have a dark side, and we cannot wisely guide our lives without acknowledging it, for the interplay between what is best within us and what is worst within us is what our lives are made of.

One further note by way of introduction: For the social scientist, the capacity to sustain pessimism is a gift beyond measure. The constraint imposed by optimism, the requirement to explain how everything will come out all right, clouds the vision. It makes it impossible to follow disagreeable ideas wherever they go, and forces us to distort them in order to arrive at conclusions that will reassure us. Pessimism imposes no such constraint.

I make no excuses for the bleakness of the image I create. In the end I believe that the truth makes us free. That will have to be optimism enough.

Chapter One

Scenes from a Sexual Holy War

If it was ever a man's world, it certainly isn't anymore. What previously were male preserves have given way to the integration of the sexes. Indeed, in many areas of society male preponderance has been replaced by female preponderance. And if it cannot be said that every element of this transformation has been taken as a cause for celebration, certainly there has not been much about it that has led many to be deeply concerned.

A story by Tamar Lewin in the *New York Times* (1998) illustrates an aspect of this. The headline reads: "U.S. Colleges Begin to Ask, 'Where Have the Men Gone?' " More than ten years ago, Lewin reports, women became the majority on college campuses, and their proportion has been increasing ever since. Although in the U.S. population as a whole there are slightly more college-age men than women, Department of Education statistics reveal that there were 8.4 million women and only 6.7 million men enrolled in college in 1996, the last year for which statistics are available. The department projects that by 2007, the gap will be even larger, with 9.2 million women and only 6.9 million men. This transformation has taken place across the full range of institutions of higher education. Women outnumber men in public institutions as well as private, and in religiously affiliated, four-year and two-year schools.

The problem that concerns the education experts is, of course, that given the widening income gap between high school graduates and those with advanced degrees, men's failure to pursue higher education will seriously limit their life choices. There is a concern that if the balance goes too far, the minority of males may feel uncomfortable. So colleges are doing what they can to give guys a break. At the same time, though, there is a danger in going too far in this direction. Lewin (1998) quotes a former college professor as saying:

"It used to be that you worried at 55 percent women, but the new wisdom is that anything up to 60 percent is O.K.," he said. "Probably nobody will admit it, but I know that lots of places try to get some gender balance by having easier admissions standards for boys than for girls. Recently, at a school where I was giving a speech, I asked 'How far down the list are you going for boys?' and the answer was 'All the way.' The problem is that if you take men who are not of the same caliber as the women, the highest-performing women leave, because the men aren't as interesting." (p. 38)

For the most part, this shift is not much to worry about, the story assures us. It is just a reflection of people's aptitudes, interests, and the choices they make. It isn't entirely clear what men are doing instead of attending college. Nor are the experts sure why, in their view, men are less committed to higher education. They do list a number of factors that may be having an influence, such as girls' greater success in high school and a strong economy that may give boys a sense that they can make their way without higher education, for example in computer work or the military. At any rate isn't it a bit sexist to think that a preponderance of females might be a cause for concern? Did we worry when there was a preponderance of men?

The idea that the absence of men from our colleges is simply a benign facet of our changing times is one that, for a number of reasons, doesn't quite add up. For one thing the idea that it is normal for a majority of college students to be male, and abnormal for them to be female, is based on the idea that men are the primary breadwinners within the family, whereas the care of children is primarily the role of the mothers. That may be a social arrangement that has given way to increased equality, but such a shift would move the proportion to 50–50. Any more of a change needs another explanation. The idea that, in the current economy, men are moving into occupations that do not require higher education, such as the military, is also questionable. In fact the same period that has shown a decline in the number of young men in college has also shown a decline in their enlistment in the military, which dropped from 34 percent in 1991 to 27 percent in 1997 (Department of Defense, 1997, 1998; Wilson, 1998). Nor does it seem to arise from the fact that women are just better suited for higher education and that in order to get men you have to go "all the way down." The fact is that men's scores on the most recent math SAT were substantially higher than those of women and were even slightly higher on the verbal SAT (Chute, 1999). [1] The SAT is one of the best measures we have for predicting college success, and these results make it difficult to understand how the claim that women are simply better suited for college can be sustained.

In deepest contradiction to the idea that the dearth of men in college is an aspect of a benign transformation is the fact that it takes place alongside other developments that cannot possibly be called benign. Among these are the increase in acts of murderous violence, such as the Littleton massacre, and the enormous rise in the rate of suicide among young males, which has increased threefold since the 1950s (Department of Health and Human Services, 1995) and which is six times as high as that of young females. [2]

IS THERE A CRISIS OF BOYHOOD?

The incidents of violence and the suicide statistics point to the possibility that the lack of young men in college is part of a much wider crisis of males in our society. In fact there is plenty of evidence to support this view, and it has become quite popular. Much of this evidence is proffered in a spate of contemporary books on the "crisis of boyhood" that are now making their way among us. Among the experts who write these books, the idea that our boys are in a perilous state is widely regarded as an established fact.

This presents us with what appears to be a puzzle. We have the view that the disappearance of men from college is a perfectly normal aspect of a benign and even beneficial transformation. On the other hand we have the view that boys are in state of crisis. These appear to be in contradiction. What is odd is that though both these views are widely held, they are not brought into juxtaposition in public discussion. The idea that the social processes responsible for the increasing female dominance in our colleges might have had something to do with the painful state of our young males is simply not an item for discussion. How could anyone fail to make this connection, even if only for the purpose of research? Especially, how could this connection fail to be made by experts on boys? Who are these experts?

I believe we may say without controversy that those who brought us the emergent female domination of college, along with the idea that it is natural and even desirable, were feminists. Certainly the fact that feminists see themselves as advocates for women is no secret, as we see from the self-statement of their division within the American Psychological Association:

Division 35—Psychology of Women promotes feminist research, theories, education, and practice toward understanding and improving the lives of girls and
women in all their diversities. Encourages scholarship on the social construction
of gender relations across multicultural context, and applies its scholarship to
transforming the knowledge base of psychology. Advocates action toward public
policies that advance equality and social justice, and seeks to empower women in
community, national, and global leadership.[3]

By extension, we might expect that those who are now telling us about the
horrors of growing up as a boy, and who would presumably be expected to
advocate for boys, might identify with their sex the way feminists do. They
might call themselves "masculinists," or something of the sort. But that is
not what happens. On the contrary they identify with feminists. This is the
Position Statement of the Society for the Psychological Study of Men and
Masculinity, Division 51 of the American Psychological Association:

The Society for the Psychological Study of Men and Masculinity (SPSMM) promotes the critical study of how gender shapes and constricts men's lives, and is
committed to an enhancement of men's capacity to experience their full human
potential. SPSMM endeavors to erode constraining definitions of masculinity
which historically have inhibited men's development, their capacity to form
meaningful relationships, and have contributed to the oppression of other people.
SPSMM acknowledges its historical debt to feminist-inspired scholarship on gender, and commits itself to the support of groups such as women, gays, lesbians and
peoples of color that have been uniquely oppressed by the gender/class/race system. SPSMM vigorously contends that the empowerment of all persons beyond
narrow and restrictive gender role definitions leads to the highest level of functioning in individual women and men, to the most healthy interactions between
the genders, and to the richest relationships between them.[4]

The debt to feminism, in theme and in ideological orientation, is clear
enough and is explicitly acknowledged. The idea that when feminism triumphed it triumphed over men and that the single-minded pursuit of the
exclusive interests of women might negatively affect the well-being of men
is not going to come from this group.
    Part of the reason, then, why this possibility is not on the agenda is that
the experts who now tell us of the boy crisis also believe that the accession
of girls to dominance is normal, natural, and legitimate. They see the rise of
girls as a reversal of previous domination and an occasion of moral triumph.
    But then what do these experts tell us is the trouble with boys? What ex-
planation can they provide that will acknowledge the boy crisis, and at the
same time preserve their allegiance to feminism? Well, to sum the matter

up, their answer is that boys are in trouble because they are expected to become men; their problems arise from the fact that they are not allowed to be woman enough.

ALL THEY NEED IS LOVE

Given the importance of feminist thought within the new psychology of boys, it is not surprising that its intellectual core would arise from the work of feminist thinker Carol Gilligan and indeed as an extension of her thoughts on girls (1996; Norman, 1997). According to Gilligan, girls, as they come into adolescence within a patriarchal world, lose their "voice," their feelings, and therefore their capacity for authentic relationship. They feel the necessity to buy into an artificial and socially constructed reality. Boys do so as well. The difference is that boys' loss occurs in early childhood, rather than in adolescence.

This difference has consequences for the ways in which the transition is made and comprehended. Specifically boys adopt the patriarchal world at the level of "concrete operations . . . (the way things are)," whereas for girls the internalization takes place at the "formal operational level . . . as an interpretive framework (the way things are said to be)" (Gilligan, 1996: p. 251). The result is that girls and women are better able to see the artificiality of social life. They are therefore conscious of an experience that for boys is likely to be inchoate, and their resistance is closer to the surface.

Still it is the similarities that are important. For both boys and girls, what they experience is that:

They are losing connection, they cannot say what they are feeling and thinking, and they are losing relationship and finding themselves psychologically alone. The division between inner and outer worlds creates a psychological instability and heightens the risk of being thrown off balance in times of stress. (Gilligan, 1996: p. 250)

With specific regard to boys, this means that:

Young boys come under pressure from without and within to give up close relationship and to cover their vulnerability—to separate their inner world, their self, from the outer world of relationships. (Gilligan, 1996: p. 250)

[B]oys are more at risk—more stuttering, more bed-wetting, more learning problems—in early childhood, when cultural norms pressure them to separate from their mothers. . . . They feel they have to separate from women. And they are not allowed to feel that separation as a real loss. (Norman, 1997: p. 50)

What we are discovering is how vulnerable boys are. How, under the surface, behind that psychic shield, is a tender creature who's hiding his humanity. I often say about my own three boys, who are now grown, that I feel that the world muffles the very best qualities in them, meaning their sensitivity. (Norman, 1997: p. 5.)

This separation, this loss of connection and sensitivity, creates a "psychological wound or scar" that remains with the boy into manhood where it forms the root of his masculine character:

To be a real boy or man in such cultures means to be able to be hurt without feeling hurt, to separate without feeling sadness or loss, and then to inflict hurt and separation on others. What is at stake is boys' manhood, boys' masculinity, their birthright in a patriarchal social order. But this conception of manhood places boys and men psychologically and often physically at risk, because it impedes their capacity to feel their own and other people's hurt, to know their own and other's sadness. (Gilligan, 1996: p. 251)

Gilligan thinks this is pretty bad news for everyone: "After a century of unparalleled violence, at a time when violence has become appalling, we appreciate again the fragility of humans. We understand better why closeness and vulnerability create the conditions for psychological growth. And we also know more fully the costs of their violation" (Gilligan, 1996: p. 258).

That's quite an indictment of masculinity, but before we buy into it, we do well to note Sommers's (2000) observation that Gilligan's assertions concerning the violent consequences of patriarchy and of premature separation from mother are entirely unsupported by empirical evidence. In fact they appear to be diametrically opposed to the research that has been done over the last thirty years and that has found that it is the absence of the father that is associated with the problem. As she puts it:

The boys who are most at risk for juvenile delinquency and violence are boys who are *literally* separated from their fathers. . . . In *Fatherless America*, the sociologist David Blankenhorn notes that "Despite the difficulty of proving causation in social sciences, the wealth of evidence increasingly supports the conclusion that fatherlessness is a primary generator of violence among young men." (Sommers, 2000: pp. 129–130)

Sommers also quotes William Galston, a former domestic policy adviser to the Clinton administration (now at the University of Maryland), and Elaine Kamarck, a lecturer at Harvard's J. F. Kennedy School of Government, in concurrence: "The relationship [between fatherlessness and crime] is so strong that controlling for family configuration erases the relationship between race and crime and between low income and crime. This conclusion shows up time and again in the literature" (Sommers, 2000: pp. 129–130).

We have a better sense of the reasons for these findings later in our inquiry when we discuss the role of fatherhood, and we also develop a better sense of where this condemnation of fatherhood comes from, given the fact that it is so much at variance with the evidence. Our present concern, however, is to see the way Gilligan's analysis plays out in the domain of education. The best known example of the extension of Gilligan's theory in that direction is the book *Real Boys: Rescuing Our Sons from the Myths of Boyhood* by psychologist William Pollack (1998), codirector of the Center for Men at McLean Hospital/Harvard Medical School, and a founding member of the Society for the Psychological Study of Men and Masculinity. Pollack's analysis may be regarded as an elaboration of Gilligan's view that boys are prematurely separated from their mothers and from their own sensitivity and neediness and that this separation is part of their socialization into the masculine role.

According to Pollack's theory, boys are forced into a narrow and outmoded definition of masculinity, a "gender straightjacket." The rules of this definition are given in what he calls the "Boy Code." Under this code, whose origin Pollack traces to the nineteenth century, boys are not supposed to acknowledge their sensitivity. They learn to feel ashamed of their needs to connect and their feelings of vulnerability. This shame undermines their self-confidence and erodes their fragile self-esteem, which they respond to by hardening themselves. This does not eliminate their needs; it simply drives them underground where they exist as permanent, painful wounds.

The gender straightjacket, and the shame that keeps it in place, have several deleterious effects. They are largely responsible for the behavioral problems we associate with boys, ranging from suicide to hyperactivity to violence. In this regard Pollack follows Gilligan in believing that boys' overly aggressive behavior arises from their wounded vulnerability. With specific regard to their academic potential, boys invest so much energy into hiding their vulnerability that they have little energy left for schoolwork. Moreover, in order to gain acceptance and avoid being shamed by their peers, boys hide their interest in intellectual and creative activities, matters that are regarded as feminine.

Taken together the various elements of the damage done by the Boy Code have been responsible for the prevalent view in educational circles that boys are inherently dangerous, emotionally dense, and unsocialized; in a word they are "toxic." As a consequence the real differences between boys and girls, such as their higher levels of energy, are not seen as normal, but as expressions of pathology. This has had profound effects on the quality of interaction. Entrenched as it is within many school systems, the myth of boy's toxicity allows teachers and administrators to become openly antagonistic to boys, pushing them toward failure at school, further ramifying the behavioral and emotional problems that Pollack decries. School officials and teachers have come to see boys as little monsters that need to be controlled, rather than as vulnerable children who need to be nurtured and whose distinctive needs require attention. Creative ways of teaching them, ways that would address their specific needs, have not been sought. Rather they have been left to sink or swim in this hostile environment. Not surprisingly they are sinking.

To sum up, Pollack maintains that the premature separation of boys from their mothers, enforced by the imposition of the gender straightjacket and the regime of shame, does lasting damage. Beneath their confident exterior is often a world of pain and need. Their attempts to detach themselves from or assuage their pain are responsible for the antisocial orientation we have come to associate with them. Our responses to this "toxicity" simply make the matter worse, and increase the toxicity. The damage caused by the gender straightjacket, together with this interplay over toxicity, are responsible for boys' academic failure and disengagement.

Yet there is hope, says Pollack. To begin with we must let boys maintain their connections with their mothers. As boys grow older and their locus of activity shifts to the school, the school itself should take on the maternal role, carefully monitoring the emotional condition of its students and listening to their cries of pain. Schools must also recognize the boys' style of learning. Then they will be able to close the gap. As an illustration of this, Pollack (pp. 248–250) cites material from a story in a British newspaper (Redwood, 1998) describing a program undertaken at a school in which the boys had fallen drastically behind the girls:[5] "An extremely creditable 78 per cent of girls at the school gained five or more A–Cs [on a standardized test], but the boys lagged behind with only 56 per cent. The disparity was particularly marked in English: 27 per cent fewer boys than girls gained grades A-C."

Leaving those boys who were already doing well in coed classes, teachers at the school placed the rest in all-male classes and organized them around the boys' style of learning;

"The most vital ingredient in the scheme's success was finding the right teacher for this group," he explains. "So I chose Rob Jeckells—a young head of house who is involved with sport, and someone to whom the boys relate very easily. We consciously planned the teaching methodology. The class is didactic and teacher-fronted. It involves sharp questions and answers and constantly checking understanding. Discipline is clear-cut—if homework isn't presented, it is completed in a detention. There is no discussion."

And Jeckells charged these boys up: "People think that boys like you won't be able to understand writers such as the Romantic poets. Well, you're going to prove them wrong. Do you understand?" Evidently they did:

The boys-only group already seems to be successful. Of boys in the same ability band last year, only seven out of 25 gained more than a C in English literature. Following recent mock examinations, Mr Jeckells believes 25 of the 34 in the segregated group will gain a C grade or better. . . . In 1996, the school had a 22 per cent disparity between boys and girls gaining five or more A–C grades; last year there was just a one per cent difference.

IS LOVE ALL THEY NEED?

So hope there is, it appears, if we follow Pollack's prescription. But before we do that we need to look at the terms on which this hope is offered. Doing that, we see that there are certain peculiarities with his account. For one thing the method adopted by the school that he cites is quite at variance with the strategy he appears to recommend. There is no listening here for these boys' pain. On the contrary there is strict discipline in which no excuses are tolerated. The role is not maternal; it is paternal.

We have occasion to reflect upon this further on. For the present it is more important to note a problem with his view that is perhaps less obvious. It is that the deterioration in the condition of boys that he addresses is recent, whereas the features he uses to provide an explanation are venerable. Even if we subscribe to his view that the Boy Code issues from the nineteenth century, it is difficult to see how the effects he ascribes to it should not have been as much in evidence then as they are now, but it appears that they were not.

This is nowhere more clear than in the image of hope that he offered us: an image of boys disproving the gender stereotype and learning Romantic poetry. This is absurd. The simple fact is that Romantic poetry, the incomprehension of which was taken to be the very symbol of male insensitivity and disconnection from feeling, was as male-dominated a field as any one can imagine. England, for example, the very home of the "stiff upper lip," which one would have thought would have been the very paradigm of the Boy Code, gave us, among others, Wordsworth, Coleridge, Byron, Shelley, Tennyson, and Keats. Take Elizabeth Barrett Browning out of the mix, and there isn't a woman who has a strong claim to inclusion.

Nor is the situation different in any of the arts. Take the nineteenth century, which according to Pollack gave us the Boy Code, and recollect the names of its artists, its composers, its writers. Their names are predominately male: Vincent Van Gogh, Paul Gauguin, Charles Dickens, Johann Wolfgang von Goethe, Felix Mendelssohn, Ludwig van Beethoven, Fyodor Dostoevski, Giuseppi Verdi, and Frederic Chopin. It is not necessary to go on.

Were there women involved in the arts during that period? Of course there were: Jane Austen, the Brontë sisters, Emily Dickinson, Clara Schumann, and many others. Yet there can be no doubt that most of the predominant figures were men. Would there have been more women if sex roles had been different? It is impossible to know, of course, but perhaps there would have been.

Yet to hypothesize that women would have comprised a higher proportion of artistic figures in the nineteenth century if the culture had been more conducive misses the important point. That point is that men of the nineteenth century, the century that, according to Pollack, gave us the gender straightjacket, created a magnificent efflorescence of art, whatever the standard of comparison. Their record of creativity simply cannot be reconciled with the image of men as rigid, insensitive, and emotionally barren.

The simple, unavoidable fact is that the "gender straightjacket," if one wants to call it that, has never been a very tight fit. Far from holding before all boys only a monolithic model of insensitive machismo, society has always revered its great artists. If it has never celebrated the fact that almost all of them were men, it didn't have to, at least until now. What Russian child does not know that Pushkin was a man? And what German child does not know this about Schiller? If the great male artists were not taken as ideals by all boys, they didn't have to be. The homage that society has always paid to its great artists would have established the worth of the artist in the eyes of boys inclined to emulate them, whether the other boys would have chosen to be artists or not.

It is hard to avoid the conclusion that Pollack, and in this he certainly follows Gilligan's lead, has taken the most vulgar stereotype of men and pronounced it to be a universal and inviolable cultural norm. The idea that the workings of the gender straightjacket, by separating men from their emotions, is responsible for their academic failure is based on this act of stereotyping.

Similar considerations apply to Pollack's account of the workings of shame, which, according to Pollack, underlies the whole gender straightjacket. Certainly shame has a negative impact on self-esteem. Indeed it is hard to disagree, intuitively, that a deep sense of shame can cause failure.

The dynamics of self-esteem are far more complex than Pollack acknowledges, however (Adelson, 1996). Part of this complexity is due to the fact that, from a dynamic standpoint, shame and self-esteem exist only in tension with one other; they define each other (e.g., Piers and Singer, 1953). For example the possibilities of low self-esteem and shame are what drive us to create the achievements that we then use to anchor our self-esteem. Anchoring our sense of self-esteem means that we are able to protect ourselves from the shame of failure, which represents the lack of achievement. Shame has its effect because it is the obverse of our ideals. "Be ashamed to die until you have won some great victory for mankind," said a plaque at my alma mater. No shame, no victory.

Again there is nothing new about this. The interplay of shame and accomplishment has been the subject matter of human self-understanding at least since the time of Homer. One may wish to question the cost involved in creating the psychological underpinning for accomplishment, but such questioning should certainly invoke quantitative considerations. How much accomplishment justifies how much suffering, one would need to consider. But, interestingly, this is not the way Pollack has approached the matter. For him, it appears, any degree of suffering is catastrophic, and no positive account of accomplishment is mentioned. It is almost as if Pollack does not believe that accomplishment exists. He seems to believe that suffering defines psychological reality.

His evident assumption is that the "genuine self" is the wounded, vulnerable self[6] rather than the self we create through our efforts, or even, for that matter, the self that is the interaction between these two elements. This is a matter to which we return in due course. For the time being, the point to be made is that it can hardly be the possibility of being shamed that is responsible for this recent downturn in the academic fortunes of boys, nor for the threefold increase in their rate of suicide.[7] Obviously if we are to explain boys' current failure, we need to explain why boys would be failing *now*, as opposed to previous times. We need some phenomenon that is contemporaneous with it.

Of the issues raised by Pollack, one stands out for being uniquely characteristic of our own time.[8] It is the idea of boys' "toxicity," together with the dynamics it generates. The idea of boys' toxicity is surely of recent vintage, and its manifestations, even as Pollack describes them, could easily account for the associations between failure and shame. Within our own analysis, however, the direction of causality is reversed. Rather than the attribution of toxicity arising from the consequences of shame, shame would represent a feeling of the toxicity of one's male identity.

Thus, although shame arising from failure to match up to a masculine ideal could not represent viable causes of boys' failure, shame arising from an attack on one's identity as a male easily could. Moreover it would serve to explain why shame, which is often the motivation behind achievement, leads only to failure in this case. It is that the ideal in this case is to be female, which is exactly what is excluded by one's identity as a male. Thus the undeniable core of truth in Pollack's association of shame and failure could in this way be preserved.

Pollack attributes the view of boys' toxicity to the dynamics of shame, and these, as we have seen, cannot be said to characterize boys of our time any more than any other. How can they account for the further dynamics that generate the view of boys' toxicity and its attendant abuse? Obviously, by themselves, they cannot. But if shame cannot account for the idea of boys' toxicity, how can we account for it and maintain its explanatory power?

The answer to this will be obvious to any observer of our times. The idea of boys' toxicity did not arise from boys' characteristics by themselves. Pollack signals what is really going on when he refers to the intensification of teacher's negative feelings toward boys as they reach adolescence, when "[a]ll the teacher's personal feelings about men and masculinity . . . come into play" (p. 241). The point is that it arose in the context of the general idea of male toxicity,[9] and may be said to represent only a specification of the general idea. Boys are held to be toxic because males are held to be toxic. Because they have certain characteristics as young males, those are said to constitute the qualities of boys' toxicity. As they become older, the manifestation of their toxicity simply reverts to type.[10]

Nor would it make good sense to suppose that increased dependence on their mothers would cure their malaise. For who, after all, holds the view of male toxicity? It is not likely that men, on their own, would have taken this view about men. The main influence here must have been from women: Many of them the mothers of boys themselves. Pollack's view is that boys' problems are due to premature separation from their mothers. Our analysis has led us into a startlingly different possibility. If the boy crisis has been caused by the female view that men are toxic, our analysis raises the possibility that boys have not been separated from their mothers enough.

THE STORY OF TOXIC MAN AGAINST MADONNA-AND-CHILD: IMAGES FROM THE SEXUAL HOLY WAR

Now we can only register the horror of what we have said. It is hard to imagine that the widespread female contempt for men to which Pollack bears witness would not have a devastating effect on their male children. Yet the very image of mothers being toxic to their sons is almost impossible for us to contemplate. It fills us with terror and immediately leads us to find a way to deny it.

"No, no, no," we want to say, women couldn't do that, mothers couldn't do that. And in this moment, as if to give us what we need in order to object to this despicable thought, as if to rescue us from this vile idea, an image of the mother rushes into our mind. It is the image of the female as warm, nurturing, self-sacrificing, devoted, and loving. She is not simply warm and nurturing in the abstract, she has someone with her, connected to her; she is loving to her child.

Consider this image. Without any attempt at originality, I call it the image of Madonna-and-child, And I note that this image of the benevolent and loving woman—the Madonna with her child—is the counterpart to the image of the toxic man that has become a staple of contemporary culture. They go, in a sense, hand in hand. They are part of the same story.

Take, for example, Pollack's book. There is nothing in it—not a single word—that expresses even the mildest demurrer about the virtues of women. It is all adulation—one might even say worship. He tells us, for example, that women know instinctively that they should not allow their sons to go off into the world too early. It is "society" that tells them they should, the Boy Code, and so on. Left to themselves, what women would do would be exactly right.

Men are pretty awful, Pollack affirms, though he thinks there are reasons, but women are morally perfect. What is more, men and women are not simply good and bad in isolation, but with regard to each other. Men's badness expresses itself as badness against women. Under the circumstances women's goodness cannot help but take the form of a fight against male badness—an emanation that has dominated the world, and whose removal will bring in the reign of women, which will make life perfect.

And so our story is fleshed out. We can now see it as the story of a struggle between men and women, seen as moral forces, engaged in what I call the *sexual holy war*. Having said that we can see that this story of the counterposition of bad man/good woman in sexual holy war is ubiquitous. One simply cannot have contact with western society in our time and not encounter it with great frequency. I am writing this, for example, at 8:30 P.M. on February 22, 1999. Two hours ago, on *NBC Nightly News*, I learned that women suffer more than they need to from cervical cancer because they are so busy taking care of others that they take no time to care for their own health. I also learned that they suffer more than they need to from breast cancer because they cannot take time off for examination, because they are concerned about appearing vulnerable in the "male-dominated" organizations in which they work. So there you have it. Women suffer unnecessarily from one form of cancer because they are so good; they suffer from another form because men are so bad.

If this were so, it would provide an important slant on the facts with which we began—the demographics of the transformation of our colleges from male institutions to female ones. It might suggest that those who are feeling good about themselves are taking the elite places to which they feel entitled, whereas those that are feeling bad and unworthy are drifting away. It will certainly tell us why this change causes as little consternation and concern as it does. The fact that women are coming into dominance and surpassing men is a good thing, one would have to conclude from the story. Men were able to have their day because of their oppressiveness. They kept women down, but now women are coming up. This is a massive social change, and if some men have to suffer, that's not so bad. They have it coming. At any rate it's certainly nothing to be greatly concerned about, and, under the influence of the story, no one is.

THE SEXUAL HOLY WAR AND THE DISTORTION OF TRUTH

This is a story that is told, but it is a strange story. For one thing, it has a rather thin cast of characters. They are stick figures. The story is powerful and compelling, but simple and stereotypic. Without nuance or subtlety, without a feeling for deeper motivation, it is fit for the comic books, for the mind of a child. It is hard to see that it can accurately represent the complexity of human life.

Is the story true? Are men so bad and women so good? Examination of the facts reveals that the story is not true, and in making this point, one hardly knows where to start. But it doesn't matter. One will traverse the whole range of issues surrounding the relationship between the sexes and find the same pattern. For example, despite the commonly held view to the contrary, most fathers are not deadbeat dads who leave their wives and children for more nubile companions (Braver, 1998). They also tend to batter their wives at no greater rate than their wives batter them (Gelles and Straus, 1990). Nor are women perfect. It is actually they that file the vast majority of divorce suits, and they do so on such grounds as "not having their emotional needs met" (Braver, 1998). There is no question that men commit the majority of violent crimes, but some women have also shown themselves capable of committing terrible violence, including serial murder (Pearson, 1997). Moreover, difficult as it is to admit, mothers commit the majority of child murders,[11] and a recent British study has shown them capable of attempting to murder their own children while they lay helpless in hospital beds (Southall, et al., 1997), apparently for the purpose of calling attention to themselves.[12]

It cannot be said that moral delinquency is a feature only of women who are identified with and in the thrall of men. A study by U.C. Berkeley sociologist Kathleen Blee (1992) shows that feminist women were a powerful, even dominant, force in the early twentieth-century incarnation of the Ku Klux Klan. In truth the objective facts suggest that morally, and irrespective of ideology, there is little to choose between men and women.

My purpose here is not simply to set the record straight. Sommers (1995, 2000) and others (e.g., Farrell, 1993, 1999; Denfeld, 1995; C. Young, 1999) are increasingly doing a good job of that. My focus here is not so much upon the facts as upon the story, and on why the story came to prevail despite the facts. My purpose here, in other words, is to ask the question of how the record got so distorted.

The way the story of the sexual holy war came to prominence despite the facts is one of the most fascinating and important phenomena of our time. The images of toxic man and Madonna-and-child did not come to be believed because they explained the objective facts as they independently appeared. Rather the images were primary, and led to a distorted view of the objective world, which then came to be believed because it supported the image. Indeed the objective situation itself became the object of attack.

To show this it is helpful to look at distortion in a specific sphere of reality. Which sphere we choose is largely immaterial, because the distortion is similar no matter where one looks. At the present time, it seems that the primary focus of the sexual holy war is in the sphere of domestic violence. We focus here in our search for distortion.

I have no doubt that, someday, the distortion of the truth by the radical feminists of our time will be seen to have been the greatest intellectual crime of the second half of the twentieth century. At the present time, however, we still live under the aegis of that crime, and calling attention to it is an act of great moral courage. Of those who have stood up and told the story, none has done so more elegantly and effectively than Christina Hoff Sommers, whose book *Who Stole Feminism?* (1995) will certainly be seen, one day, as a classic of our time. My account of feminist distortion in the sphere of domestic violence will rely heavily on her work. As good a place to start as any is with the Super Bowl hoax of 1993.

SUNDAY, BLOODY SUNDAY

"A day of dread" for American women, Dan Rather called it on the day before the big game. As such he was repeating what had become received wisdom about Super Bowl Sunday by that time. The story had begun the previous Thursday when a coalition of women's groups held a news conference in Pasadena, California, the site of the game, to announce that Super Bowl Sunday is "the biggest day of the year for violence against women." Forty percent more women would be battered on that day, said Sheila Kuehl of the California Women's Law Center, basing her claim on a study done at Old Dominion University three years before. A media watchdog group, Fairness and Accuracy in Reporting (FAIR), had bolstered the credibility of the claim, and had sent out a massive mailing warning "Don't remain at home with him during the game" (Sommers, 1995: p. 189).

The next day, psychologist Lenore Walker, author of the influential book *The Battered Woman*, and, remarkably, head of the American Psychological Association's Task Force on Violence and the American Family was interviewed on *Good Morning America*. She said that she had put together a ten-year record showing that violent incidents against women increased sharply on Super Bowl Sundays. On the day after that, a story by Lynda Gorov (1993) in the *Boston Globe* maintained that women's shelters and hotlines are "flooded with more calls from victims [on Super Bowl Sunday] than on any other day of the year." Her specific reference here was "one study of women's shelters out West" that "showed a 40 percent climb in calls, a pattern advocates said is repeated nationwide, including in Massachusetts" (Gorov, 1993: p. 189). Gorov quoted experts who would enlighten us on the causes of this. For example, Nancy Isaacs, a specialist on domestic violence at the Harvard School of Public Health, said that "[I]t's a day for men to revel in their maleness and unfortunately, for a lot of men that includes being violent toward women if they want to be." Specifically, "It's 'I'm supposed to be king of my castle, it's supposed to be my day, and if you don't have dinner ready on time, you're going to get it.' " (Gorov, 1993: p. 13). The story was picked up not only by *CBS News*, but by the *New York Times*, and just about every other authoritative source. NBC even issued a pre-game public service announcement reminding men that domestic violence is a serious crime.

The only problem with the story was that it was not true. This was revealed in a January 31 *Washington Post* story by staff writer Ken Ringle (1993), the only reporter who bothered to check the story out, who found out that none of the claims held up: "Despite their dramatic claims, none of the activists appears to have any evidence that a link actually exists between football and wife-beating." For example, while interviewing sociologist Janet Katz, one of the principal authors of the Old Dominion study cited at the original press conference, Ringle asked about the study's reported linkage between violence and football games. She said, "That's not what we found at all." In fact, to the contrary, an increase in emergency room admissions "was not associated with the occurrence of football games in general." Checking with Lynda Gorov, Ringle was led on a wild-goose chase. To begin with he found out that she had never seen the study documenting the 40 percent increase, but got it from FAIR. FAIR, in turn, claimed to have gotten the figure from Lenore Walker, who then referred Ringle to a Denver psychologist and authority on battered women named Michael Lindsay. Lindsay "[a]dmitted he could find no basis for the report. 'I haven't been any more successful than you in tracking down any of this,' he said. 'You think maybe we have one of these myth things here?' " (p. A1).

A myth indeed, and the Super Bowl hoax was not the only instance of it.

LYNDON AND ASHTON

Writing in the *Sunday Times of London* during the O. J. Simpson trial, Neil Lyndon and Paul Ashton (1995) noted the climate of our era: "Campaigners have already been filmed outside the court claiming that: All women are at risk: all women are unprotected.' " They added:

The existence of domestic violence on a large scale has become an unquestionable fact of our age. As Rosalind Miles has written, in an exemplary passage of feminist reasoning: "The patriarch at bay usually has to look no further than the ends of his arms ... beating the wife, 'teaching her a lesson' or 'just giving her a reminder' becomes 'what your right hand is for.' "

They noted that evidence for the existence of domestic violence as a broad phenomenon has never been very solid. Before 1993, for example, records were not routinely kept by British police forces of complaints about or recorded incidents of domestic violence. Under the circumstances, therefore, "[T]he true extent of wife battering was, therefore, an open field for speculation, guesswork and statistical jiggery-pokery." Looking at the figures that had been advanced, they concluded: "How they jiggery-pokered. How they speculated and guessed."

The story of this jiggery-pokery is a fascinating one. To begin, they note, with perhaps a bit of hyperbole, that over the past twenty-five years, "as many figures for domestic violence have been published as there are numbers in the national lottery." Yet, without hyperbole, they observe that none of the figures was small and that all appeared to confirm the existence of a vast and menacing problem.

Taking figures for London as a general example, Lyndon and Ashton tell us that in 1990, a spokesman on domestic violence for the Metropolitan police told them that it received "about 25,000 calls a year" reporting incidents of domestic violence, a figure that was "an extrapolation for London as a whole drawn from research in specific areas." They calculated that it would represent 1.44 percent of all women in London living with a partner. That would mean that one woman in every seventy living with a man in London would have been reporting domestic violence to the police.

Yet high as that number was, it appeared to represent an understatement. Lyndon and Ashton tell us that the research on which it depended was conducted by a feminist criminologist, Dr. Susan S.M. Edwards, and the figure she had actually given in her London Policing study was more than double the number supplied by the Metropolitan police: " 'The number of women who officially reported violence to the police in the Metropolitan police district alone in one year was estimated at 58,000.' That figure would have represented 3.35% of women living with a partner, or one woman in every 30." Even that figure was not high enough, according to Sandra Horley, director of the Chiswick Family Refuge and, according to Lyndon and Ashton, one of Britain's leading experts on domestic violence. According to Horley, even that terrible number was too low:

In a letter to *The Independent* in 1990, she wrote: "The Metropolitan police receives approximately 100,000 calls a year from women who are trying to escape male violence."

This would represent 5.8% of women living with partners in London, or one woman in 17: an appalling number, representing a sickening general incidence of violence.

Miles took Horley's figure even further. In her book, *The Rites of Man*, published in 1991 and, according to Lyndon and Ashton, respectfully reviewed, she wrote that: "In the London area alone, more than 100,000 women a year need hospital treatment after violence in the home." They note that this, truly, is a terrifying statement. If one woman in every seventeen living with a man in London needs hospital treatment for injuries inflicted by her man, they observe, the true figure for incidents of domestic violence, including those unreported to the police and untreated by hospitals, must be colossal. It would follow that the feminists and the violence lobbyists must be right about the degree of horror.

It turns out, however, that when, in 1989, the police forces in England and Wales first got around to publishing their own numbers, the figures were considerably smaller. For example, the number of domestic violence incidents recorded by the Metropolitan police in 1993 was 11,420:

That figure is equal to 0.66% of all women living with partners in the capital, and less than half the figure of 25,000 reported incidents previously given to us by the Met. It is less than a quarter of the figure given by Edwards, whose work has been sympathetically received by the Metropolitan police. It is less than one eighth of the figure given by Horley, whose Chiswick Family Refuge has been supported by public funds.

As for the 100,000 figure given by Miles for women receiving treatment in London hospitals after domestic violence, we can now see plainly that her figure is clearly a fiction. (Lyndon and Ashton, 1995)

A fiction. A myth, perhaps. And note again what happens when scrutiny is applied to the basis of the claim:

When we telephoned [Miles] to ask where she had got the figure from, she said at first that she could not remember; and when she was asked to comment on the discrepancy between her figure and the Home Office's, she terminated the interview because "there is someone at the door."

Next day, she remembered "reading it" (the figure of 100,000) in the *Evening Standard* the year before the book was published; but she could give no date, author, context or origin for this item of scholarly research.

Explaining the discrepancy between its previous estimate and the published facts, a spokesman for the Metropolitan police said: "I can't explain that at all, but 25,000 is a wrong figure."

Defending her figure of 58,000, Edwards told us: "You should not regard my higher figure as representative of the number of cases of domestic violence which should be regarded as crimes."

Eh? Come again? Why would 58,000 London women a year be calling the police if not to report criminal violence? "Many women," she said, "report incidents of violence which do not actually constitute a crime." In that case, one might ask, why should anybody think of them as being battered women? (Lyndon and Ashton, 1995)

Horley was not available to be challenged on her figure of 100,000.

As we can see, just as with the Super Bowl Hoax, the figures seem simply to arise in the imagination, and then are asserted as if they are objective facts. In addition, responding to the anticipated defense that violence against women is greater than that reported, since women do not report many incidents, Lyndon and Ashton add another wrinkle that may be of interest to us:

If, however, anybody wants to argue about the hidden extent of our domestic violence, the figures which have just been published put them and their case even
deeper in trouble.

Of the 11,420 domestic violence incidents in the Metropolitan police area in
1993, how many would you guess involved the same individuals more than once?
How many complaints were of the threat, rather than the reality, of violence? How
many of those incidents were reported by men who were living with men? How
many incidents of domestic violence were reported by men living with women?

They add:

You would have to guess the answers to these questions because the facts are hard
to find. For instance, Scotland Yard acknowledges that: "Every district has its share
of repeat or persistent callers but the number are unquantifiable."

We cannot know, therefore, how many reported or recorded incidents of violence involve the same individuals more than once. Similarly, Scotland Yard cannot say how many callers are complaining about the threat rather than the reality
of an act of violence; but that 68% of reported cases of domestic violence constituted "mental cruelty" or "threats of force." (Lyndon and Ashton, 1995)

More interesting to us is that:

Of those incidents, a proportion are not women reporting that they have been
bashed but men reporting that a woman, or another man, is bashing or threatening
to bash them. If, as we have repeatedly been told for 25 years, women are reluctant
to tell the police about violence in the home, we can be certain that men will be
even less eager to report such shameful incidents.

According to one estimate recently published in the *Los Angeles Times*, American men are nine times less likely than women to seek the protection of the police
from a violent partner at home.

Our analysis of Britain's figures confirms this picture. Women are eight times
more likely than men to report an incident of domestic violence to the police, yet
it now appears certain that the most likely victims of domestic violence are not
women but men.

A Mori survey recently commissioned and published by the BBC programme,
Here and Now, showed that 5% of women living with men had experienced an incident of violence from that man; but 11% of men living with women said that
they had experienced an incident of violence from their woman.

It therefore follows from this survey that men are more than twice as likely to be
the victims of attack in the home, though they are eight times less likely to report
it. (Lyndon and Ashton, 1995)

PARITY IN BATTERING

Men assaulted by women? Now there's an image that does not fit well into the neat bifurcation of toxic man/Madonna-and-child. Yet there is good evidence for it, and much of it comes from the Western side of the Atlantic. Claims such as the following cited by Sommers (1995: p. 193) will be familiar to many readers:

In the United States, a man beats a woman every twelve seconds. (French, 1992)

An American woman is beaten by her husband or boyfriend every 15 seconds. (*New York Times*, April 23, 1993)

Every twelve seconds, a woman in the United States is beaten by her husband or lover. (*Mirabella*, November 1993)

Most people not familiar with the social sciences will not realize what must go into such statistics, if they are to have any basis at all. They cannot be based on official U.S. government statistics, because the government keeps track of crimes, not domestic violence as such. Instead they must be based on large-scale, extragovernmental, empirical research. This is extremely expensive and must be carried out by highly trained professionals, of whom there are few. Furthermore there are few sources of funding available, outside of the U.S. government, which makes no secret of what it is funding. The result is that it is usually not difficult to say where the results come from, if they have any basis at all.

In fact much of this material comes from the work of Richard J. Gelles of the University of Rhode Island, Murray A. Straus of the University of New Hampshire, and their coworkers. Their National Family Violence Survey, funded by the National Institutes of Mental Health, has now run in three waves. It constitutes the most extensive database in the field, and it is often possible to tell how such statistics are derived from it. Generally this is achieved by ignoring two features of Gelles and Straus's research. First Gelles and Straus clearly differentiate between degrees of severity, and statistics like those discussed earlier typically are achieved by ignoring that distinction—lumping insults together with knifings. More interestingly they achieve their shock value by ignoring the fact that, according to this research, violence is just as likely to be perpetrated by women against men as by men against women.

This latter finding came as a great surprise to Gelles and Straus, but it made itself known through their research. For example, the data supporting the figure of a woman being beaten every fifteen seconds equally supports a claim that a husband is beaten every fourteen seconds. To be sure Gelles and Straus note that women are more likely to be injured in such exchanges,[13] but their finding that women are as likely to be violent, and indeed to initiate such violence, has since become one of the best replicated findings in all of social science.[14]

Most recently, as of this writing, the U.S. Department of Justice (Moffitt and Caspi, 1999) published findings from a long-term longitudinal study of men and women in Dunedin, New Zealand, which found that women (37 percent) were even more likely to have perpetrated domestic violence than men (22 percent).[15] Among the other interesting aspects of this study were that:

Risk factors in childhood and adolescence for male perpetrators included poverty and low academic achievement. Female perpetrators showed risk factors of harsh family discipline and parental strife [but not poverty or low academic achievement]. Both male and female perpetrators also had histories of aggressive behavior.

The strongest risk factor for both male and female perpetrators and victims was a record of physically aggressive delinquent offending before age 15. More than half the males convicted of a violent crime also physically abused their partners.

Domestic violence is most prevalent among cohabitating [rather than married] couples.

Sixty-five percent of females who suffered serious physical abuse and 88 percent of male perpetrators had one or more mental disorders (as defined by the American Psychiatric Association in the *Diagnostic and Statistical Manual of the American Psychiatric Association* ["DSM-III-R"]). (Moffitt and Caspi, 1999: pp. 1–2)

The idea that the male perpetrators of domestic violence are uneducated, mentally disturbed people from disadvantaged backgrounds who have a record of violent crime outside of their domestic relationships, which tend not to be based on marriage, obviously does not accord very well with the idea that violence toward women is a normal aspect of masculinity in our society. Nor does it support the idea that the middle-class women who are the target of this propaganda are deeply at risk.

Yet for our purposes, what is equally of interest is that findings of parity in domestic violence were often known to those who broadcast findings concerning male-to-female violence, and were deliberately kept from the public. This is a fact that emerged with particular clarity in a recent issue of Canada's best selling newspaper, the *National Post* (Evenson and Milstone, 1999). The article begins "[w]omen are just as violent to their spouses as men, and women are almost three times more likely to initiate violence in a relationship, according to a new Canadian study that deals a blow to the image of the male as the traditional domestic aggressor."

Evenson and Milstone also note that the most surprising aspect of the study (Kwong, Bartholomew, and Dutton, 1999) is the source of the data, a survey of 705 Alberta men and women conducted in 1987. It turns out that, although the original researchers asked men and women the same questions, they published only the responses of the women. The responses of the men have only now been reported.

Thus it was originally reported that roughly 10.8 percent of men in the survey pushed, grabbed, or threw objects at their spouses in the previous year, and 2.5 percent committed more severe acts, such as choking, kicking, or using a weapon. As we now know, 12.4 percent of women in the same survey committed acts of minor violence, and 4.7 percent committed severe violence. In fact the symmetry here was contained within the data of the survey:

The violence is seldom one-sided. Of those surveyed, 52% of women and 62% of men reported that both partners were violent.

When questioned about who initiated the most severe conflicts, 67% of women believed they had started it; only 26% believed it was their male spouse

But the symmetry was unreported and that had its effect:

When the original Alberta study was published in the *Canadian Journal of Behavioural Science* in 1989, it was taken up by feminist groups as evidence of the epidemic of violence against women . . . the one-sided Kennedy-Dutton study was cited extensively in a 1990 House of Commons committee report *The War Against Women*, which ultimately led Brian Mulroney, the former prime minister, to call a two-year, $10–million national inquiry into violence against women. The inquiry's 460–page report made 494 recommendations aimed at changing attitudes in governments, police departments, courts, hospitals and churches. It also led to a torrent of lurid news features about battered women.

Evenson and Milstone observe:

Publication of the "other side" of the violence study provides a sharp illustration of how social science is manipulated to fit a particular agenda.

"It happens all the time. People only tell one half of the story," says Eugen Lupri, a University of Calgary sociologist whose research shows similar patterns of violence against men.

"Feminists themselves use our studies, but they only publish what they like. As some feminists say, it's counter-intuitive. We would not expect that to be true; and if things are not expected to be true, for some people they are not true."

And they add:

Even the federal government appears to turn a blind eye. In 1993, Statistics Canada began to keep track of assaults by men on women in its Violence Against Women survey. But it does not measure the female-to-male violence. "At the time, it was decided that since violence against women was more prevalent, we would only keep track of that," explains spokesperson Shelley Crego.

Ms. Crego said this decision was based on police reports, noting women complain more frequently of assault by men than vice versa.

But:

In her article, Dr. Kwong implies this creates an incorrect picture. "It is important to keep in mind that, within the criminal justice system, any of the physical acts endorsed by these respondents would constitute assault," she writes.

Explaining the selectivity of their focus, the original researchers said they were "primarily interested in male-to-female violence at the time." Yet allowing such "interests" to distort their report of their findings raises serious questions about whether, under color of doing science, they were in fact doing political advocacy. It must be seen to represent flagrant and willful disregard of the facts,[16] and a stunning violation of scientific procedure.[17] The withholding of evidence concerning parity in battering has distorted public discussion and has had a dramatic impact on what people believe. It is difficult to avoid the conclusion that that was precisely its intent.

DEMONIZING THE MESSENGER

For our purposes, however, of equal interest to the disregard for objectivity is the response from feminists when such revelations have been brought into the open.

For example, returning to the Super Bowl hoax, Ringle's story was followed up in a February 2 report by the *Boston Globe*'s Bob Hohler, who fully supported his conclusions and got some reactions to it from some of the figures involved. Interestingly, while they generally backed off from the story, they did so in a way that enabled them to maintain the image in general. Thus:

One expert, Joan Stiles, public education coordinator for the Massachusetts Coalition of Battered Women's Service Groups, told the *Globe* that the Super Bowl story "sensationalized and trivialized" the battering problem, and damaged the cause's credibility. Lundy Bancroft, a training director for a Cambridge-based counseling program for men who batter, said, "I disbelieved the 40 percent thing from the moment I heard it." Bancroft also suggested that the campaign to pressure NBC to air the domestic-violence spot "unfairly stigmatized" football fans. "There is no stereotypical batterer," he said. (Sommers, 1995: p. 191)

As we have seen, the general framework of belief about domestic violence rests on material that is no more substantial than the Super Bowl hoax.

Most interesting of all, however, was this response from Lenore Walker:

Lenore Walker was furious with Ken Ringle for criticizing her research. She attributed his unfriendly stance to male pique at not being able to get through to her on the phone the day he was writing his story. As she explained to the *Boston Globe's* Bob Hohler: "He [Ringle] felt as if he was entitled to talk to me; because he did not get what he was entitled to he got angry and decided to use his pen as a sword as a batterer does with his fist when he does not get what he thinks he is entitled to." (Sommers, 1995: p. 192)

Walker's response here may be taken as paradigmatic. The fact is that the attempt to destroy the validity of objective disagreement by demonizing its proponents, and indeed to subsume it under the category of violence against women itself, is standard practice here. This is from Sommers's account of the way Gelles and Straus's research was received:

Battery and rape research is the very stuff of gender feminist advocacy. Researchers who try to pursue their investigations in a nonpolitical way are often subject to attack by the advocates. Murray Straus reports that he and some of his co-workers "became the object of bitter scholarly and personal attacks, including threats and attempts at intimidation." In the late seventies and early eighties his scholarly presentations were sometimes obstructed by booing, shouting, or picketing. When he was considered for offices in scientific societies, he was labeled an antifeminist. . . . In 1992 a rumor was circulated that Murray Straus had beaten his wife and sexually harassed his students. Straus fought back as best he could and in one instance was able to elicit a written apology from a domestic violence activist.

Richard Gelles claims that whenever male researchers question exaggerated findings on domestic battery, it is never long before rumors begin circulating that he is himself a batterer. For female skeptics, however, the situation appears to be equally intimidating. When Suzanne K. Steinmetz, a co-investigator in the First National Family Violence Survey, was being considered for promotion, the feminists launched a letter-writing campaign urging that it be denied. She also received calls threatening her and her family, and there was a bomb threat at a conference where she spoke. (Sommers, 1995: p. 200)

One need not stop here. The attempt to suppress the message of the equivalence of violence in relationships through the demonization of those who bring the message is abundantly evident. As a final example, consider this from an article by Scott Sleek (1998) in a recent issue of the APA (American Psychological Association) *Monitor*:

For years, Irene Frieze, PhD, wanted to keep rather quiet about her unexpected findings on dating violence. She was worried about how the mainstream media might spin her results, and how they might be interpreted by the feminist groups that had long lauded her work.

Why the hesitancy? Frieze, a psychology professor at the University of Pittsburgh, and her colleagues had found in surveys of 300 college students that women appeared more likely than men to start physical altercations with a dating partner, usually in the form of slapping, shoving or pushing.

Frieze certainly wasn't the first person to make such a discovery about women's role in relationship violence. In fact, many psychologists, including noted feminist researchers, have collected similar results with far larger sample sizes. (Sleek, 1998: p. 130)

But:

When a Pitt public relations officer learned of the data last October and decided to issue a press release on it, Frieze's reservations proved accurate. The National Organization for Women denounced the research as fraudulent, while a radio station exaggerated her results as showing that women "cause most domestic violence." (Sleek, 1998: p. 130)

SCAPEGOATING THE "DEADBEAT DAD"

A similar story may be told with regard to the image of the "deadbeat dad," the irresponsible father who abandons his family and refuses to pay child support. This image is so familiar to us that we do not even think to question it. Like so many of the other aspects of the contemporary denigration of men, it turns out to be a fantasy, and unsupported by the facts. An extensive recent federally funded[18] study by Sanford Braver (1998) makes this plain. Men, it turns out, have not caused family breakdown by divorcing their wives. On the contrary, a substantial preponderance of divorces, from 63 to 67 percent (Braver, 1998: p. 133), are initiated by women. Nor is it the case that men are evicted from their families by women tired of their violence and abuse. In fact the most important reasons given by females, and the only ones ranked as "very important" by more than half, were "[g]radual growing apart, losing a sense of closeness" and "[s]erious differences in lifestyle and/or values." "Violence between you and your spouse" ranks only sixteenth on the list, mentioned as very important by only 20 percent (Braver, 1998: p. 139) of divorced women.

What is more, the idea that men refuse to pay child support also turns out to be a myth. Until Braver's study the idea came from research that lumped married men together with men who had never been married, and only questioned women. Men who had not married had obviously not undertaken a commitment to support their children, because that is what marriage is. And asking only women whether their ex-husbands have paid introduces an obvious bias. In fact, when Braver asked men about their payment of child support, he found that they claimed to be scrupulous in their payments. Wisely suggesting that the truth lies somewhere in between, Braver went on to ask what percentage of their support payments were made, and found that, even by the mothers' accounts, they were paid 68 to 69 percent of what they were owed, a figure far less alarming than is typically supposed.[19] Again, looking at the reasons that men did not pay, he found that it was almost entirely due to unemployment. The wives of men who were fully employed during the year said they paid 80 percent of what they owed, while the men reported that they paid 100 percent (p. 33).

Here again what we find is that the myth of the "deadbeat dad" is a variant on the fantasy of "toxic man." And here again we find the same pattern of abuse directed at those who question the myth. Thus Braver, who began his research as much convinced of the "deadbeat dad" idea as anyone else, reports:

[O]nce I began to uncover and point out evidence that tended to exonerate fathers, some researchers were mistakenly led to infer that I myself must somehow be antifemale, antifeminist or antimother. . . .

The truth is the direct opposite: I have long identified with the goals of the women's movement to increase opportunities for women (and men as well), to treat the genders equally, and to end male domination in families. But somehow even to speak in defense of fathers is taken by some as the equivalent of bashing mothers. (pp. 13–14)

Along these lines Braver tells the story of an academic conference he attended at Arizona State University in 1988. He was in the audience during a panel discussion, which was moderated by one of the country's most respected demographers. One of the members of the panel spoke about her research on child support and during the question-and-answer period another member of the audience raised a question about Arizona's supposedly poor record in child-support collection. Braver recalls that this gave him what he thought was a good opportunity to share his findings about the problems that arise from trusting official records. He continued:

I raised my hand and was given the opportunity to address the audience member's question. I explained how the official database statistics can be misleading and how I had taken the trouble to interview both mothers and fathers. I then repeated [the results partially reported earlier].

At this point, the moderator stood up and said, "You know, I've heard about your findings. Our panel was discussing this very issue, of differences between mothers' and fathers' answers, over lunch. And what we concluded was if the mother tells you one thing and the father tells you something else, then the father is a God damned liar."

Braver adds:

I was so flabbergasted, I could think of no response and sat down.

I have yet to see any data that fathers either don't remember events as accurately as mothers or simply lie more. In the absence of convincing data that supports this view, those holding it are merely expressing their own prejudices, biases it would not be acceptable to express toward any other group. I can't imagine this man standing in a public setting and proclaiming that any racial, ethnic, or religious group—or even mothers, for that matter—were a bunch of "God damned liars." (p. 35)

THE ELEVATION OF THE SUBJECTIVE

So what is one to make of this? What we have, clearly enough, is a case in which a set of assertions is promulgated, widely and loudly, as empirical facts in support of a vision of the world as a war between the sexes. But the assertions turn out to be distortions: myths, fictions, perhaps even fantasies. Moreover, as we have seen, the attempt to correct the distortions is not allowed to have its own impact, but is itself defended against in the name of the good side. It is subsumed under the war between the sexes itself, and is seen as simply a movement by the "bad" side. And this strategy has been largely successful.

One must conclude from this that the order of understanding has been reversed in this case. These subjective views are not, for those who promulgate them, ways of interpreting the facts. Rather the subjective views come first, and then the facts are given weight in accordance with whether they support these views. Thus the subjective has been raised over the objective.

Now one may object that this is an old story, and tells us nothing but that human beings can be biased. In a sense this is true, but it does not give sufficient recognition to the peculiarities of this case. Of course we know that people have biases. For that very reason, we have fashioned means to limit the damage they can cause. The whole institutional structure of criticism, from freedom of speech to peer review, has the intention of safeguarding us from our limitations in this regard. What we see in this case is that this institutional framework has broken down. A set of subjective views has emerged as sacrosanct, beyond criticism. It has been hermetically sealed off from the world. The result is that a vicious bias has triumphed over fact.

If the images of toxic man, of Madonna-and-child, of the sexual holy war, are views that are not based on facts, then what can they be based on? If they are not the best we can do to give meaning to the facts, what can they mean? Where do they come from and how do they claim their authority? From where do they get the power to override and even banish the facts? And how do they gain this power even among people like Pollack, who see themselves, with perfect sincerity, as the passionate defenders of the most innocent objects of this vilification? These are the questions that are of interest to us in the chapters ahead.

NOTES

1.

	Math	Verbal
Men	532	502
Women	509	495

Part of this difference is certainly due to the fact that more women took the test than men. Still, these data do not support the view that colleges are getting their male students from "all the way down."

2. In 1995, 4,132 males in the age range 15–24 killed themselves, versus 652 females in the same age range (Anderson, Kochanek, and Murphy, 1997).

3. Available on their web site *http://www.apa.org/about/division/div35.html*.

4. Available on their web site: *http://web.indstate.edu/spsmm/posstat.html*.

5. For some reason Pollack does not provide a reference to the article. It is also cited by Sommers (2000), who does. Quotations presented here are from the original, and are not significantly different from those given by Pollack.

6. See, for example, Pollack's usage on page 5.

7. The demand that men be more sensitive is arguably a feature of our time. If Pollack is correct, this demand is in conflict with the demands of the Boy Code that require that boys deny their sensitivity. Could the boys' failure be due to their state of confusion? This is not a claim Pollack makes explicitly, but it may be useful to consider how it would fit with the rest of his case. The answer is that it would be a hard case for Pollack to make. According to Pollack the requirement that boys be sensitive is unqualifiedly positive; increased sensitivity, on the part of society as a whole, is much of the answer to boys' problems. What we can see, on that level, is that the demand for sensitivity is at the same time permission

and encouragement to be more sensitive. But the two work against each other, says Pollack. That would mean that, in Pollack's view, increased sensitivity would undermine the Boy Code and its deleterious effects. It is hard to see how the salutary effects of this increased sensitivity would not easily outweigh the confusion of responding to it in the context of the Boy Code. Confusion, then, cannot be held to be the cause of boys' failure.

8. Another contemporaneous issue that certainly deserves consideration in this regard, though it is not mentioned by Pollack, is the rise of fatherlessness. Of course girls grow up in the same fatherless families that boys do, but it certainly makes sense that fatherlessness might impact boys more than it does girls, at least in certain ways. My point here is that the rise of fatherlessness has not taken place in a vacuum, but has been largely the result of a cultural configuration that regards fathers as, at best, unnecessary and, at worst, malevolent. It is the analysis of this cultural configuration toward which our inquiry is directed. For recent examples of this configuration, see "Deconstructing the Essential Father" (Silverstein and Auerbach, 1999). This is the lead article in an issue of the American Psychological Association's presumably scientific journal *The American Psychologist,* despite being stunningly selective in its reading of the research literarure and overtly political in its intent. The various web sites connected with the National Organization for Women continue to be a treasure-trove in this regard. Witness, for example, their recent attack upon Congress for passing a resolution in favor of Father's Day, even despite the fact that our lawmakers thought it necessary to rename the holiday "Responsible Fathers' Day" (Jensen, 2000).

9. For anyone unfamiliar with this genre, it may be useful to provide a few examples. The imagery of male toxicity varies in the subtlety of its presentation. On the subtle side, for example, we have Gilligan (1982), who, while observing the form of equivalence, identifies men with their dark side and women with their ideal side, and sees male motivation as dominated by aggression and selfishness; women's motivation, by contrast, is seen as arising from a sense of connection, and is organized around caring, nurturance and the creation and maintenance of relationships.

Moving away from subtlety, we get this from Andrea Dworkin (1993: p. 214):

In everything men make, they hollow out a central place for death, let its rancid smell contaminate every dimension of whatever still survives. Men especially love murder. In art they celebrate it, and in life they commit it. They embrace murder as if life without it would be devoid of passion, meaning, and action, as if murder were solace, still their sobs as they mourn the emptiness and alienation of their lives.

This from Robin Morgan, former editor of *Ms.* magazine (1989: pp. 138–139):

The phallic malady is epidemic and systemic . . . each individual male in the patriarchy is aware of his relative power in the scheme of things. . . . He knows that his actions are supported by the twin pillars of the State of man—the brotherhood ritual of political exigency and the brotherhood ritual of a sexual thrill in dominance. As a devotee of Thanatos, he is one with the practitioner of sado-masochistic "play" between "consenting adults," as he is one with the rapist.

This from Gloria Steinem, founder of *Ms.* magazine (1993: pp. 259–261):

Patriarchy requires violence or the subliminal threat of violence in order to maintain itself . . . The most dangerous situation for a woman is not an unknown man in the street, or even the enemy in wartime, but a husband or lover in the isolation of their home.

And from Marilyn French (1992: p. 182):

As long as some men use physical force to subjugate females, *all* men need not. The knowledge that some men do suffices to threaten all women. Beyond that, it is not necessary to beat up a woman to beat her down. A man can simply refuse to hire women in well-paid jobs, extract as much or more work from women than men but pay them less, or treat women disrespectfully at work or at home. He can fail to support a child he has engendered, demand the woman he lives with wait on him like a servant. He can beat or kill the woman he claims to love; he can rape women, whether mate, acquaintance or stranger; he can rape or sexually molest his daughters, nieces, stepchildren, or the woman he claims to love. The vast majority of men in the world do one or more of the above. (Emphasis in original.)

Obviously if these insults were directed at the membership of any other group, whether ethnic, religious, national, or anything else, they would immediately be labeled "hate speech," and all right-thinking people would condemn their very utterance. That they are not, but are instead regarded in mainstream quarters as informed and respectable opinion, is a fact that is near the focal point of our inquiry.

10. Christina Sommers's recent book *The War against Boys* (2000) provides a wealth of material illustrating the way the denigration of males has become a dominant theme of education in our time. Summarizing, she says:

More and more schoolboys inhabit a milieu of disapproval. Routinely regarded as protosexists, potential harassers, and perpetuators of gender inequity, boys live under a cloud of censure, in a permanent state of culpability. Martin Spafford, a high school teacher in London, has made observations about British boys that apply to American boys as well. . . . "Boys feel continually attacked for who they are. We have created a sense in school that masculinity is something bad. Boys feel blamed for history, and a school culture has grown up which is suspicious and frightened of boys." (p. 57)

This often reaches the level of the ludicrous:

In 1997, Nan Stein [a director of the influential Wellesley College Center for Research on Women] did a national survey of domestic violence/sexual assault experts who present programs in public schools. She asked them what they liked least about the educational materials they had to work with (guides, handouts, videos, and so on). Stein reported that among the most common complaints were that "males are never positively portrayed" and "males are never shown in a positive light." However, she did not see this as a reason to change the message: when boys object, it only shows the "need for materials to defuse male resistance." She seemed not to notice that the instructors, not the boys, were the ones objecting to the materials. (p. 58)

11. In July 1994 the Bureau of Justice Statistics of the U.S. Department of Justice released a Special Report called *Murder in Families*, detailing the results of a survey of family homicides in thirty-three urban U.S. counties. The report cov-

ered only convictions. It said, in part: "In murders of their offspring, women predominated, accounting for 55 percent of killers."

12. This is the so-called "Munchausen Syndrome by Proxy." The Southall research group remotely videotaped the interactions of parents with thirty-nine children who had been brought to the hospital due to the suspicion that they were being seriously abused. In thirty-three of these cases, a parent was observed attempting to kill the child, primarily by suffocation. The research paper, along with subsequent news accounts, uses the neutral term "parent," but a perusal of the case descriptions suggests that the bulk of them were female. A colleague reported that in an interview on New Zealand National Public Radio, Southall acknowledged that in all but one of these cases, the perpetrator was female—either the mother or, in one case, the grandmother. Looking for a better source for this, I wrote to Southall. He did not answer the precise question, but said, in a letter dated February 16, 1999: "In the setting of Munchausen Syndrome by Proxy it is our experience that the vast majority of perpetrators of abuse are women."

13. If this is true, the greater strength of men would largely explain it. On the other hand, the finding could be due to an increased tendency for women to report injury (Cook, 1997). In any case, it is a matter of public record that in the worst cases of domestic violence, those resulting in death, typically about 40 percent of the victims in the United States are men (Department of Justice, 1994).

14. Fiebert (1998) documents ninety-five studies (seventy-nine of them empirical and sixteen reviews and/or analyses) and recently by the British Home Office (1998) in a study based on the British Crime Survey of 1996.

15. These attributions were reported by the respondents about themselves, and there was a high level of correspondence (70–80 percent) between individual's self-reports and the reports of their partners.

16. As of this writing, there has not, to my knowledge, been a hint in the major U.S. media of the research showing the parity of domestic violence. This is true even in the context of "Violence against Women" legislation, whose supporters have used, and continue to use, bogus information. The suppression of this information continues apace, and it continues to have a powerful effect.

17. Compare the lack of response in this case with the treatment of an incident in which an ideologically driven researcher, attempting to show that high voltage power lines can cause cancer, withheld contrary data. Robert P. Liburdy, a cell biologist at the Lawrence Berkeley Laboratory, an arm of the Energy Department, was found to have published two papers with misleading data. Investigators said Liburdy eliminated data that did not support his conclusions. After the investigation he resigned quietly from the laboratory in March and has agreed to withdraw his research findings. That story was reported in an article on page 1 of the *New York Times* (Broad, 1999). It takes nothing away from the importance of fraud in cancer research to say that fraud in research into family violence is also important.

18. Braver says that the research was funded by more than $10 million in grants, primarily from the National Institute of Child Health and Human Development and the National Institute of Mental Health.

19. Fathers report paying 84 to 92 percent of what they owe. Again the truth is likely to lie somewhere in between.

Chapter Two

The Sexual Holy War and the Meaning of Work

Our consideration of the state of relations between the sexes has led us to a series of questions. What is the meaning of the ideas of toxic man, Madonna-and-child, and the sexual holy war? How did sexual difference come to be formulated as a Manichean struggle between the forces of goodness and those of badness? How did these ideas become so powerful among us? Where did they get their power? These are matters that the present chapter begins to address. In the end I show that these ideas represent a conflict, not between men and women, but between deep and primitive levels of the psyche, and that they derive their power from their depth.

Before continuing with our inquiry, however, something needs to be added. It is the observation that the picture of the sexual holy war is a comprehensive image. The images of toxic man and Madonna-and-child are not limited to the ideas of men as wife batterers and deadbeat dads, with women portrayed as helpless victims and abandoned mothers. On the contrary the sexual holy war is thought to play itself out in matters well beyond the realm of interpersonal relations. Its picture of male perfidy and female perfection pervades the whole range of ideas we have about social reality.

The imagery of the sexual holy war is nowhere on better display than within our ideas of work and work organization. Feminist conceptions of work and work organization deliver the view that the ways in which men are seen to have organized work, while enjoyable enough for them, given their warped and oppressive natures, are destructive and debilitating for

Madonna and her children. What is more, these deleterious aspects of work are unnecessary, because a form of work and work organization based on women's ways of doing things would be beneficial, in each and every respect, and for everyone (e.g. Ferguson, 1984; Calás and Smircich, 1991; Cheng, 1996).

What it is important to note, at this point, is that this Manichean perspective makes it impossible to understand the functioning of organizations. At best we could know whom to celebrate and whom to condemn within an organization, but these are questions that exist only within the crudest of moral orders. An understanding on the level of social science, in which institutions are understood objectively, in terms of how they function, and recognized for their benefits as well as their deficiencies, is precluded.

If we may generalize beyond the range of work organizations, what we can see here is that the distortions involved in the image of the sexual holy war are likely to propagate themselves as distortions within the whole range of our self-understanding. Sexuality and sexual differentiation, I would acknowledge, are critical to an understanding of every aspect of social life. That is why a distortion in these matters can have the most profound negative impact on our self-understanding and on our capacity to make sense of our lives.

So it is generally and so it is with regard to the understanding of work and work organization. Constraining our understanding of work and organizations to fit within the imagery of sexual holy war makes a nuanced and realistic understanding of these institutions impossible. And this has finally set the stage for our work within this chapter.

In this chapter I address the questions with which we were left at the end of our first chapter. What does the imagery of the sexual holy war mean and where does it get its power? I also want to show what is lost by confining our self-understanding within the boundaries of the sexual holy war. I do this by providing what I think is a richer and more realistic understanding of the place of sexuality and sexual differentiation within the dynamics of work and organizations.

As we pursue our inquiry, we find that, with regard to the differentiation of the sex roles, the idea of a simple moral dichotomy between the sexes is impossible to reconcile with the complexity of work and work organization. Indeed an interesting paradox emerges. The critics of men have shown that men and their works are imperfect. And men are imperfect, to be sure. Yet nothing is perfect, and once we get over the idea that anything is perfect, we may begin to see that imperfections are often only one aspect of something that, viewed from another perspective, has positive consequences of the most important sort. Men's imperfections are tightly bound up with the sources of their achievement.

Understanding this will put us in a position to see something further about the costs of holding a Manichean view. For it will become apparent that the idea of female perfection, although it has its own place within the traditional female role, raises real problems for women's assumption of the responsibility of working for a living.

The tendency to idealize and demonize precludes an understanding of the intricacy of human psychology and of human depth. Yet human complexity must be understood if we are to live our lives wisely. And it is necessary to live our lives wisely if we are going to live them well.

For our purposes it is necessary to develop a theoretical basis. The core of my analysis will be adapted from an examination of Freud's psychology of development by the French psychoanalyst Janine Chasseguet-Smirgel (1986). It will be necessary to begin with Freud's account.

FREUD

Early in the course of development, for both the boy and the girl, the relationship with the mother is the mainstay of emotional life. As of yet, the child does not experience its mother as living in her own world, with her own agenda, but experiences the mother's power in the service of its desires as being the extension of, as the complement of, those desires. We may say that the child at this stage experiences itself as the center of a world, we may call it the *maternal world*, that is lovingly structured around it. Freud's name for this experience is "primary narcissism" (Freud, 1914), or, borrowing a term from Romaine Rolland, "the oceanic feeling" (Freud, 1930).

Primary narcissism cannot last, for there is a real outside world that is not the infant's mother. It is indifferent to the child and entirely outside of the child's control. Within the context of this indifferent outside world, the child is vulnerable and helpless. It defends against this helplessness in the only way it can, through the wish to reunite with, to fuse with, its loving mother. The mother will hold us, comfort us, and make things all right. Her limitless power to take care of us is experienced as omnipotence. Reinforced by our mother's love, we will no longer be helpless and powerless. We will again be the center of a loving world. Thus the desire to return to the original narcissistic state develops as a way of coping with the anxiety of being helpless in the face of the world's indifference.

The omnipotent mother, whose love will make life perfect for us, is a child's fantasy. But according to psychoanalytic theory, childish fantasies do not disappear, they remain with us in the unconscious, where they can have the most profound effects. For instance, as I have said, the "oceanic feeling," so important in the spirit of religion, is one of these effects. In general our idea of a positive direction in life, of a place that we can "get to," in which the tensions and limitations of our lives will disappear, and in which we can simply be ourselves and be loved for it, is formed out of this image of fusion. Freud (1914, 1921) referred to our fantasy of ourselves as fused again with the primordial, omnipotent mother as the "ego ideal." Chasseguet-Smirgel describes the fantasy this way: "In my view, this fantasy corresponds to the wish to rediscover a smooth universe without obstacles, roughness or difference, identified with a mother's insides to which one can have free access, the representation, at the thinking level, of a form of unfettered mental functioning with the free circulation of psychic energy." And she follows this with: "The father, his penis and reality itself must be destroyed in order for the paradise world of the pleasure principle to be regained" (p. 30).

We return to this point later. For the time being, note that, so far, the developmental pattern has been identical for boys and girls.

For Freud the cause of male and female divergence is anatomical, resting in the fact that boys, but not girls, possess a penis (Freud, 1925). The recognition of this fact gains significance at the stage of the Oedipus complex, at around the age of six. At that point the boy child's desire to be with the mother develops a focus that is experienced as explicitly sexual. Conceiving the father as a rival, the boy entertains the fantasy of destroying him. But he comes to understand that in a struggle with his father he will come off badly. Specifically the little boy is afraid that the father will castrate him and thus end the rivalry. It is to allay the fear of castration that the child learns to anticipate the punishment of the father by internalizing him and learning to punish himself for doing things that the father would otherwise have punished. In this way the superego is created. At the same time, an implicit promise is made that, if the boy grows up and becomes like the father by following the injunctions of the superego, he will be able to have a position like the one the father appears to have with mother. Then he will attain the ego ideal and be again the center of a loving world. This, for Freud, was the genesis of the male role (1923).

The female role is conditioned by the lack of the penis. The little girl, taking her father as a rival, soon discovers that the competition is already over; she has already been castrated. The realization that she lacks a penis leads the girl to envy those who have this organ. She turns toward the father, with the idea in mind that someday he will give her one. But over time, typically, and in disappointment, the little girl gives up the idea of having her own penis and comes to take a passive role toward the father, and toward men in general. Behind this lies the hope that ultimately one of them will give her a boy child whose penis she may possess as her own (Freud, 1931, 1933).

A number of points stand out from this account as worthy of remark. Among them are the denigration of female power that is involved and the claim that females are determined by their anatomy to be passive toward and dependent on males—objects rather than subjects. Material of this sort has, of course, been seized upon by countless feminists as evidence of a bias against women.

One can very easily understand their concerns and sympathize. On the other hand, as Mitchell (1975) has pointed out, the fact that women do not like such reasoning does not, in itself, make it false. A far more serious attack upon Freud has been developed by Chasseguet-Smirgel (1986)—an attack that has no less legitimacy than Freud's work itself, because it takes place within the basic framework of the logic of psychoanalysis.

CHASSEGUET-SMIRGEL

The central feature of Chasseguet-Smirgel's analysis[1] is her observation that the image of the female that arises in Freud's theory—weak, passive, dependent—is the exact opposite of the *maternal imago*, the primordial image of the omnipotent mother that we all carry around with us in the unconscious and that establishes, for all of us, the definition of the female. Our inquiry has already made us familiar with her. She is the root of the image of the Madonna.

The maternal imago structures the very root of our personality. She mediates ourselves to ourselves and provides the basis for our sense of self-unity and goodness. Self-love, that is to say, begins with our mother's love for us, and, at the deepest level, that is what it remains (Freud, 1914).

She is a fantasy, an infant's image, yet one that maintains a central place within our minds even as adults. She is a female figure, not a real woman, but she lies behind our deepest idea of the female: deeply connected to us, her love will enable us to accept ourselves and feel safe and substantial. There is no weakness or passivity in this image; she is the opposite of the female in Freud's theory.

For psychoanalysis an opposition of this sort cannot be a mere coincidence; rather it must be a dynamic opposition. The theoretical conception, obviously a secondary development, must have arisen because it is the opposite of the archaic image. This is the central logic of Chasseguet-Smirgel's reasoning.

For her the image of the female in Freud's theory must have arisen to deny the power of the mother that Freud, and men generally, feel exerted over them by women. Along with this would go the images of weakness, passivity, and dependency—all following the logic of denying the opposite. But why should the image of the primordial mother exert such power that Freud's whole theory of women would arise to deny it?

The answer is contained in the nature of our relationship to the maternal world. As we have seen, the chief emotional constellation for the male, as well as for the female, consists in the wish to return to narcissistic fusion, to be again the center of the maternal world. The mother is the object of our desire. She will take care of us entirely. But as the object of our desire, as the perfect source of love, she also represents our helplessness before her. It is this helplessness that men need to defend against by denying the power of women. For the closer the man comes to being the center of the maternal world, the more defenseless he becomes in the face of her wishes and whims and the less capable he is of resisting being cast out and abandoned.

What we need to see here is that if being within the circle of her love means we have a place within the universe, it follows that outside of it we are just flotsam and jetsam. This is a matter of being or nothingness. Without her love as a bedrock, we lose our sense of our own substance. Her capacity to accept or reject, therefore, or a capacity that can be successfully asserted in her name, has got to be the strongest power in the psyche. The more men approximate the infantile relationship with the mother, the weaker they become and the stronger she becomes.

This is the root of the man's desire: to be comforted and taken care of by the loving mother, conceived as omnipotent. At the same time, though, it is the source of terror, for the mother is, after all, an other. Her love, on which the man counts for his emotional sustenance is, that is to say, her love. The man has no power over it. Leaving himself to be comforted and cared for by her means he is also in the position of complete dependence on her. Yet she is completely outside of his control. So the deeper his love, the deeper the dependence, and the more helpless he becomes. Now we can see the core of men's emotional orientation toward women. *It is complete, profound, and overwhelming ambivalence.*

The helplessness of the man before the primordial mother must be contrasted with the condition of the woman. For women, too, the central focus consists in the return to being the center of the maternal world. But for the girl a natural alternative is open that is not open to the boy. She can imagine becoming a mother and being the maternal world for her own child.[2] By being the mother, identifying with her child, and experiencing the child's feelings for her, she can be both nurtured and nurturing, helpless and omnipotent, loved and loving. The woman can project the attainment of the ego ideal in a form that does not lead to her total helplessness. She can directly identify with the omnipotent, primordial mother. Moreover her route to the ego ideal is natural and organic. She can maintain the fantasy that, simply by being herself, she can attain the ego ideal.

As the presence of androgynous male religious figures such as Jesus and Buddha indicates, it is possible for males to also see themselves in this condition of self-fusion. Nonetheless, as Chasseguet-Smirgel (1986) notes, it is not going to be as easy for the boy to do this as the girl, and this will structure the difference between the sexes.

The result is that the boy cannot approach the idea of fusion with the mother with the same degree of equanimity as the girl. The girl can identify with her power, can include herself in the circle of love, but the boy cannot. For him, overcoming the difference between himself and mother means subordinating himself to her. But she is a separate person, and therefore he puts himself at risk in doing so. There is, therefore, at the deepest core of male being, a deep and powerful ambivalence. Men live in terror of the thing they love the most. Women do not have the same degree of ambivalence. At least in fantasy, they *are* the ego ideal. *They* are the thing they love the most.

MASCULINITY AND CULTURE

According to Chasseguet-Smirgel, who assumes the same traditional family structure that Freud did, both the boy and the girl child, in order to defend themselves against their helplessness before their mother, project her power onto the father. In this way, by identifying with the father and coming to be like him, they hope to be able to gain power over the mother. Of course, as we have seen, for the female who projects her role as a mother, this will be only a secondary solution. For the male child, however, it is the predominant way out of his feeling of helplessness and generates the traditional male psychology of work.

In order to gain a proper understanding of the traditional male psychology of work, it is necessary to slightly revise Chasseguet-Smirgel's account of the projection of paternal power. For it is easy to see that it cannot be the power of the primordial mother that the child projects onto the father. That would only make the child feel helpless and dependent on the father as well as the mother. It must be a different power.

This is the thesis I wish to assert. The child projects upon the father a power equal to the power of the primordial mother but different from it. In effect the child projects upon the father a countervailing power with regard to the mother. It assumes that the father has standing with the mother that enables him to be with her without being dependent and helpless before her as the child is, that is, without either impinging on or being subordinate to her power. As she is idealized, so he is idealized. The child assumes, in other words, that the father is doing something that causes the mother to admire him, to idealize him, and that that is the basis upon within she allows him to be with her and within the family.

What could it be that the mother, conceived as the primordial mother, would admire and idealize? What could be the basis of the father's power? Shortly I consider some answers to this question, but to begin with let us note that it is an open question. There is no answer that is naturally built into the family constellation in the way that the role of the mother is. This is where culture enters into the configuration.

Culture may be said to be our created heritage. It may be thought of as organized around our ego ideals. But remember that the ego ideal represents what someone must do in order to gain a place within the maternal world. Women, to the extent that they identify with the primordial mother, already have a place within the maternal world. Men are different in that they must do something in order to attain it. The idea of what they need to do is not given for all time, but is created and developed. This process of creation is cultural development itself, and culture may therefore be thought of as what men have imagined they had to do in order to gain the admiration of women.

In the most fundamental sense, it is the fantasy of the maternal world that defines the concept of worth. Men's job is to give substance to this fantasy. Separated from the maternal world to which he wishes to gain entry, the man's function is to engage the indifferent world and transform it in a way that enhances the maternal world. Taking indifference and bringing it within the sphere of love, he transcends the mundane, transforming the ordinary into the special, moving toward the realization of the ego ideal. It is the response of the woman that validates this transformation. Thus men have to create and implement practices that make sense to and represent the female within the maternal world. They must move toward the realization of the maternal world, the ideal world over which, he and she agree, she presides. By doing this, they seek to be able to claim for themselves, through the admiration of the woman, centrality in the maternal world, whose very possibility they have brought into existence.

It is easy to see how work, conceived as economic activity, would fit into this psychology. If the man does work that creates improved material circumstances for the woman and the children with whom they identify, he can push back the boundary of the indifferent outside world and create room for the free play of fantasy and love. He can expand the sphere of the maternal world, to which he may then be admitted. But it is also easy to see that other solutions are possible. For example the man may take the role of defending the group from other groups, who are seen as preventing the realization of the maternal world. In either case what we see are attempts at heroism, attempts at proving oneself worthy of inclusion in the maternal world. In this way we may define the traditional male role.

For an understanding of the psychology of the sexes, what needs to be seen is the way the sex roles, being based on a fantasy, are unstable and subject to undermining. As work, insofar as it differs from making a home, has been the male province in the sexual division of labor, I concentrate primarily on showing how the instability in male psychology plays out in the domain of work. Nonetheless, as we also see, instability in the female role deeply affects the ways in which women orient themselves toward work in this world of changing sex roles.

To begin with let us recall that the male psychology of work has its roots in the idealization of the female. That idealization is its deepest premise. His job is to take a corner of the world and make it into a place where her goodness can prevail, where there is room for her to be her ideal self. Then the story goes on, she will admire the man for making this ideal world possible, and her admiration will bring him into it. But what if she does not acknowledge that? What if she finds no room in this world for herself, as she would like to be? Or what if she does not acknowledge his contributions? Then there would be no ground for granting him admiration. If that happened the male role would dissolve into the air. The male role only serves its purpose to the extent that it is valued by the female, but that is based on her acceptance of the image of herself that it offers, and on her appreciation of his role in the creation of it. If she rejects either of these, she will experience his role as pointless, and it will fail.

This puts male psychology into a terrible bind. Within this psychology the male's standing with the female is always tenuous, his role always subject to being rejected and repulsed. For the male to lose his place with the female nothing more is required than that she cease to buy into the fantasy he has attempted to realize, or into his role in the creation of it. All she needs to do is say, "I am not happy," or "I am not impressed," or "You're a jerk." There is nothing he can do about that because the whole drama is a fantasy; yet it is a fantasy in which her place is essential, but his place is contingent. So from within this fantasy, she can say to him, "You're a jerk," and she will always be right. He is, after all, only a man. But he cannot say to her "You're a jerk, too," because then the basis of their interaction would be undermined, and along with it the basis of his sense of meaning.

This is a point whose importance cannot be overemphasized. The scorn with which many women declare men to be jerks is based on women's feelings of inherent superiority. But on what is that sense of superiority based? As we began to see in the first chapter, it is not based on facts. Rather the facts that are adduced to prove it are themselves selected based on the feeling of superiority. What I am suggesting here is that the feeling of superiority arises from a fantasy, and a fantasy that men and women collude to preserve.

This realization points to an instability in the psychology of women that corresponds to the instability that we have seen in the psychology of men. It is that the maintenance of the image of female perfection has been dependent on the work that was done by men. In order to maintain their image of their omnipotence, they were reliant on men to create the conditions that represented the expression of their power. That is not to say that they cannot, in the present, do the same work and thereby become independent of men. I have no doubt that they can. *But they cannot do it and maintain the image of their omnipotence at the same time.* For, according to the fantasy, their expression of their perfection should be effortless, a spontaneous expression of their desire, and work is anything but that.

Instability can be a productive force of immense power. It is precisely the instability of the male sex role that has driven the achievement for which men have been responsible in the sphere of work. We turn to this complex process shortly. For the present it is equally important to note that the instability in the female role has been responsible for the maintenance of family life that has been her own great achievement. She has had to keep two contradictory images in her soul and it has been her capacity to sustain this conflict from which she has created the complex sense of purpose that has kept this whole grand game in operation. She needed to identify with the omnipotent mother, and through that identification to maintain the love that was the family's emotional sustenance. At the same time, she had to maintain an understanding of the limits of that omnipotence, of its dependence on material circumstances that were not subject to her omnipotent control, in order to appreciate the mutuality in male-female relationship and keep the familial bonds intact. It may well have been her capacity to manage this complex understanding that led to the deeper sense of emotional nuance that women have had than men.

But instability is unstable, after all. It always presses for its own elimination. It was the abandonment of complexity, in favor of the simplicity of the fantasy of the omnipotent ego ideal, that has brought us to the condition of sexual holy war in which we find ourselves today.

Before getting to that, it is worthy of note that the complexity of these dynamics are entirely missing from the image of sexual holy war. Complexity is especially lacking in the idea that male psychology is simply determined by the need to control the female. What we can see now is that the truth is much more complex. Men do not so much want to control women, as to be secure in women's love. The attempt to gain admiration is the man's way of maintaining for himself a position of importance in the woman's life without threatening her omnipotence. It is within the context of this omnipotence that the male role arises, and by that token the male can only control the female by undermining himself and his own rationale. If the female is not omnipotent, and therefore capable of rejecting the male, she is not the object of male desire. The premise of the woman's freedom to accept him, and therefore her freedom to reject him, is the psychological root of the whole drama. This is why the status of the male with the female is always in question and is never a foregone conclusion. Ultimately the power in the relationship of male and female rests with the female precisely because it is the omnipotent female that is the underlying object of the male's love.[3]

In the next section, I wish to show how the work role may be understood as the way that male psychology works its way out in our culture.

THE MEANING OF MALE WORK IN WESTERN CAPITALIST CULTURE

The first aspect of the psychology of work in our culture that may be illuminated by an understanding of male psychology is its *external focus*. In order to appeal to the female, the man must do something. And he must do something that appeals to the female. He cannot appeal to her as himself, because that would mean he could as easily not appeal to her, leaving him open to abandonment. It is through his work that he can make himself appealing to her and at the same time avoid the totally arbitrary caprice of personal attraction and affection. This means that men's work activity is focused on something outside of themselves, on something that exists independently of themselves. Existing in the world, it is able to exist in the world of the female, and indeed to mediate his relationship with her. The meaning of work therefore is invested in the product, and in what the product is intended to achieve,[4] and it is to the productive process that the self is subordinated. This focus outside of the self is, above everything else, the reason why culture has been so much the product of male activity.[5]

There is a distinction that is worthwhile making in this connection. Within the dynamics of this focus outside the self, we may perceive an interesting dimension. The content of the work men do may be seen to vary in accordance with the degree to which it conforms to external demands. At one extreme it can be entirely defined by external expectations, so there is little specific room for individual initiative. An accountant, for example, submits numbers to analysis based on precisely defined rules so that, at best, the product will not vary at all from accountant to accountant. At the other extreme, the work may be highly idiosyncratic, depending largely on the workers' sense of what it should be like. At this extreme we have the artist, whose work consists very much of making an expression of who he is. Hirschhorn (1999) distinguishes between a psychology of work based on Csikszentmihalyi's (1997) concept of "flow" and one based on Lacan's (1977) concept of *jouissance*. Hirschhorn uses the former to explain the feeling of pleasure we may derive from work, and he uses the latter to explain passion. In the former we manifest a response in a work situation that has been sufficiently well-learned that we do not have to think about it, but can simply "flow" with it. By contrast the psychology of passion involves a transgression of convention. It manifests a choice by the individual to be himself, to impose himself on the situation—a choice that is undertaken with desire, but also with a high consciousness of the risk of rejection that is involved. It is of interest to note that the need to create something outside of the self is present in both of these cases, and therefore that the passion of artistic production is very much a part of male psychology, and not incomprehensible within it, as Pollack (1998) seems to suggest.

It goes without saying, however, that most people do not take the risk of being themselves, but adapt to external demands. They are not passionate about their work and the self that they comport at work may be said to be self-estranged. I discuss this concept at a later point.

Related to the external focus of male work is its *compulsive character*. As we have seen, men need to feel secure in the love of the primordial female. The meaning of work is that it attempts to assure that security, but men cannot acknowledge this. For one thing it grows out of a fear of women that itself cannot be consciously acknowledged. For another the very premise of women's freedom is what drives the whole dynamic.

What follows from this is that the psychological significance of work consists in the fact that one can use it to assert control over something in the face of the fact that what one really wants control over is denied and unthinkable. It has, therefore, the symptomatology of a compulsion, a reaction-formation, which is invested with energy through the denial of a powerlessness that cannot be consciously accepted (Schwartz, 1982; Sullivan, 1953).

This compulsive character of male work is another feature that has resulted in the fact that so much of cultural creation has been male activity. To the extent that female identity revolves around identification with the primordial mother, this compulsion is not present. Females whose identity is cast this way have no need to appeal to the primordial mother while at the same time denying their dependence on her. In their fantasy they already *are* the primordial mother. But achievement, as McClelland (1961) discerned, arises from the *need for* achievement. It does not result, for the most part, from the *desire to* achieve. Without the need to achieve, the achievement in the form of a product is likely to be lacking.

Indeed what holds true in the objective sphere of achievement may even hold true in the subjective sphere of the feelings of self-esteem that men derive from work. The needs for self-esteem, as Maslow (1970) noted, arise from a deficiency. The male project consists in the overcoming of a deficiency. It is an interesting speculation on life's ironies that the feeling of strength arises from the need to overcome weakness (Adler, 1951).

At any rate, the compulsive character of male work has a number of dimensions. Perhaps the most obvious characteristic of male work that arises from this compulsivity is what I call the *displacement of affect*. As we have seen, the aim of male work is to be loved and admired by the female. But the recognition of the strength of this need places the male in great fear of abandonment and destruction. It cannot be acknowledged consciously and therefore shows up as an autonomous, unexplained, unquestioned drive to achieve something, to create something, whose meaning can only be understood by reference to the unconscious. So it is that the meaning of male work lies in a different direction from its apparent goal.

A second characteristic is that compulsivity lends itself to what may be called the *imposition of order*, as represented by men's history of attempts at understanding what is going on and of creating structure intentionally in accordance with that understanding. In these ways the levels of uncertainty and chaos are reduced.

Taking the displacement of affect together with the passion for order allows us to understand a third characteristic of compulsive male work, which may be seen in its reliance on *impersonal rules*, the heart of what Weber (1947) characterized as bureaucracy. In part, such rules arise from the necessity to feel in control, but we also need to observe that the obverse of impersonal rules would be feelings. As our reasoning has shown, men's feelings are displaced. Consciously they are with the work; unconsciously they are with the female. Men do not associate with each other according to feelings simply because their feelings for one another are of limited importance to them.[6]

A fourth aspect of male work that is revealed by this analysis is its orientation toward *competition*. The point here is that the object of the work cannot be acknowledged because of the dependence and helplessness that it invokes. But there must be some way of gaining a sense of success, or at least of progress in order that the whole project not seem futile. This is where competition comes in. Competition gives men a way of measuring "progress" by using comparative means. Men can measure their rate of progress against one another, and therefore avoid having to ask themselves the forbidden question of what the work is all about. Moreover the notion of "winning" comes to make sense in this connection. Winning the contest provides them with a marker enabling them to pause, even though briefly, in their drivenness. Men are racing headlong in a direction defined by the fact that what they want, but dread, is in the opposite heading. At the extreme they cannot imagine pausing, even if only temporarily, without some such artificial means.

The characteristics of male work that I have described here have all come to stand as features of the male dominance of the workplace (e.g., Ferguson, 1984). As such they have been taken as being features of the work environment that exclude women and, because excluding women is seen as being basically the only thing men do (see, for example, Cheng, 1996), have come to be seen with scorn, and as features that will be overthrown when women take their rightful place as the creators of a new meaning for life. Yet reflection suggests that such derision is inappropriate, because these characteristics have a productive side as well.

For example, the compulsiveness and displacement of affect, even though they may easily lead to one's immediate needs being ignored and not met, nevertheless leads to the mobilization of energy in the service of production for the satisfaction of other people's needs, and hence creates the basis for social exchange. The capacity to give meaning to work that is of no intrinsic interest cannot help but have an impact on the quality of work one does, even if it is not pleasurable, just because it needs to be done. Indeed it can generate an entirely new kind of pleasure, rooted in the sense of accomplishment. And competitiveness may be offensive to some, but the economic world is competitive: firm against firm, country against country. When we recognize that competition concerns the drive to do things better than others, we can see that the continual improvement it demands has had its effect in the rise in standard of living that has marked the modern world. That rise in standard of living has made it possible, finally, for large groups of people to live beyond poverty. This has never happened before, and did not happen all by itself. Consistency demands that those who have scorn for its prerequisities must either express a willingness to give it up, or a reasonable and concrete plan to replace them. Neither of these has been seriously advanced.

Again the imposition of order has been found by some to be offensive, but the absence of order is not an idyllic flow of a benign nature of which we are part. It is the flow of a chaotic nature that is indifferent to us and ready to eliminate us without hesitation.

It must be the impersonality of male work that, more than anything else, has been criticized by feminists (e.g., Ferguson, 1984; Gilligan, 1982). Interaction in male work activity is ordered by rules, rather than by feelings. As I have said, this is partly the result of the passion for order but it is also because men's feelings are elsewhere, with the female. Of course one can easily lament this lack of feeling, but it is worthwhile to note that it is this unemotionality that makes possible the application of logic and rationality to the design of work.

The virtue of rationality is a point that many feminists miss because they contrast rationality with feeling and they identify feeling with warmth and love. Rationality must be contrasted, not with feeling directly, but with irrationality, and feeling must be seen to encompass not only warmth and love, but coldness and hatred. Envy, jealousy, rage, and resentment, after all, are also feelings. And it is when the complex play of our conflicting emotional forces is allowed to overcome reason that irrationality comes to dominate our affairs. We need to bear in mind that bureaucracy itself arose in opposition to nepotism and favoritism, whose distorting effects on organizational functioning will be familiar to many.

Impersonal rules mean that workers must do their work in a certain way. Yet this is an inevitable feature in any circumstance wherein what has been learned in the past is being applied in the work that is being done in the present. Indeed this work may be getting done by people who never participated in the messy and time-consuming process that led to the learning they now apply. Management thinker Peter Drucker (1993) has even maintained that it is the application of knowledge to work that has been primarily responsible for the remarkable increase in standard of living during the twentieth century. Again, order is a prerequisite for the fact that workers can count on the work of others being done in a certain way. Insofar as the different jobs are component parts of the same whole, this makes it possible for them to get their own work done. It is actually quite a wonder that, by virtue of their defined tasks, people can work in coordination with people they may have never even met. Reflection reveals that this is an absolute necessity for the development of large-scale formal organization.

Externally oriented, order imposing, compulsive, displaced, competitive, unemotional—these are the characteristics of work done from male psychology. It is easy to see how at least some of these characteristics, when carried to an extreme, could result in the kind of domination of content by form that Weber (1958) called the "iron cage." Yet, on the whole it seems difficult to evade the judgment that the work men do within this context would be generally salutary. What is produced is creative, in a very broad sense, and the overcoming of deficiency that it represents is worthy of respect. Moreover, and most important, because its orientation, even if partly unconscious, is toward an ideal female and their children, it seems deeply expressive of love and affirmative toward life.

Under the circumstances it is difficult to see how the males who are defined through this approach to work have come to be seen as toxic, as the oppressive creatures that many have come to see them as being. In order to understand how this came about, we need to go further in our exploration of the sex roles. Until this point we have based our inquiry in the relationship between the female role and fantasy. We have identified this fantasy as part of the sexual holy war, specifically as the image of Madonna-and-child. To get to the image of toxic man, we need to explore what lies outside of fantasy. But what lies outside of fantasy is reality. So our inquiry needs to move to the exploration of the relationship between reality and the male sex role.

THE SEX ROLES AND REALITY

The original nexus of child and mother is the stuff of which fantasies are made. Our idea of the maternal world represents a bond with an apparently omnipotent, loving mother, a mother who is experienced both as the whole world and as a complement of the self. As we know, this is the fantasy of Madonna-and-child. There is no room here for anything that is alien to the self, and in fact the primordial mother arose in the first place as a defense against what is alien to the self. This means that the maternal world is in conflict with reality.

Reality is, first and foremost, the world that is outside of ourselves, a world that is indifferent to us. It may be thought of as what makes our fantasies fantasies, as what makes it possible to make a mistake.

As Chasseguet-Smirgel has argued, following Freud, this is the aspect under which the father first appears. This is the critical element necessary for understanding the origins of the idea of the sexual holy war. The father is the part of the parental complex that is not the mother. He has a relationship with the mother that excludes us. We are not the center of the mother's world because part of her world is wrapped up with him. In contrast to the perfect maternal world, the father appears as a blockage, a threat, and an invading presence.

This circumstance has affective consequences of the most profound sort. For it seems to the child that, were it not for the father, it could resume a perfect union, a fusion, with the mother and have complete and perfect contentment (Chasseguet-Smirgel, 1986). The father is seen as preventing this. In this way he becomes the personification of pure evil. This is the core of the idea of the toxic male.

Looking at it this way, we can see that the objectionable aspects of this apparition do not issue from the father as such. They arise from the fact that he represents whatever it is that interferes with the fantasy that a life can be lived in fusion with the perfect mother. In a word he introduces the fact that the world does not exist to satisfy our desires. It is unconnected to us and indifferent to us. The father brings to us the fact of this disconnected real world and its indifference. In fact, as we ultimately see, the repudiation of the father is rooted in the repudiation of reality itself.

For the present, carrying on with the revised Freudian conception, we note that, within the traditional family, the male and the female roles embody different orientations toward reality because of the sexes' different orientations toward the ego ideal.

To the extent that she identifies with the primordial mother, the female orientation toward the ego ideal is formed from the fantasy of being both parties in the infant/mother matrix. To this extent the woman encounters indifferent reality as if it were an anomaly. Indifference begins and remains foreign to her—incommensurable with her idea of the maternal world.

The traditional female role is marked by a profound emotional identification with her child, a dissolution of boundaries and an immediacy that needs to be understood in terms of the logic of mothering. Specifically its function lies in the comfort and warmth that it brings to the child. As the child experiences the mother as the whole world, so the mother's love for the child gives him or her the experience of being the center of a loving world. Later on, as Freud noted, it also adds to the closeness of the relationship of male and female, but this is only insofar as the woman takes the man as himself an infant. Generalizing we can see that what may be called the female style, being warm and nurturing, and even nice and placating, is itself an outgrowth of the identification with the primordial mother and the attempt to deny the difference between the infant and the mother.

The original male orientation toward the father, as the representative of alien reality, is the same as that of the female. But the impossibility of the little boy becoming its own mother leads to a different relationship with the father. As we have seen, the child projects a power equal to the primordial mother's onto the father, making the assumption that the father is doing something that the mother values and through which she finds him appealing and worthy of her company. Identification with that role then becomes, for the male, the conception of the route back to the mother in the attainment of the ego ideal. But the father's place is at the family's boundary with external reality, and hence dealing with external reality becomes the definition of the male role.

This, then, is the traditional differentiation of sex roles. The female role involves identification with the primordial mother. Oriented toward herself as the ego ideal, she maintains the possibility of dissolution of boundaries within a loving world, which the developing child needs. The complement of this role is that of the male, who engages indifferent reality and keeps it, so to speak, at arms' length, so that the world consisting of her and their children can be a safe and loving one. As we have seen, this provides the meaning of the male work role. To get a deeper sense of this role, it is useful to see what the psychology of engaging indifferent reality amounts to.

WORK AND ITS DISCONTENTS

If the world were our mother, we could simply be ourselves, do what we want, and be loved for it. But, for the man, although returning to the maternal world is his unconscious goal, the route to its attainment is through engaging the external world. This means, above all else, that he cannot simply do what he wants, or at least that he does not expect to be loved for doing what he wants. His belief is that he must do what he needs to do in the face of indifferent reality, not what he wants to do, if he is going to be loved.

Dealing with indifferent, external reality means the decentering of the self. It means placing oneself within the framework of impersonal exchange relationships and reciprocal demands that define what it means to be a member of society. It means the internalization of these external demands to form obligations (Schwartz, 1983). Taken together what we see here is the formation of the modern superego (Freud, 1923, 1930).

The superego is the psychological underpinning of[7] work within modern capitalism. It is the basis of the moral element that Adam Smith (1759) recognized was necessary for the capitalist economy to do its progressive work. But it comes with a price. Consider Freud's (1923) formulation for this dynamic: "If I were the father and you were the child, I should treat you badly." What this suggests is that work energized in this way is not likely to be pleasurable.

This is easy enough to see. The person must deny his wants, his desires, and his impulses, the satisfaction of which would be what would give him pleasure. These must become a source of anxiety for him. It is this anxiety that drives the compulsive, externally oriented work activity that we have already discussed.

It drives him to make his way in a world that is not oriented around his impulses. He must *estrange himself* from himself, construct a self for the purpose of work that is not his own self, but is defined by the constraints and demands of the outside world. Yet these constraints and demands are out of his control. They are uncertain and can be known only in a limited way, and yet knowing them is vital for him, if he is going to be able to cope with the world. From this it can be seen that although he needs to understand and engage the world, he cannot, in any more than a limited way, have certainty about it or safety within it. The result must be that his experience with it must be a source of self-estrangement, insecurity, and stress.

We can see that the male role involves insecurity and stress arising from uncertainty in a number of different dimensions. I do not wish to provide an exhaustive list, but a few of these dimensions seem particularly noteworthy. First of all there is the physical dimension. The person is a physical being in a physical external world, which is not organized around him and poses the possibility of danger, of threats to his body.

The physical dimension of uncertainty may be the most palpable cause of stress in the workplace, but another form of uncertainty, although far from obvious, may be equally important in understanding the dynamics of the sexual holy war. I refer to what I call *moral uncertainty*.

As we have seen, the impetus behind the work role, as it has been defined by men, is to transform the indifferent world into a place where fantasy can reign. The worker stands at the boundary of the fantasy of love within his family and the outside world. The problem is that the outside world is also made up others who are trying to maximize their own fantasy realms.[8] This puts the person who is trying to maximize his income in the position of being seen by others as representing a blockage to their own maximization, making the person prone to the feeling of guilt.

Guilt is the way that one, through the superego, treats oneself badly. In one's imagination, one finds oneself condemned, and unworthy of love, by those whom one has brought into oneself, and undertaken to take seriously, on their own terms. To some extent we can avoid feelings of guilt by participating in relationships where the terms of exchange are clearly defined and everyone knows what is going on. But these rules are social conventions. They exist only by consensus. Yet the consensus is never complete; it is always changing, and therefore subject to individuals' self-enhancing judgments of their own entitlement.

What is more, the very basis of the consensus can be repudiated. A system based on the idea that one's rewards should be in accordance with what one puts in, for example, can be opposed by the idea that everyone should have equal rewards, or that rewards should be bestowed in accordance with one's previous deprivation, and so on. This means that the moral basis on which one justifies what one has is always in question. It puts any person who has anything at all, which by definition means anyone alive, in the stressful position of being subject to guilt.

Certainly the most obvious form in which uncertainty occurs in work is *economic uncertainty*. Work is rarely done in such a way that the person who produces something is the same person as the one who uses it. Rather most work takes place in a complex matrix of social exchange called the market, in which producers and consumers interact through the medium of money. However, the market is extremely dynamic, and no one's place within it is assured. As the dynamism of the market increases, so economic insecurity is increasingly a cause of stress.

Different work roles and different workers, of course, differ in the level and type of uncertainty that they involve, or choose. But working life is never free of stress. In the traditional breakdown of sex roles, men have dealt with this stress by giving it a meaning. It is something they have put up with for the sake of their families, and from which they have retreated to the homes that they have made possible.

THE POWER AND POLITICS OF THE SEX ROLES

The sex roles that we have defined have not existed in isolation, but have articulated with one another and made each other possible. These sex roles have been dependent on one another, and this mutual dependence is what has given them their stability. Mutual dependence means mutual power (Emerson, 1962), and we need to see the sources of power in this relationship.

Family life requires a degree of stability if it is going to serve as a place of comfort. Hence it falls to the person, or persons, who are earning the money for the family to absorb the stress and insecurity of the workplace in ways that permit a relative stability in income.

By taking on the role of dealing with the uncertainties of the workplace, even at the cost of stress, men have traditionally created a dependency on the part of women. This has certainly been a source of power. But the power men have gained in this regard has itself been an attempt to generate a countervailing power to that of the female, without which it would be meaningless. As I have said, union with the female, given meaning by her association with the primordial mother, is at the core of men's motivational structure. There is no unilateral power in the traditional relationship between men and women. Both have had power. It is now necessary to show how these dynamics of power have played themselves out in contemporary sex relationships.

Men have always been wounded in their engagements with the world. They have always estranged themselves and borne the brunt of stress. They have taken on these burdens to create a home under the aegis of their women. The home was intended to be the place where their self-estrangement and stress were relieved, where they could simply be themselves among the women and children they loved, and which made it possible for them to reengage the world. To the extent that women have valued what men have done, and offered the promise of the maternal world to them, women have offered healing of the wound that work entails. In this way, even given the fact that his desire for her has been matched by his fear of her, the pain of the work that he has done has been given sense.

If she believes that the male role is hard, that men who undertake it estrange themselves from themselves, that it is full of stress and that the only reason men do it is for love, she knows that she has power here. She believes that she can make the man's life meaningful or meaningless by the gift or withdrawal of love. The psyche contains no greater power than that, because it creates the very possibility for all other forms of power. Understanding this she believes that the dependency she feels on the man is part of a mutual dependency. It is her belief that the wound he undergoes for love of her makes sense only if it is healed by her love, that makes her love for him consistent with her own sense of power in this connection. As Benjamin has observed (1988), it is only the sense of power that makes possible the free giving of love, and the free giving of love is what the whole project is all about.

We know that there are potential instabilities built into this arrangement. Both of them may be seen to arise from the possibility of the breakdown of mutual dependence. Mutual dependence means that one is subject to the power of another, yet, as we have seen the ultimate aim, for all of us, is fusion with the omnipotent primordial mother, who is not subject to the power of anyone.

The threat to the traditional division of labor arises from the fantasy of attaining this omnipotence, or, rather, from the belief that this fantasy is attainable, that omnipotence is possible. This belief arises from two related sources, one issuing from what has traditionally been the male role and the other from the female.

HIERARCHICAL OMNIPOTENCE

The primordial mother, whose omnipotence underlies the power of the female, is, after all, a fantasy. We may imagine her in the form of a woman, but she may underlie other images as well. Any fantasy of the ego ideal will involve a projection of the primordial mother. And, historically, other entities have served that function. Success, the nation, the revolution—any idea we have of an ultimate cause—are images of fusion with the primordial mother. In our society one representation in particular is worthy of mention in our present connection.

Characteristic of the modern organization has been the attempt to draw its members into itself as a basis of meaning. For this purpose it utilizes the uncertainty that work entails and the promise of relieving its stress through progress up the organizations' hierarchy. As I have argued elsewhere (1990; also see Jackall, 1988), this involves the generation of an image of the organization, and the high officials who represent it, as omnipotent and perfect: identical with their roles in a perfect organization, free of uncertainty, and entirely capable of coping with the world. I call this image, in which the organization itself represents the ego ideal, the *organization ideal*. Central as it is to the organization's motivational structure, the maintenance of this image becomes increasingly central to the role of the manager, as he rises within the corporation, and support of the manager's presentation of this image increasingly becomes central to the role of his subordinates.

Now, the creation of this image, by itself, does not alleviate self-estrangement, uncertainty, and stress. In fact, by creating a poorly delineated official view of the world, to which one must conform, it may increase uncertainty, especially of the moral sort, and the attendant stress. Nor does it necessarily decrease economic uncertainty, often only raising the level of income at which one feels it. But for those who have bought into the organization ideal, the uncertainty and stress they experience do not bring the image into question. Rather they provide additional impetus to advance further up the hierarchy, where the image, they believe, will be realized. This increase in investment in the organization is likely to be justified by a further buttressing of the idea of the organization ideal.

As the level of an individual's power increases, both in reality and potentially, it becomes increasingly likely that the individual will break away from the real demands of his situation and its uncertainties and indulge himself in the fantasy of his omnipotence. For them attaining the highest level of the organization would mean the end of self-estrangement. It would mean being identical with an omnipotent organizational role, and hence omnipotence. They would have embraced their own self-estrangement and redefined their selves in terms of the organization. Such individuals have, in effect, redefined the organization's highest levels as the maternal world. For such persons the use of the family to alleviate self-estrangement and stress becomes limited. They have, in effect, married the organization. In this fantasy, which is more real to them than reality itself, they would not need anybody. At the extreme their emotional dependence on real women would be undone, and the woman's power in the relationship eliminated.

What we see here is one cause of the breakdown of the sexual division of labor, and one that we can say has its origin in the male role. We discuss this further in the next chapters. For the present I turn to the source of the breakdown that arises from the female role. More than the male fantasy of hierarchical omnipotence, it is the origin of the idea of sexual holy war.

MATERNAL OMNIPOTENCE

The traditional male role consists in men separating themselves from their desires and creating an estranged self, defined by its obligations. They do this to keep reality at bay, and reduce uncertainty and stress within the family. If the man is successful, the female can maintain her own identification with the primordial mother and preside over a home where love can circulate freely. The problem is that if the work of the male is sufficiently successful in distancing reality, the idea that reality is different from fantasy can become lost. Reality would then, so to speak, lose its reality. If this were to happen, the meaning of the male role would become lost as well. If the woman should come to the conclusion that coping with reality is not a cause of pain and stress, she would have to conclude that what the man does is not the expression of an estranged self, but is a selfish expression of his desire. Then the basis for her positive valuation of him would be lost and the whole process would unravel. Her belief that he has separated himself from himself and is in pain from stress would evaporate,[9] and the need of the man, limited as he is, could come to be seen as a selfish demand. The only reason women would satisfy it would be the dependency that men (e.g., MacKinnon, 1989) have imposed on them.

Moreover, if the reality of reality were lost, there would be nothing keeping the female identification with the primordial mother from becoming total. If that were to happen, she would identify herself with the sense of omnipotence that the figure of the primordial mother contains. Under this identification she would be swallowed up by narcissism. She would imagine that she could make life perfect simply through her love and goodness, just by being herself. She would come to experience the boundaries of the family, not as a barrier for keeping indifferent reality at bay, but as a prison confining her potential. Whatever causes of imperfection or limitation that existed in the world would be thought to exist only because her capacity to make things perfect is being stifled.

In comparison to her fantasized omnipotence, she would not experience the actual power she has over the man as power. At the same time, her image of the magnitude of his power over her would be measured by the limitations that he has apparently placed on her omnipotence. In comparison with her goodness, its sources would seem to come from pure evil.

The result of all of this would be that the interdependence and the balance of power between men and women would break down. The female's reliance on the male would come to seem to her to be a process of oppression in which, not only she, but also the whole world, comes under the domination of evil. Throw off this evil and her natural goodness will guarantee that the world will be the maternal world. Appropriate the work role, which has traditionally been the major source of men's power over women, and the basis of this power will be massively diminished. Obviously what we have here is the psychological basis of the sexual holy war and the place of the workplace revolution within it.

There is a problem here, one may imagine. Throwing over the traditional sex role differentiation and taking on the work role for herself should rapidly dispel the myth in which it originated. Going into the workplace should lead her to exactly the self-estrangement and uncertainty that men have engaged, which has caused the stress from which they have suffered. Should this not dispel the idea that they were simply performing their work roles out of their own selfish desire? Would this not inevitably lead to a reappreciation of the traditional arrangement?

The answer is that it would, if it could be assumed that engaging reality would mean having to take it seriously on its own terms. But the whole premise of her omnipotence is that constraint, limitation, indifference, are forces of evil. This is a view that can be maintained if it is assumed that when these features of the world are met with in the workplace, they are not there as inevitable features of the workplace. They are there, rather, because men put them there. This reattribution of work's discontents is the subject matter of the next chapter of our inquiry.

NOTES

1. Chasseguet-Smirgel's analysis is in many respects similar to the analyses of Chodorow (1978) and Dinnerstein (1976). These latter writers, it seems to me, do not sufficiently appreciate the complexity of the psychodynamics arising from

male ambivalence. In a word, they understand only the dynamic of separation, without understanding that separation is not an end in itself, but rather serves to provide an opportunity for reunification.

2. It is important not to see this as a categorical distinction and therefore make too much of it. Freud was quite clear that there was considerable overlap between the psychology of men and women, and Chasseguet-Smirgel follows suit. Girls certainly identify with their fathers and form the superego. Moreover identifying with mothers who had previously identified with their own fathers serves the same function, and one can go down the line as far as one wants with this. Again, men can identify with their mothers. To a large extent, the difference I am suggesting is not so much qualitative as quantitative. Nonetheless there is an element of identity that is involved in the question of whether one identifies with one's mother or one's father, and this is a source of one's sexual identity, even when the mother or father one identifies with has strong elements of the other sex.

3. In this context we can see the origins of male violence against women. Contemporary feminist theory regards it as an attempt to control women, as political, as simply a tactic in a strategy of subjugation. This view rests on a profound misunderstanding of the male ambivalence toward women. The feminists see one component of this ambivalence, but to see only one component of an ambivalence is to see much less than half of the whole matter, because each half is given meaning only by its relationship to the other. The basic ambivalence here is between fear and desire. The violence is the product of the fear, but the fear is strong only because the desire is strong. Male violence against women is not a cold-blooded, rational attempt at control. It is hot, it is passionate, and it is, above all, desperate.

Men love women; women are the most important things in their lives. Masculinity, the pursuit of the male ego ideal, the metric of a man's life, is given meaning by that desire. When it seems to become impossible, the meaning of a man's life is lost; whatever he knows to do to pursue it, he knows will be to no avail. Yet there is nothing he can do that he knows will work. Men know that violence against women is absurd, but it is the frustration of understanding that absurdity and hopelessness that drives it. It is mute and stupid because it understands itself to be beyond language, reason, and rationale. Male violence against women is not an expression of the essence of masculinity, but of its breakdown.

Exploration of the psychology of female violence against men will have to wait for another occasion.

4. A few years ago I was at a conference at a university that was simultaneously holding a conference of ministers. I was sitting next to a couple of them at lunch. I can still hear one of them saying to another, in the voice of someone who had lost patience with others who could not understand the simple truth that was so obvious to him, "We're human *beings*, not human *doings*." Of course, in the eyes of God, who loves us just as we are, we may well be human beings, but

in the eyes of our fellow humans, who for the most part have no reason to give a damn about us, our only importance lies in what we do.

5. Anyone looking at the vast efflorescence of women's cultural products during our time cannot avoid the observation that the vast bulk of them lack external focus and focus exclusively on themselves. Such self-absorption is rarely a characteristic of great endeavors.

6. There are important apparent exceptions to this, but the deviations here are more apparent than real. For example male feelings of rivalry among each other are often quite profound and powerful. But it is easy enough to see that underlying the feeling of rivalry is desire for the female, who is, after all, the object for whom the rivalry is being conducted. More difficult is the case in which, as we discuss later, men working together in extremely harsh circumstances, such as combat, often develop feelings for each other that are quite considerable and that, by all accounts, form the basis of their association. One may say in such cases that the group becomes its own mother. The need for the mother, for the female, is so profound here that men must create it and project it onto their own association.

7. Foucault, who describes this internalization most vividly in his description of the "panopticon" (1979), both sees its place in the capitalist order and recognizes that it is not fun. His denial of cultural progress is partly due to the fact that he does not see the achievement involved in this. Specifically he does not sufficiently credit the idea that this internalization is not of capricious persons, but of rules that the authorities themselves are bound by—rules that are themselves required to make sense. This process that underlies legal-rational authority (Weber, 1947) sets limits on the individual, but greatly expands the possibility of freedom for the individual within those limits and for the collectivity concerning the specific limits themselves. Foucault's evident preference for drawing-and-quartering over modern penal incarceration, which is also used in support of his denial of cultural progress, may make more sense to those who share his preference for sadomasochistic sex (Eribon, 1991) than it will to others.

8. In the case that primarily concerns me, the fantasy is that of a human being with real or imagined relations with other human beings. But there is no reason to stop there, as the proponents of animal rights insist.

9. Actually this reduction is often intentional. In this way we may understand the "macho" image that some males try to project. It arises from two sources. First is the necessity to shield the female from anxiety, which he could not do if he were to bring it in with him into the family constellation. Second is the fact that his denial of pain and anxiety is an attempt to maintain his own image of heroism, which is the dramaturgical device through which he validates his presence in the maternal world, and denies his dependence on her, as we have seen earlier.

Chapter Three

Feminist Reattribution of Work's Discontents

The view that the adverse features of working life are the result of male domination is by no means monopolized by a feminist fringe. It has penetrated well into the mainstream. An example here is a well-received book by Elizabeth Perle McKenna (1997) called *When Work Doesn't Work Anymore: Women, Work, and Identity*. Her work serves us well as an illustration of the process of reattribution.

MCKENNA'S COMPLAINT

A graduate of Yale, McKenna worked in book publishing for almost twenty years, rising to such positions as associate publisher of Bantam Books and publisher of Prentice-Hall, Addison-Wesley, and William Morrow/Avon Books. As her career developed, she increasingly felt a conflict between its demands and "having a life," especially as it revolved around her family. At a certain point, her upward progress came to an end. Then she began to take her conflict seriously and wound up quitting her job.

My answer to this increase in internal friction was to ignore it as long as possible. But when I finally experienced a big reversal in my work, I had nothing to fall back on but denial. (p. 12)

Believe me, when I left my job, I had no idea that this hidden drama had been brewing just below the surface, informing my discontent. I thought I was unhappy because the management had changed or one thousand other things. (pp. 13–14)

Now if McKenna's point were that the demands of career and personal life create conflicts that one must resolve by choosing one over the other, there would be nothing either exceptional or objectionable about her ideas, but that is not her point: "We don't want to be asked to choose between two parts of ourselves any more than we want to be asked to choose between outdated, old-fashioned, and gender-based lifestyles" (16).

Her point is, instead, that such conflicts are occasioned by the fact that work organization has been dominated by men, especially men with wives at home, and has been structured to serve their interests. This orientation is what caused McKenna's conflict, and the conflict of many women in her position. These women are the intended audience and beneficiaries of her thoughts:

This is a book for women who feel that the way they work better fits a man with a wife at home to take care of life. (p. 17)

The working world remains a segregated place. A place built for men with full-time wives at home to take care of the rest of life. (p. 39)

Again the question is whether the situation would be the same for a woman who had a husband at home "to take care of life"? Is McKenna saying simply that, relieved of having to "take care of life" by having a wife at home, men can devote more time and energy to their work, and hence set standards of work productivity with which women, who want to "have a life" as well as work, cannot compete? In that case the matter would be symmetric for a woman who had a man at home. Yet this is not what McKenna has in mind. For her there are differences between men and women that go beyond the energy their living arrangements make available for work:

We didn't see that achieving the success of our mentors actually meant that we would start complying with a certain system of behavior that governs the way most businesses work. . . .
    This set of rules reflects the male culture that created them, and achieving any real success is very hard without obeying them. We may not have been aware that there was a cultural difference at work in our climb up our organizations but, once we had been working for a while, found that we didn't quite agree with some of these rules. (p. 48)

This, of course, sets the stage for McKenna's treatment of the self-estrangement inherent in the work role, an approach that, predictably, blames self-estrangement on male dominance:

[I]f we want our careers to flourish, we start to find that how we act and what we privately feel are not always the same. We quickly learn that if we are to have any chance at competing for the good jobs, we go with what our office cultures dictate, even if it goes against our best interests. We find out that saying what we think and doing what we believe is right does not necessarily produce good results. If a woman wants to succeed, by the time she gets to her first job performance review, she has learned two things: 1) Her first job is the right behavior—right by what the prevailing culture says is right—and 2) if she wants to get ahead, acting right is more important than being right. (p. 49)

There is no sense here that all of this is as true for the man who wants to succeed as it is for the woman. Nor will it appear to anyone familiar with corporate life that the demands for McKenna to play-act were in any way extreme:

It's not that I was a macho female from nine to five and a real femme from five to nine. I was more or less the same, somewhat outspoken, opinionated woman at work and at home. Like many of the successful women I interviewed, I considered myself a feminist and felt I had an obligation to speak out and not hide my light under a business suit. But as time went on, as I became responsible for more than myself, that more gutsy, abrasive side quieted down. I often found myself faced with the option of being what I considered "right" or getting the resources I needed to do the job correctly. I could either make a stand, or save the energy, keep the confidence of the person who hired me, and be able to publish a book well or hire another person. In my quest to have it all I put away part of myself. (p. 67)

Here again, there is no sense at all on McKenna's part that she has simply discovered the dark side of corporate organization (Schwartz, 1990; Jackall, 1988). As a result, her perfectly normal response to this requirement:

But this double life takes a slow toll on us. We start to resent our work for asking us to dissemble and we start to lose self-esteem for doing so. (p. 67)

is easily dragooned into the service of the sexual holy war. Thus she gives us this from Elizabeth Debold, one of the authors of *Mother Daughter Revolution*:

"What naturally happens when you overlay yourself and develop a false sense that goes against core values and connections is depression. This is a totally predictable result because what you are doing is dampening, silencing, and subduing a whole part of who you are." What happens, Debold says, is that over time the rage at having to trade in whole parts of ourselves builds up so much that it could blow up the world. "The submerged parts of yourself that you roped into a really fragile balance start to move around. We get furious at our bosses, our coworkers, our mates, our children. We start to feel that at any time the lid might blow sky high. But we keep saying, 'Things are fine, the problem's just me,' because to engage in the bigger problem, the institutionalized problem, is too overwhelming, too enraging. Women don't yet have a decent way of analyzing this and the working world hasn't changed enough so that there are real alternatives." (p. 80)

Elizabeth Debold points out that if the depression can turn into anger, good things can come of it. "The woman's movement was founded on rage," she notes. "The question is how do you take that rage, that energy, that sense of 'I can't believe this!' and use it? If you can't use it," she concludes, "it feels like it will just corrode your insides." (p. 81)

THE REATTRIBUTION OF WORKPLACE UNCERTAINTY

As self-estrangement is transformed from a characteristic of the situation to a condition caused by men, so is the uncertainty that feminists find in their work roles. They do not have to understand it as a characteristic of indifferent reality. They can see workplace uncertainty as a part of men's oppressive rule, to be overcome as they defeat men in the sexual holy war and re-create the world through the blessing of the love that arises from their natural, authentic goodness. If they define uncertainty in this way, their affective response to it will not be insecurity and stress, but rage against men for having caused it.

This would feed into the massive program to scapegoat men that, as we saw in the first chapter, has become a major component of contemporary culture. The scapegoating program is multifaceted, and we now examine some of its manifestations as they are defined by the forms of uncertainty that can be encountered in work.

To begin with relatively simple matters, men's physical uncertainty can be redefined as the concomitant of something men have chosen to do: a result of their own aggression, of the machismo that serves to show how tough they are. Women's physical uncertainty would come to seem an anomaly, the result of male domination of the workplace, and to be overcome when the workplace is redefined to take the needs of women into account. In a paper delivered at the International Society for the Psychoanalytic Study of Organizations, Recinello (1996) observed that when women entered the workplace, they were placed in dangerous jobs, and cited the Triangle Shirtwaist Factory fire as an example. But the fact that the Triangle fire is remembered, as opposed to the many losses incurred by men in the workplace, itself testifies to the anomaly of women being in a situation of danger.

The National Institute for Occupational Safety and Health estimates that, even in this era of government oversight, between 7,000 and 11,000 lives are lost in the workplace. Farrell (1993: 416–417), using U.S. government statistics, notes that 94 percent of injury-related occupational deaths occur to men and that every day almost as many men are killed on the job as were killed in combat during an average day in the Vietnam war. The more hazardous the job, he notes, the greater the percentage of men, and he gives these examples:

Fire Fighting	99% Male
Logging	98% Male
Trucking (heavy)	98% Male
Construction	98% Male
Coal Mining	97% Male

He contrasts these with the least dangerous jobs, which are typically held by females, giving these examples:

Secretary	99% Female
Receptionist	97% Female

The simple fact is that women have not moved heavily into jobs that are physically dangerous, and so the degree to which women have to redefine their physical uncertainty is limited.

The matter becomes much more interesting with regard to moral stress. Farrell (1993) has argued that the sexual division of labor has also been a division of moral responsibility. Men's job has been to preserve the innocence of women by taking the moral responsibility on themselves. This view accords with our thinking. Men have created the capacity of women to maintain the maternal world, in which love circulates freely and no one is held guilty. In order to do this, men have accepted the burden of guilt. Farrell addresses this matter in terms of the defender role. Men, in their role as soldiers, are the ones who kill in order that women do not have to kill. But the point applies to economic activity as well. In order to maximize love within the family, men have undertaken activity which has made them feel guilty, or been held guilty by others, or in which they simply have been guilty.[1]

The burden of guilt that men have assumed has come to serve as their own indictment. Although the man's situation has lent itself to moral ambiguity, the woman's conception of her innocence, ironically made possible by the man's assumption of guilt, can be absolute. From the standpoint of that innocence, women can look upon morally compromised men with the disdain of the morally superior.

Nor will it help for a man to say that he is not guilty because he is operating within the established rules. For women can rejoin that the rules have, after all, been established by men, and therefore bring with them men's iniquity. They might say, for example, that the rule that work should be rewarded in accordance with its productivity is only a smokescreen for the powerful to abuse the weak. And they might suggest, instead, a rule in which everyone is rewarded equally. A man might respond that, within a rather short period of time, society will lose the ability to reward productive behavior, with the result being that there will be much less of it. But this response may not carry much weight. If one gives up the idea of an objective reality, one loses the idea of consequences. Then rules come to be assessed on the basis of purely subjective criteria and on the basis of whether one likes them, and those who introduce even the notion of reality into the conversation are met with moral revulsion.

The point is that although men stand at the boundary between the fantasy of the maternal world and external reality, women, to the extent that they identify with the primordial mother, do not. For the woman who defines herself in terms of this identification, the whole world should be the maternal world; her desires, selfless as she assumes them to be, define what is morally good. What is morally bad is what contravenes her desires. Ultimately this is reality itself, and its representative—the man. What we can see from this is the way stress caused by moral uncertainty can become transformed into self-righteous moral rage against men for having corrupted the world. Men are not guilty because the world is the way it is, they can say. The world is the way it is because men are guilty.

For one thing, men are selfish. For example, despite the fact that it was her husband's income that made it possible for her to quit her job and write her book, McKenna offers this general comment on the nature of men: "Our personal lives, too, aren't exactly what we pictured growing up. . . . Even if we had wanted a prince and the prince had come along, chances are he needed our income just as much as he needed his own" (p. 27).

Generally what McKenna finds to be the morally questionable aspects of the workplace seem to relate to men's atavistically toxic, animal nature:

. . . an unwritten set of rules directs her fate—a Darwinian system that weeds out those with no stomach for politics, competition, or monofocused ambition. The rules of the system were designed to help men distinguish leaders from followers, and to determine who ran the pack as top dog. (p. 51)

Women, in their moral superiority, will set it right. Thus:

We started to know that if running our offices had been up to us, we would probably have included some different criteria in our definition of business success. Women who have reached a level of achievement say that if they were *really* in charge, if things were *really* up to them, work would operate very differently. They would reward collaboration, not competition, among co-workers. They would share information and their definition of success would depend more on the quality of what was produced than on the system that produced it. Conventional business success, measured in terms of power and hierarchy, would cede to job sharing and teamwork. As Anna Quindlen put it, "If women were in charge, we would feminize the way things work. Not just because we are right but because it would make things better for everyone." (pp. 48–49)

In all of this we find an analysis that authorizes the transformation of moral uncertainty into a political program to feminize the workplace so that it would reflect women's morally superior nature.

Perhaps the most important form of insecurity for women, given that their primary reason for entering the workplace was economic, is economic insecurity. Due to their capacity to affect the formation of public policy, the ways in which they redefine economic insecurity and stress are also, therefore, profoundly important.

THE REDEFINITION OF ECONOMIC UNCERTAINTY

One important way of redefining economic insecurity is to explain it away as the result of "sexism" in the workplace. Here it is asserted that women's economic insecurity is caused by discrimination on account of their sex, without which they would be better off than they are. Sometimes this takes the form of the supposition that women make less than men for the same work. This charge is made despite the fact that this would make organizations subject to expensive lawsuits, and despite the fact that if women would do the equivalent work more cheaply, it would be hugely profitable for them to replace the men with women (Sowell, 1985). Not surprisingly specific examples of such discrimination are rarely cited.

More commonly the complaint is raised at the aggregate level. Here it is charged that women are discriminated against as a group, as shown by their aggregate earnings. Currently the popular figure is that women make only 75 cents for every dollar that men make. Serious research by economists has revealed the fallacy here. In fact, among people age twenty-seven to thirty-three, women who have never had a child earn about 98 cents for every dollar men earn. Women make less than men because of historical circumstances arising from the traditional sex role differentiation, such as lower levels of education, and from choices that they have made: to interrupt their careers for child rearing, to work in specialties that make fewer demands on one's time, and so on (Furchtgott-Roth and Stolba, 1999). These clarifications, however, rarely emerge into public discourse. In all of this, what we see is the attempt to redefine economic stress as something that is not inherent in women's working life, but something that is caused by men and that can be eliminated by eliminating the power of men.

The Glass Ceiling

A particularly interesting case here, though one that contains elements of moral uncertainty as well, is the idea of the *glass ceiling*. The glass ceiling represents the idea that some groups, specifically women in this case, are blocked in their chances for promotion because they are women—that there is a only a certain point to which they are allowed to rise.

Now, in any specific instance, it is entirely possible that a woman's career progress is stalled by features related to her sex. This may be due to old-fashioned prejudice, or it may be due to a considered judgment, right or wrong, that the female qualities that she possesses are not what is required at the higher level. As far as these acts of discrimination are concerned, whether the discrimination is rational is the sort of thing that the marketplace is good for sorting out. Obviously an organization that makes poor use of the talents of its employees will be at an economic disadvantage compared with one that does not. Charges of employment discrimination, therefore, always merit the exploration of alternative explanations.

An article by Trost (1990) in the *Wall Street Journal* observed that women managers did not quit jobs because of their families, but because they felt blocked in their advancement. Moreover women were much more likely to feel they were blocked than were men. But people's own judgments of their worth are not always the most valid indicators, and therefore when a charge of discrimination is made, it often makes sense to look at other factors that may have been responsible for that feeling.

In the case of the glass ceiling, an interesting possibility presents itself. First of all consider the imagery of the glass ceiling. The image here is of a state of perfection that you believe you can see, but that, despite any visible barriers, you can't get to. But we know this idea. It emerges from the organization ideal and the fantasy of hierarchical omnipotence, which we discussed in the previous chapter. Hierarchical omnipotence is a fantasy of perfection that one locates at high levels of the organization. We discuss it again in the next chapter, but at this point it is useful to note that the organization demands it as a performance. Someone who bought into this picture and accepted it would be surprised to discover that whatever level she had reached in the organization, her subjective experience would not match the perfection she expected to find. She could use this discovery as a further goad to motivation, or it could mean the beginning of disillusionment with the idea of "success" itself. The idea of toxic man creates another possibility. She can conclude that, because of her sex, she is not being allowed to rise to the level where the real goodness is; that she is being blocked, thwarted, and kept from participation in the bliss that she still believes is there.

This is the kind of language the women interviewed for the article used to describe their condition. They said they did not find "job satisfaction," "respect," "really meaningful work," and so on. In other words they were not finding the subjective dimension of their work to be what they expected.

This view was given credence by one of the interview subjects:

"The reasons I left had nothing to do with family," says Gloria Webster, who used to be a financial analyst for a multi-national chemical corporation. In her 14 years there, Ms. Webster says, she won regular promotions, yet could never break into management. Though she had supporters and good training opportunities, she says she finally "hit what I felt was my glass ceiling," feeling blocked as a woman by "people who didn't want me to succeed in any way." (p. B2)

The critical passage here is the expression "could never break into management." What strikes me as odd about this is that virtually anybody above the rock bottom of the organization can think of himself or herself as management. I know, for example, many first-line supervisors who think of themselves in this way. Webster, with fourteen years of regular promotions in a staff function, could surely think of herself as management if she were so inclined. Indeed the author of the article sees herself as addressing the problems of managerial women. Thus, she says, "managerial women who quit tend to do so not because of family obligations, but because they feel blocked from advancement." Trost entitled the article, "Women Managers Quit Not for Family but to Advance Their Corporate Climb."

On the other hand, as Jackall (1988) pointed out, consistent with the theory of the organization ideal, managers always experience themselves as on the margin and never able to feel sure of their status. They are never free of stress, and a large component of this stress is certainly the economic stress that concerns us. Jackall attributes this to what he calls the "probationary" character of management.

Managers experience the stress of this probationary feeling without being able to talk about it or otherwise allow it to be known by others. Indeed, as even McKenna bears witness, the performance of their organizational roles is built around denying it. To the outside observer, they may easily appear to have a sang froid that the observer lacks. It is perhaps this that Webster was thinking of when she talked of being "management," but this simply means that the performance has worked. She has not seen the stress that lies behind it. If she had she would have known that in corporate life, especially at high levels, nobody wants you to succeed—not because you are a woman, but because you are competition. A focus outside their sex would perhaps help to make the nonsexual nature of this experience manifest, but the attribution of their stress to men can preserve women from its contrast with their omnipotence. This may serve as reason enough for many of them to maintain it.

Finally with regard to economic uncertainty, we should mention that by maintaining their identification with the primordial mother, women can retain the option of being mothers. To some extent this enables them to entertain the idea, realistic or not, of leaving the workplace or of lessening their involvement. That idea, by itself, will often be effective in limiting their stress. In general, though, the idea of being mothers enables them to shift the burden of economic uncertainty to the fathers of their children. Adopting that role permits them to see their economic uncertainty as being caused by men who are not living up to their responsibility. This will not necessarily relive their uncertainty, but remember that the cause of the redefinition is not so much to relieve it as to maintain the fantasy of their goodness and omnipotence. In effect it authorizes a shift in response from stress, which threatens the sense of goodness and omnipotence, to rage, which does not. And for this purpose, all that is necessary is to find a scapegoat, someone to blame it on. This may take the form of rage against a "worthless" or "lazy" husband, or one who is not, when everything is taken into consideration, pulling his weight.[2] When the marriage is strained to the breaking point, for this or other reasons, and comes apart through divorce, this dynamic helps to generate the campaign against "deadbeat dads" that we discussed in the previous chapter.

WHERE WE ARE

In our time the distinction between reality and fantasy has become lost, and, along with it, the understanding that reality calls upon us to do what we do not want to do, and the association of work and stress. The result has been that the entire conception of male activity has changed and, with it, the meaning of the sexual division of labor. If men have simply been doing what they have wanted to do, if their activity has been pleasure, then it is evidently something that women have been deprived of and excluded from. The traditional differentiation of sex roles has come to be seen as a structure of aggression, subordination, and oppression. Under the circumstances women could assume that breaking down the sex roles, especially with regard to work, would be a righteous world-historic liberating act.

Yet work does involve engagement with reality and therefore is a sphere in which self-estrangement often must be undertaken and uncertainty encountered. Consistent with their revolutionary perspective, women could redefine self-estrangement and uncertainty as being caused by male oppression. But they were not caused by men, and women's attempts at redefinition, therefore, must involve distortions of reality. Inevitably this must mean that their orientation toward work must reflect these distortions and be inadequate for their own purposes of self-understanding. As a result work is likely to be a source of profound uneasiness for them, in which their sense of why they are doing what they are doing is unclear and their disorientation is palpable. Expecting too much from it, they will be continuously dissatisfied with what they have got. And there will be no way of reconciling themselves to their disappointment, short of giving up the illusions that gave birth to their enthusiasm for work in the first place. To be sure they can increasingly experience rage and scapegoat men, but that is likely only to make matters worse and to further distort their sense of what they are doing.

The altered conception of sexual relations revolves around archaic conceptions of the mother and father. The father, as we saw, appears within the infant's world as an alien force who excludes the infant from the nexus of infant/mother that is the substance of fantasy. If the father, whom as we have seen represents reality, represents the objective world that is indifferent to us, can be delegitimated, if his power over the mother can be seen as aggression and as serving only his own interest, liberation from the father can be seen as the route to the maternal world. In other words the repudiation of reality would become a righteous, legitimated, liberating act. As Chasseguet-Smirgel (1986) wrote in a passage quoted earlier: "The father, his penis and reality itself must be destroyed in order for the paradise world of the pleasure principle to be regained" (p. 30).

What lies behind the sexual holy war, the war between Madonna-and-child and the toxic man, is precisely this attempt to destroy the father, his penis, and reality itself in order to realize the infantile fantasy of fusion with the mother. What we can see from this is that the conflict between the sexes that characterizes our time is not really, at the deepest level, a conflict between the sexes. It is intrapsychic—a conflict between two ideas, ideas that themselves emerge from two levels of mental functioning. One of them is organized around the figure of the primordial mother, a projection of our infantile desire for boundless love within a universe made to our order. Freud called it the *pleasure principle*. The other is based upon our capacity to take the external world, which is not loving and does not revolve around us, into account. Freud (1911) referred to this as the *reality principle*.

This leads us to two conclusions whose importance cannot be overemphasized:

- First it is only because these two principles are represented by the (female) mother and the (male) father, and only to the extent that men and women are identified with these sexual roles, that this conflict develops the aspect of a sexual war.

- Second we can see that there not only is a difference in kind between these two principles, there is also a developmental difference. A reversion to the primordial mother, the embodiment of the pleasure principle, is a deep and profound regression.

The pleasure principle, revolving around the primordial mother, is developmentally prior to the reality principle, which defines the role of the father. Its operation is therefore less subject to rational control. Again the primordial mother is the whole world to the infant, in a way that the father is not. She exists in a world in which the existence of an external world has not been comprehended. Indeed she is used to defend against the external world. Her power is therefore experienced as limitless, and it is directed against the very idea of an indifferent external world. For these reasons the pleasure principle is more emotionally powerful than the reality principle.

It follows from these considerations that what underlies the sexual holy war is something far more dangerous than even a war between the sexes. It is nothing less than a revolt of the primitive and the emotional against the mature and the rational. It is driven by the most powerful forces within the psyche. The self-confidence of these primitive forces is not put to the test of coping with reality, and therefore is boundless. Being prior to a sense of limitation and a capacity for self-reflection, it is profoundly antagonistic to both of these. Seeing itself as identical with all of the goodness in the world, it sees everything that differs from it as corruption and oppression. With a sense of perfect righteousness, it undertakes to remake the world in its image, and its scope is limitless. Get over the sense that, since it is represented as female, it is benign, and one can see that its potential danger is immense. An illustration of this danger is provided in a paper by Calás and Smircich (1991), to which we now turn our attention.

CALÁS AND SMIRCICH

Published in the academic journal *Organization Studies*, "Voicing Seduction to Silence Leadership" is a work that helped take the sexual holy war into organization theory and demonstrates its danger. Fascinating and infuriatingly brilliant, it was written with a postmodernist[3] disdain for referential language. It has to be understood through the feelings it evokes. I try to convey these feelings here.

Calás and Smircich attempt to make a case for substituting female leadership for the male leadership that has been dominant in our organizations, as represented by the organization theory created by male authors. They begin by quoting a passage from the postmodernist writer Jean Baudrillard:

Everything is seduction and nothing but seduction.
   They wanted us to believe that everything was production. The leitmotive of world transformation, the play of productive forces is to regulate the flow of things. Seduction is merely an immoral, frivolous, superficial, and superfluous process: one within the realm of signs and appearances; one that is devoted to pleasure and to the usufruct of useless bodies. What if everything, contrary to appearances—in fact according to the secret rule of appearances—operated by (the principle of) seduction? (567)

On this basis Calás and Smircich maintain that leadership is nothing but seduction. Because seduction is sexual, obviously, in their view, it can be gendered—divided into male and female forms. They further maintain that, in the past, it has been male seduction, and they illustrate this by various "readings" of the management literature which reveals this male orientation. They counter these, in some cases, with attempts at providing a female form.

In brief Calás and Smircich tell us that male sexuality is homosexual, with men interested in nothing but themselves. Their interest in women is only to use them to bolster their own grandiosity. Men's apparent sexual interest in women is only a cover for power and domination.

Executive thinker Chester Barnard's leader, for example, turns out to be a homosexual "priest," who cannot acknowledge his homosexuality and covers his seductive activity with moralization about the organization's purposes. Participative management theorist Douglas McGregor's foray into democratic management is seen as a joke among upper-class homosexuals about bringing the lower classes into the ruling strata, with no real intention of doing so, the punch line consisting in the humiliation of the lower class who find themselves exactly where they started.

Next comes organization theorist Henry Mintzberg, whose leader is a fickle narcissistic swine who seduces to show his power and creates organization as a demonstration of his potency. The violence of his seduction is thinly disguised and manifest upon resistance from the victim, at which point seduction essentially turns into rape. Of course women can have narcissistic sexuality as well, but when they do it is "the response of women resigned to the inevitability of violence in sexualization" (p. 588).

Finally, Peters and Waterman, authors of the best-seller *In Search of Excellence*, while adopting the gender-neutral language of their own time, nonetheless maintain the narcissistic swinishness of Mintzberg's leader. Calás and Smircich reveal this by setting it off against a feminine form in alternate rereadings of their text. A few examples follow:

Peters and Waterman with a [Male Subtext]	Peters and Waterman with a [Female Subtext]
Leadership is many things. It is patient, usually boring coalition building [or the game of courting your prey].	Leadership is many things. It is patient, usually boring coalition building [or the careful sewing of a family quilt].
It's building a loyal team at the top that speaks more or less with one voice [so that she, at the bottom, can be kept silent in her pain].	It's building a loyal team at the top that speaks more or less with one voice [full of cacophonies, and always sustained by cries and laughter].
It's being tough when necessary, and it's the occasional naked use of power [you pitiful thing, daring to oppose me, feel all the weight of my rage].	It's being tough when necessary, and it's the occasional naked use of power [you won't snatch my children away from me. Don't even come close, I'll kill you first—] (p. 590).

In the end the essentially homosexual reference of Peters and Waterman's work is revealed to Calás and Smircich when Peters and Waterman turn to James McGregor Burns's concept of "transformational leadership," which likens the leader to the pedagogue:

> And suddenly we remember Gallop's . . . commentary on Luce Irigaray's readings of Freud, which remarks that there is a certain pederasty implicit in pedagogy . . . because a greater man penetrates a lesser man with his knowledge. This (male) homosexuality in the structures of society includes everybody. It is the male standard of knowledge—the apparently sexually indifferent logos, science, logic—which measures all members of the structure along a predefined agreement over what knowledge is. And that is all the knowledge to be had about "leadership." (p. 591)

Thus there is nothing new here, but only an "old satyr" returning us "back, in a flash, through the parlors and gymnasiums permeated by sexual/homosexual jokes . . . to make us repent and pray 'in-the-name-of-the-Father' kneeling in front (in whatever way) of 'Barnard-the-priest' " (p. 592).

Asking "is this homosocial, elitist, monologic leadership the desired seduction for the organized life of the present. . . . An organizational life of companies without offices . . . behind the screen of PCs and VTRs?" (p. 593), they raise the question whether another seduction, a feminine seduction, is possible.

Attempting to gain an image of female seduction that would be beyond the male form, with its "homosocial *domination* and *servitude*" (p. 594; emphasis in the original), Calás and Smircich realized that "our images of 'seduction' also emanated from a male dominated culture." Looking for a term that would be less "univocal," they turn to the notion of pleasure: "Pleasures beyond leadership-seduction may provide the bases for other types of social relations and newer forms of organizational knowledge" (p. 594). Their models of the idea of pleasure as the basis for social relations are utopias written by female authors: Charlotte Perkins Gilman (1915/1979) and Marge Piercy (1977). In these utopias men are either not present at all, having killed themselves off in wars, or have become quasi-women, developing the capacity to breast-feed. It will suffice to say, although to be sure this point is brought out more fully in the novels themselves, that life in these worlds of women is perfect, as far as their inhabitants are concerned. Oppression and limitation have been eliminated along with men and their masculinity. Even here, however, Calás and Smircich demur, because the structure of these worlds is given by the negation, the opposition to, the traditional male form. But the opposition to the male is by that token defined by the male. And at any rate, opposition is, after all, a structure of (masculine) logic.

Turning to their own offering of pleasure, Calás and Smircich tell us that this is what they have been giving us all along. They have been playing with us and enjoying themselves in the process. And if they have not said anything substantial, that has also been by intent. Their idea of pleasure is the evocation of the ephemeral which they have accomplished through this writing exercise.

Rather than *fixing* ourselves in the text (the typical imagery of "universal-truth-knowledge" in modern metaphysics) we prefer the imagery of a transient subject, never to be captured, always on the move, as so many points of pleasure on a woman's body. And as we write these words we recognize that this is all that we . . . have been doing so far. But, at the same time, this form of writing ourselves in the organizational text has provided us with the pleasure of resistance and activism . . . while maintaining an awareness—so often forgotten in the dominant order—of the limits of human agency. (598)

CONTRA CALÁS AND SMIRCICH

Calás and Smircich's article despite, or because of, its charm, is exactly the kind of thing that men are afraid of, a realization of their worst fears. It is a rejection of the validity of their whole project, spoken in the name of the woman they love and fear the most, and to whom those projects were directed—the primordial mother. Let us note the way their article expresses the points that have already been discussed.

To begin, and most central to what they are doing, there is the unrelieved haughtiness, mockery, and contempt in their tone, belittling men and all their efforts and getting the idea across that there is nothing that men can do that women would have to take seriously.

Moving to matters of substance, the purpose of their invocation of Baudrillard's claim that everything is seduction and not production is again to deny the meaning of men's works. It claims that men's work has had no lasting or valuable outcome. The same goes with the assimilation of leadership, which has an aim outside of itself, something that gets accomplished, with seduction, which has no goal beyond itself. In both cases there has been nothing about what men have done that could serve as a basis for admiration.

The claim that working life is an expression of male homosexual desire[4] is an interesting one, and calls for extended discussion.

To begin with let us note the truth upon which their claim leans for its credibility. As I noted in Chapter 2, there is a sense in which male activity can sometimes lead to disengagement from the female. The high official may take the organization itself as his maternal object. He may be said to "marry" the organization, and because the other officials of the organization are also likely to be male, he may be said to be "marrying" them.[5]

Such emotional relations have been called "homosocial" by some (e.g., Kanter, 1993), but homosocial does not mean homosexual. Homosexual means that the bodily impulses are mobilized, but the body is not present in these homosocial relations. They are asexual, not homosexual. These are relations that are based on identification with organizational roles, and involve abandonment of the body. They are mediated through the organization itself, which is why women who identify with their own organizational roles can fit into this pattern in exactly the same way. Yet Calás and Smircich not only miss this point, they also miss it in a malign way. Their purpose is not to understand organizations, a goal that they do not further even in the slightest, but to attack men.

Given the disapproval in our society toward male homosexuality, an attitude that currently has the name "homophobia,"[6] and of which they were surely aware when they wrote, their charge of homosexuality must be seen as something that they knew would be taken as offensive. It will be found offensive because it plays upon a very deep anxiety. Freud (e.g., 1940) maintained that people are constitutionally (biologically) bisexual, and he wrote often of the repression of homosexual impulses. This suggests that the construction of a heterosexual identity involves the repression of one's own homosexual affect. Freud also said, in his paper "Analysis Terminable and Interminable" (1937), that among men the capacity to get at one's desire to be passive toward men marks the distinction between terminable and interminable analysis, which is to say that the desire to be passive toward men is the deepest content of the unconscious.

Now if one can assume that the male desire to be passive toward men is at the heart of homosexual affect, it follows that, for heterosexual men, their own homosexual impulses are their deepest and darkest secrets. As we have seen, competition among men is implicitly competition for the female. Accepting one's desire to be passive toward men would mean accepting one's loss in this competition and hence having to give up the fantasy of fusion with the mother. This would suggest *why*, for heterosexual men in our culture, homosexual impulses are the deepest and darkest secrets—they pose the threat of castration, which is the permanent loss of fusion with the mother (Chasseguet-Smirgel, 1986).

Looked at in this way, Calás and Smircich's "reading" is an act of aggression against men and an offensive within the sexual holy war. It is an attempt at symbolic castration, which apparently seems to them to be a liberating and subversive act, an act that has given them "the pleasure of

resistance and activism." This idea that the castration of men would be tantamount to liberation means that masculinity is oppression, which is the
fundamental premise of the idea that men are inherently toxic.

Further analysis of Calás and Smircich's defamation reveals several related effects. First and perhaps most obvious, is that it simply reiterates the
point about male activity not creating a product, only this time with regard
to biological productivity. Second and most important, it denies that
women have any need to feel appreciated through male achievement, let
alone appreciation for it. Male work, they are saying, has no place within
the heterosexual division of labor—an exchange matrix whose validity
their aspersion of homosexuality is meant to deny. Third, it means that
women can spurn men's sexuality without violating the natural order of
things, which is helpful if one wants to see oneself as the expression of a benign nature and of life. Finally the denial that men are heterosexual means
that women do not have anything that men desire. But if they do not have
anything that men desire, women have no power over them. In their trans-
actions, then, women may be seen as pure victims, without any responsibility for their condition at all.

Taken together these assertions amount to the claim that the so-called
works of men have only been exercises in self-gratification. Certainly they
were not for the female, who was only abused and oppressed by them. And
far from involving the rending of the self, their only purpose was pleasure
and self-glorification—and indeed the glorification of a self that, because it
created no product, simply expressed an essence of domination and violence. Women had no need for any of this as was shown by the idea that the
absence of men would produce utopia, in which pleasure and natural female spontaneity would create whatever is necessary and desirable.

It is this idea, that pleasure is all that is necessary and that to follow the
desires will lead only to more pleasure, that is the direct voice of the primordial mother and the root of the repudiation of reality. For it assumes
that the world naturally responds positively to our spontaneous move-
ments and that it is not an alien and independent entity that needs to be
acknowledged and taken into account. It is as if, in Calás and Smircich's account, we are connected to the world through an umbilical cord. The
world, in a word, really is our mother. It is only men, who contribute nothing, that stand between desire and its gratification.

It is this view of the world that lies underneath Calás and Smircich's repudiation of logic and definitive language. If the world is structured to give
us pleasure, then any idea we have of it is good enough and equivalent. If
the structure of things naturally comports itself to our most pleasurable fantasies about it, there is no need to watch one's step, to avoid making mis-

takes, to do one's best to understand the structure of things. Indeed there is no need even to maintain a consistent vision of the world, which means that we can use language purely evocatively, as Calás and Smircich claim the right to do.

If this were the case, the life of men would indeed be contemptible. Unable to gain their pleasures simply by being themselves, they need to mold the world and bring it into their orbit. It clearly grows out of, and is an expression of, a profound weakness and, set against the assumption of female perfection, self-sufficiency, and strength in its absence, it would certainly be a proper object of disdain. Because all of their activity grows out of this contemptible base, there is nothing that they can do that would assert any legitimate claim on the affection of women, and nothing that women could find appealing. Their assertions of themselves with regard to women thus seem as impositions and aggressions; the world that they have created and in which women live seems a realm of oppression and a reversal of the natural order of things, in which the lesser rule and have power over the greater. Get rid of them and life will be perfect.

Under the circumstances we have to see Calás and Smircich's claim to be "maintaining an awareness . . . of the limits of human agency" as disingenuous. For taking male limitation as contemptible reflects only an awareness of *male* limitation. The fact is that there is no corresponding expression of female limitation to be found here. It seems rather that women never do anything that is less than perfect except when it is caused by men. Indeed there is no sense that women *have* to do anything at all, other than just be. Omnipotent and all-loving, they can make things perfect simply by their presence. The assumption that women are the primordial mother is unmistakable here. It is only against the backdrop of this assumed female self-sufficiency and perfection that such contempt for male limitation makes sense.

Thus the whole question turns on the nature of reality. If there is no self-subsistent, objective reality with which we must cope, then Calás and Smircich are correct: all is fantasy and pleasure and the only question is whose fantasy and pleasure. Under these circumstances the idea of an indifferent reality comes to seem a male invention to justify their own innate oppressiveness. The male necessity to create order, to organize, to understand, to accept the bounds of logic, to use words in a consistent way, turn out to be actions in expression of a warped and crippled nature. But if there is a world "out there," even if we cannot, with our limitations, fully grasp it, then the cultural achievements that men have created are all the more admirable *because* of their limitations.

Turning back to our original point, if there is no world "out there," then the father is an intruder into the nexus of mother and child, who holds the mother in subjection through violence; if there is a world out there, then the idea that all we have to do to claim the mother, to make life perfect, is to get rid of the male, turns out to be a fantasy. Recall Chasseguet-Smirgel's description of the ego ideal. Compare it with Calás and Smircich's vision and their attack on maleness:

In my view, this fantasy corresponds to the wish to rediscover a smooth universe without obstacles, roughness or difference, identified with a mother's insides to which one can have free access, the representation, at the thinking level, of a form of unfettered mental functioning with the free circulation of psychic energy. The father, his penis and reality itself must be destroyed in order for the paradise world of the pleasure principle to be regained. (p. 30)

This brings us to a point at which theorizing develops a practical edge. Calás and Smircich appear to hold the belief that fantasy and desire can serve to generate effective organization as well as realistic perception. Thus, as a guide for organizational theorizing, they offer this: "What other pleasures for the 'organizational text' can our friends and colleagues inscribe . . . ? What is your pleasure?" (p. 598). But organization does not emerge effortlessly and spontaneously from the soil of fantasy and desire. If it did, every child would be an entrepreneur. Even established organizations, when they eschew reality and turn their processes toward the generation of fantasy, can lose their viability and their capacity to survive (Schwartz, 1990).

If there were no real world, wishing, as the old song says, would make it so. The fact, of which we all have sufficient evidence, that wishing does not make it so is the reason why the idea of reality emerged in the first place. So it is not the male that stands in between desire and its realization, it is reality itself. If abandoning the constraints of reality for the pursuit of pleasure is the course established by giving free reign to the primordial mother, one can easily understand why reasonable people would be afraid of it.

More concretely, if there is a world "out there" with which we need to cope, Calás and Smircich's vision will be less than helpful in suggesting ways for us to steer through it. Certainly their vision will not help us in organizing. For the writing exercise that they have been engaged in, which they offer as their model of organizing, has been an attempt to remove univocality, to oppose consistency in meaning. As organization theorist Weick (1969) has taught us, the process of organizing is just the opposite. It is the reduction of *equivocality*—the creation of specificity. For it is univocality that makes coordination possible, and organization without coordination is not organization at all.

As a basis for organizing, giving up the idea that reality imposes constraints, and substituting the spontaneous pursuit of pleasure, is not going to maximize the possibilities for human freedom and enjoyment. It will not increase the free flow of creative energy and the pleasure of spontaneity. What one can expect from it instead is unemployment and a deteriorating standard of living. Push it further and it becomes poverty, social disintegration, and, ultimately, chaos. Students of organization, and not only students of organization, need to keep this in mind.

NOTES

1. An example of this is provided by the HBO television series *The Sopranos*. In this series the main protagonist, a Mafioso, keeps the details of his activities from his wife. She knows perfectly well what line of work he pursues, and fully enjoys the standard of living it makes possible, but by exempting her from the particulars, he lightens the burden of her guilt.

2. The major study purporting to show that, when housework is taken into consideration, women do more work than men (Hochschild, 1989) has recently come under serious methodological criticism concerning the adequacy of its data and the interpretations drawn from it (Farrell, 1999). Using data from a number of publicly available sources, including those to which Hochschild refers, Farrell finds that conclusion is not supported. Women may work more inside the home, but the additional work that men do outside the home more than compensates. For example, an analysis of Bureau of Labor Statistics data revealed that in families with children under eighteen, working men work more outside the home than working women (45.4 versus 34.6 hours). He also reports the results of a University of Michigan study (Juster, 1985) that found that when work inside and outside the home are added, working men worked four and one-half hours more than working women (61.4 versus 56.9). Farrell also raises questions about whether Hochschild's methods accurately measure the type of housework that men do.

3. A brief discussion of postmodernism awaits within the next chapter.

4. What is striking and significant about Calás and Smircich's claim is not the idea that men have homosexual affect, an idea that no Freudian would deny, but the idea that men are *exclusively* homosexual. That strikes me as being sufficiently bizarre as to stand in need of analysis in its own right.

It is also worthwhile noting that it is only male homosexuality that arouses Calás and Smircich's disdain. Female homosexuality, as displayed for example by the characters in one of the utopian novels they offer as a model, does not come in for similar ridicule. More than that, it is part of their approved model of social relationships.

5. As we shall see later on, something not dissimilar happens with the combat soldier.

6. This term is actually quite interesting. The term phobia generally relates to an extreme aversive reaction, but one that is fairly well detached from the rest of the personality. It makes it seem as if an aversion to homosexuality is an isolated attitude, representing nothing more than narrow-minded bigotry and prejudice against those who are unlike us in their choice of sexual partners. Yet, as I am trying to show here, aversion to homosexuality is an expression of the fragility of the male sexual identity and the role that emerges from it. It is by no means isolated. The current orthodoxy that equates sexual orientation with a mere matter of taste in partners simply denies that there is a male role associated with and arising from heterosexuality.

The idea that aversion to homosexuality should simply be extinguished through public shaming is frightening in its own narrow-mindedness. Whether it will undermine the male role is an open question. But, as an expression of the toxic-man ideology, it seems dedicated to that purpose. The discrepancy between the simple-mindedness of the premise upon which this strategy rests, and the awesome complexity of the potential consequences, is simply stunning.

Chapter Four

The Sin of the Father

As we have seen, at the heart of the denigration of men lies the subordination of the objective to the subjective. This recognition enables us to draw a link between feminism, which is arguably a fairly narrow intellectual current, and postmodernism, or poststructuralism, which is considerably broader. Associated with the various writings of Derrida, Foucault, Lyotard, Deleuze and Guattari, and others (including Calás and Smircich, of course), postmodernism may be thought of as holding that there is no objective external world. Knowledge is only language and language is only about other language. There are no grounds outside of language for being able to say that one idea is any better than any other. What a society believes is a function of who rules within the society. The rulers make discourse that serves their interest seem the vehicle of "objective" truth and, in so doing, marginalize the languages of others.

The attack upon the father is the point at which feminism and postmodernism come together. Typically called the patriarch, the rule of the father is seen as the most long-lived and pervasive structure of oppression. According to this view, the father has oppressed and marginalized all those who are not like him, fashioning the discourses of "civilization" to support and obscure this oppression. Under cover of this camouflage, he has pursued only his selfish interest, not caring at all for anyone else. More than just controlling, he represents control itself, and were it not for his domination, freedom and self-expression would have reigned. Were it not for him, the different voices that he has silenced would have been able to create their own discourses, making a world full of difference and multifarious beauty. So terrible is this tyrant and the social order he created, that resistance to it can provide a basic direction for an individual's life.

Now this is a substantial indictment and a skeptic might wonder at its balance. Surely there have been malignant fathers. These fathers have sinned, this skeptic might agree, but have there not been benign and even beneficent ones, as well? If it is fair to say that civilization has represented patriarchal domination, certainly it has also manifested concern for the well-being of the groups he has led. How does one account for the unqualified character of this denunciation? To make sense of it, one must assume that the evil he has done has so far outweighed the good that it is not necessary even to measure the latter.[1]

What was this evil? What did the father do, or what was he believed to have done, that was responsible for this absolute condemnation? Surely this cannot have been just the collection of sins that fathers have committed, on the order of the sins that all human beings commit. It cannot have been just the sins of fathers. It must have been more than that. Let us call it the Sin of the Father. What was supposed to have been the Sin of the Father?

Our inquiry has put this question in a different light. It has brought us to the view that the ideas of toxic man, Madonna-and-child, and the sexual holy war are external representations of intrapsychic phenomena, and that what is under attack is the traditional role of the father. It is easy enough to see the idea of the Sin of the Father as an aspect of this, but doing so raises its own question. For these intrapsychic phenomena are timeless. They have always existed and will always exist. Why have they arisen in this form in our own time, rather than before?

My contention is that one cannot answer the question of the Sin of the Father without a comprehension of the meaning of the accusation itself, and the meaning of the accusation cannot be understood without an understanding of its context. For the idea of patriarchal evil cannot be understood in isolation. It did not emerge out of no place. Rather it expressed and represented a social dynamic of the time. Understanding it, then, must require understanding that social dynamic and seeing the place of the idea within it. That is the purpose of this chapter. I examine the roots of the belief in the badness of the father, looking at its social origins and its psychodynamics, trying ultimately to reveal its meaning. My course of investigation requires the elucidation of the connection between the father and the corporation man, a figure who is deeply involved in this play of meanings. I proceed from there to an analysis of his family. In the end we will be better able to understand the nature of the Sin of the Father.

THE ALIENATED STUDENT

By general agreement, postmodernism, and the associated assault on the father, began in the late 1960s (e.g., Best and Kellner, 1991). But focusing on its representations as they arose in the protests of the time overlooks the possibility that there were broader cultural factors present. It would be the continued influence of these factors that would account for the persistence of the postmodern assault after its immediate cause was eliminated. That is the assumption I make. I look at postmodern expression, and the attendant antagonism toward the father, as a broader cultural force that had its origins in the postwar period, and in the fifties especially, to which the protests of the late sixties gave direction, but not birth.

In doing this, in a sense I am retracing my own steps. For the critique of the patriarch has had a deep resonance with me, even if it has also, more recently, deeply disturbed me. Trying to understand it, and my reactions to it, I am trying to understand myself. I am also trying to understand my father, and my relationship to him, as a way of finding, and creating, within myself, the capacity to be a father in my own right. My starting point is a book that has often felt to me, despite differences in detail, like a dissection of my own psyche. This was a study by Keniston (1960) of what he called "the uncommitted," a group of alienated students at Harvard University.

By "alienated" Keniston meant "the rejection of the roles, values, and institutions [the alienated individual] sees as typical of adult American life" (p. 25). As he points out, there is, a priori, no reason to suppose that such a rejection would entail an entire outlook on life, but that was, in fact, what Keniston found: "[t]he rejection of the dominant values, roles, and institutions of our society . . . was almost always a part of a more general alienated ideology, embracing not only attitudes toward the surrounding society, but towards the self, others, groups, even the structure of the universe and the nature of knowledge" (p. 56).

Keniston describes this outlook in some detail, stressing especially the "deep and pervasive mistrust of any and all commitments, be they to other people, to groups, to American culture, or even to the self" (p. 56). For our purposes the most interesting characterizations were those which clearly presage the postmodernism of our time. In order to illustrate this, I quote passages from Keniston and associate them with postmodern themes.

Alienated Students	Postmodernism
The universe itself is basically empty and meaningless. (p. 61)	Denial of objective reality
In such a pessimistic, anxiety-provoking, and "dead" universe, truth necessarily becomes subjective and even solipsistic. The alienated are true to the logic of their position, and almost to a man accept the subjectivity and even the arbitrariness of their own points of view. (p. 62)	Subjectivism, relativism
Whatever sense of meaning a man may have must inevitably be his own creation. (p. 62)	Social constructionism
Above all, they have contempt for those who "blind themselves" to the "realities" of existence by "pious optimism," shallow consolations, and the easy acceptance of the traditional verities of our society. Part of the difficulty in communication comes from the unreliability of appearances. Not only do the alienated generally agree with a statement like "Beneath the smiling face of man lies a bottomless pit of evil," but they affirm that all appearances are suspect, whether of men or institutions. Thus, nothing can be accepted at face value, every appearance is likely to be deceptive, and every surface conceals opposite potentials beneath it. (p. 63)	Deconstruction
The ethical corollary of anger, scorn, and contempt is self-interest, and in the alienated we find a special form of egocentricity (p. 66) which involves the need to use others for one's own purposes—and the converse conviction that the same principle governs the actions of one's fellows, even when these are disguised under some other principle. (p. 67)	Reduction of social process to self-interested politics
All place primary emphasis on experience and feeling, on the search for awareness and the cultivation of sentience and perceptiveness . . . and they further emphasize the importance of expression of this experience.	Authenticity

Almost to a man, they emphasize what I will call "aesthetic" goals and values . . . those goals and values whose primary source is the self, and whose chief aim is the development of sentience, awareness, and feeling. (p. 71)

In such an outlook, reason must play a secondary role to feeling.

Resistance to reason and "logocentrism"

In the struggle for emotion, passion, and feeling, the enemies are two: first, excessive rationality and self-control, and second, social pressures which limit independence. (p. 72)

Resistance to external and internalized social control

The individualism of the alienated is . . . a solitary and lonely individualism of the outsider, the man who lives physically within his society but remains psychologically divorced from it. (p. 73)

Marginality

The enemy is the entire status quo—not merely pernicious aspects of the social order which must be changed to permit improvement, but the entire social and cultural ethos. (p. 78)

Generalized rage against society

The result is a diffusion and fragmentation of the sense of identity, an experience of themselves as amorphous, indistinct, and disorganized. . . . Insofar as they have any clear sense of self it is almost entirely defined by what they are against, what they despise, by groups they do not want to belong to and values they consider tawdry. (p. 186)

Fragmentation of identity, negative self-definition

Fear and dislike of competition . . . leading to an almost complete repudiation of the competitive business ethic of American society, to a dislike of and avoidance of social situations with a competitive quality, and to the continuing view that competition and rivalry, though ubiquitous, are destructive to all concerned. (p. 176)

Abhorrence of aggressiveness, competition

A central legacy of childhood for most of
these alienated young men was the deep
conviction that adult men—as epitomized
by their own fathers—were not to be emu-
lated, and the further belief that adulthood in general was disastrous insofar as it
meant becoming like their fathers.
(p. 178)

Repudiation of the father

In [their] fantasies . . . we find [an] exaggerated dream of the blissfulness of early
mother-son relationships, of the capacity
of truly maternal women to provide *totally*
for men, of the complete absence of distinctions between self and object. (p. 189)

Appeal of fusion, apotheosis of
the maternal, rejection of the distinction between subject and object

For many alienated students, the refusal of
adulthood extends to a *rejection of adult
sexuality*. . . . These youths find what our
society defines as a "normal" sexual relationship between man and woman frightening and difficult. Some of these
[difficulties] are common to late adolescents, . . . but these are heightened by their
fundamental aversion for "aggressiveness," for "initiative," for "activity"—all
qualities culturally defined as part of the
male sex role. (p. 199)

Difficulty in developing male
heterosexual orientation

An especially crucial aspect of the failure
of acculturation among the alienated is . . .
their systematic *undermining of repression
and denial*, two of the most common adap-
tive techniques in our society (and probably in all societies). (p. 197)

Fascination with the "dark side"
of life and society

If it may be granted that Keniston's alienated students represented
postmodernism in its embryonic form, the question then turns to where
this outlook came from and what were its psychodynamics. This is a subject
that Keniston explored primarily by interviewing the students about their
family lives, and exploring their psychodynamics through the use of the
Thematic Apperception Test. His explanation, whose theoretical framework was heavily influenced by Eric Erikson, moves the subjects' relations
to their fathers from one of the themes of their alienation to its center.

According to Keniston the theme encountered over and over among
these students was a peculiar family constellation in which the father was

seen as weak, damaged, and emotionally distant, and the mother was seen as vigorous, powerful, and vital. There was also a typical family history.

In this history the parents came from traditional families, characterized by strong fathers whom they idealized. But, products of their times, they sought to go beyond these families, in the sense of creating new roles for themselves that would help them to express themselves more fully. They began their marriage with these high ideals, including beliefs in the possibility of new roles for women, but lost their way. The father gave up his early ideals and settled into a career that would enable him to make as much money as possible. He became, in a word, the corporation man. The mother gave up the ideal of a career that would permit the full expression of her talents and became a housewife.

As time went on, he became increasingly invested in his career, separating himself physically and psychologically from the family. She thought less and less of him. He did not, in her view, sufficiently support her in the realization of her ideals. Nor was he very much of a man. Certainly he was not the man her father was. She took their son as an emotional substitute for the husband, drawing him very close to her, sharing her disappointment in her marriage and her husband, and assigning to the son the responsibility of fulfilling the ideals that were missing in her life. The problem was that as she drew the son close to her emotionally, and made him responsible for her fulfillment, she simultaneously undercut the father who would ordinarily serve as the son's model of valued achievement. The result was that the son became what Keniston called a "pyrrhic victor in the Oedipal struggle." He was able to maintain the fantasy of a perfect fusion with his mother, but lost the possibility of forming the superego.

In order to get a full idea of what this would mean, it is necessary to return to our discussion of the Oedipus complex. In doing so I am going to add a bit to Keniston's account, based on the more contemporary understanding of the powerful role of the mother that we developed in Chapter 2. It does not in any significant way conflict with Keniston's own interpretation.

As we saw, the infant's early experience of life is primarily structured by its relationship with its mother, who is experienced as omnipotent and as a source of boundless love. The fantasy of the return to fusion with her structures our lives, but for the boy and the girl this fantasy, the ego ideal, is experienced somewhat differently. The boy, unlike the girl, can project fusion with the mother only at the cost of losing his own identity, and of being swallowed up and engulfed in the process. To deal with this he comes to see the father as one who has earned a place with the mother, who is able to maintain a place with the mother without being destroyed because he is admirable in her eyes; he has done something that she values.

As I have argued in Chapter 2, what the primordial mother is understood as valuing is a sphere in which the expression of her nurturing power could be given its freest expression, a sphere of love in which the desire of her loved ones would be satisfied. The role of the father is that of expanding the sphere of the mother by engaging the external world, and removing the indifferent and alien elements of reality that limit the free and safe expression of the mother's love. To be sure the father can never do this. Reality remains reality. Still the conditions of life can be made more congenial, and threatening reality can be made less threatening. These can count as progress toward the ego ideal. Such progress is both energized by this fantasy and helps to keep the fantasy alive, and the maintenance of the fantasy is what is necessary for hope.

Now a father who can be seen as doing this would be one to emulate. This emulation could be projected to result in a similar relationship for the boy: an adult male who would be valued by an adult and powerful female on the basis of her appreciation of his accomplishments. The internalization of this image of the father, in which the son undertakes the responsibility to participate in the world on a similar basis, is the classical root for the superego.

The father's emulability assumes that the mother appreciates the father. The devaluation of the father by the mother would tend to cause this edifice to collapse. If the mother does not admire the father, and especially if she engages the son with the fullness of her emotionality into this project of devaluation, the son will not be able to project an image of himself that would enable him to see himself as equal to the powerful figure of the mother. He will not be able to order his life with a prospect for independent, valued identity. He will be able to retain the fantasy of fusion with the primordial mother, but not without the experience of that condition as rendering him totally dependent and swallowing him up. Indeed her bringing him into this devaluation project would tend to reinforce that fantasy of being rendered dependent and engulfed, because that is exactly what has happened.

If, in addition, she holds the father responsible for her lack of fulfillment, and implicitly makes the son responsible for the reinforcement of her grandiose idea of herself, she will have made the son's independence from her into an act of abandonment, an injury to her, the son's only connection and hope. He must, therefore, as the bedrock of whatever identity he can have, follow her lead, not move from her project, never even question her claim that, were it not for the father, her life, and their relationship, would have been perfect. In all of this, he relinquishes any possibility he has of an emotional life as a competent male adult, substituting instead the idea that male adulthood is the root of his problem. No wonder he is alienated.

What we see here are the psychodynamics that underlie the alienated/postmodern worldview. Nothing good can be said about the father or his works, because that would involve a betrayal of the mother. Thus the social forms in which more socialized individuals transact their identities must be seen as artificial. They must be denigrated and "deconstructed."

No capacity to project an image of a valued self into the future means that the metric of one's life can be based only on one's experiences of the moment. These are, of course, volatile. From this would arise the idea that people only deceive themselves to think they have some idea of an objective "truth." Because one's experiences of the moment are the only reality one can acknowledge, any blockage of them, any interference with their free expression, would be seen as an intolerable act of oppression. Resistance to this oppression would be experienced as an identity one could legitimately have; it would be hard to think of any other. Commitment would be impossible because commitment always means an acceptance of limitation. In the absence of any possible goal that would justify the acceptance of limitation, commitment could only be seen as the internalization of oppression. Value in the world would have to consist in the freely given love of one's authentic self, as defined by one's feelings of the moment, a fusion that only the mother's love for the child could approximate. Any limited acceptance by a specific other would be experienced in the context of the fact that the concrete relationships one has had have been devastating. Only the fantasy of relationship, relationship in purity, could be allowed.

The lack of engagement with others in social forms or relationships means that the self is always experienced as isolated, marginal, and ephemeral. It cannot connect itself with any others or any thing. This would be believed to be true for others as well as for oneself, even though they deny it. Any connection, therefore, would be seen as only a subjugation brought about by brute force. Those who seem to experience such connection would be seen as covering over that brutality by a fantasy of how wonderful the brute is and how much he deserves to be loved. In this process of covering over, the voices of the dominated and oppressed, the discourses which express why they should be loved, are suppressed and silenced. Competition and aggressiveness, one would believe, are to be spurned. All they do is establish such dominance. But there is nothing of value that could legitimate the supremacy of any one over anyone else. All that could possibly be of value was what previously was—fusion with the perfect mother who loved one exactly as one was. That was a perfect world, one would suppose.

The father would be seen as the one who destroyed it. "And he wants to be loved for that?" the alienated would say. "Screw him, his sex, his discourses, and his ways. Let us reject him and turn to the mother. Undefiled by the father, she will give us everything we need and want."

As we have described this matter, the Sin of the Father has been explained away. In this view, there is no great Sin of the Father, but rather the Sin is a construct, primarily of the mother, to explain her lack of fulfillment. The son bought into this because he had to, or face her rage. And he could not face her rage because his connection with her gave him the only identity he could have.

Now obviously this analysis constitutes a very serious accusation. It attacks a whole strain, one might even say the dominant strain, of contemporary thought. One needs more to accept it than what has been given. Specifically, it seems to me, one needs to develop it in three ways. First one needs to go more fully into the charge itself, to take it more seriously, to look for the truth in it before dismissing it. Second one needs to look at it from the alternative point of view. What had the mother to say about all of this? The third charge, which in the end I will accept, is that the account here has been excessively reductionistic. Surely postmodernism represents more than the expression of this peculiar family configuration. Surely there is something taking place at a deeper level.

In order to develop my claim, then, I look first at the substance of the charge: What did the father actually do that might properly have resulted in this denigration? This involves taking a look at the purported sinner himself: the corporation man. Second I look at the matter from the other point of view, from the point of view of the mother. It turns out that she has been very well spoken for in a book which gave rise to contemporary feminism, *The Feminine Mystique* by Betty Friedan. What we see there is the same landscape I have already described. Finally I try to place this family drama in broader perspective, attempting to show how broader social forces are playing themselves out through this configuration.

THE SIN OF THE CORPORATION MAN

In this section I want to examine the charge against the father. As the alienated student saw it, and here he joins the disdain of the mother, the father's sins were threefold. First he was a sell-out, a phony, a man not to be admired. Second he abandoned the family, removing himself physically and psychologically. Third he was responsible for the limitations imposed on the mother, which were reflected in her terrible unhappiness. About the third charge, I respond in the section on Friedan. About the first two, my argument is that, although there is a great deal of truth to these charges, they do not add up to the attack upon the patriarch. The reason is that the corporation man, the phony, the absent father, was no hypermasculine macho man who suppressed and dominated everyone else. On the contrary, he was a strictly androgynous guy.

As an ideological construct, the hypermasculine macho man, despite Pollack's (1998) claim that he is still the model of masculinity, had long ceased to exist by the time the corporation man sold out. He was the product of social forces that were, not one, but two generations back from the forces that molded the fathers of the alienated students. As Bendix (1956) has argued, Spencerian Social Darwinism, the ideology that within corporate organization corresponded to the macho man model, had given way by the twenties to the model of the Taylorite "scientific manager" who subordinated his individuality and arbitrary authority to impersonal methods. These methods defined his own job as well as they did the jobs of those under him. It is still possible to see patriarchy in this, and certainly the Foucauldian critique of discipline, with its emphasis on the subordination of the self to an internalized system of abstract rules (Foucault, 1979), refers to this form of organization. However, the emphasis Taylor and his followers placed on the common good and on the idea of finding the appropriate job for each individual worker represented positive valuations both of community and diversity that the patriarch is supposed, by the postmodernists, to lack. Again, along with the involvement of the industrial psychologists who were to assist in the alignment of individual workers and jobs came an understanding that workers had attitudes and feelings, betokening a surprising sensitivity on the part of the supposedly heartless patriarch.

The idea of patriarchy becomes attenuated to the breaking point as management ideology shifts toward the "human relations" model, the model that dominated managerial ideology at the time the fathers of Keniston's alienated students were "selling out" (Bendix, 1956). For the ideal manager in the human relations model was a character who was striking in his androgyny.

The model of the worker that formed the center of the human relations movement was of an individual built out of sentiments, a subject rather than an object. The ideal manager was a person who held "Theory Y," rather than "Theory X"; that person believed that work could and should be motivated through those sentiments, rather than through external control (McGregor, 1960).

For Mayo, the central principle of worker motivation was "the desire to stand well with one's fellows, the so-called human instinct of association"

(Mayo, cited in Bendix, 1956: p. 313). The art of management required the engagement of these desires with the organization's tasks:

Mayo's view of the managerial task may be defined as the endeavor to provide an organizational environment in which employees can fulfill their "eager human desire for cooperative activity." The major objective of management is to foster cooperative teamwork among its employees. (Bendix: p. 317)

It thus required sensitivity to sentiment and an understanding of its logic (Roethlisberger, 1943). If we may follow authors like Gilligan (1982) in the presumption that sensitivity, concern for connection, interdependence, belonging, and so on are feminine characteristics, there is no way of denying that the ideal model of the manager in the human relations approach had a highly developed feminine side.

Nor would it be correct to assume that human relations ideology was in any way characteristic only of a fringe movement within a generally patriarchal management caste. On the contrary, it was quite broadly based, as Bendix illustrates with a passage from a 1953 *Fortune* magazine description of the General Electric training program: "If the task of the manager is not work so much as the managing of other people's work, it follows that getting along with people is far and away the most important skill of all" (p. 320).

Indeed even the broad emphasis in the "scientific" literature of the time on such qualities as "consideration" and "socio-emotional orientation" (e.g., Fleishman, Harris and Burtt, 1955) reveal the importance placed at the time on the "feminine" side of the personality. One might add that this literature was so inconclusive (e.g. Korman, 1966) that it is impossible to disregard the claim that it was driven more by ideology than by science.

Ferguson (1984), who observed clearly the feminine aspects of the behavior of subordinates to their bosses, failed to see that, as approved behavior, the display of feminine characteristics was also supported in the other direction. This was exemplified in the classic novel about organizations of the period, *The Man in the Gray Flannel Suit* (Wilson, 1955).

THE MAN IN THE GRAY FLANNEL SUIT

Tom Rath, the book's protagonist, enters the corporate world after service in the infantry during World War II. In the following scene, he visits the apartment of Ralph Hopkins, head of the United Broadcasting Company, for whom Rath has been hired to write a speech. Note the femininity of Hopkins's display, with its apparent concern to please, its informality, its concern to establish bonding, its apparent deference, its support of the other.

The door was opened almost immediately by Hopkins himself. He was smiling and looked more affable than ever: "Come in!" he said. "So nice of you to come!" . . .

"Won't you sit down? Hopkins said. "What can I get you to drink?"

"Anything. What are you having?"

Hopkins walked over to a table near one of the windows on which stood a small forest of bottles, a trayful of glasses, and an ice bucket. "It looks as though we have quite a collection here," he said, as though that were the first time he had seen it. "I think I'll have Scotch on the rocks. Will that suit you?"

"That'll be fine."

Hopkins took a pair of silver ice tongs in his hand and delicately dropped ice cubes into a glass. After splashing whisky over them, he placed the glass on a small tray, ceremoniously walked over and handed it to Tom. "Thanks," Tom said, figuring he was getting served by the highest-paid bartender in the world. "Is there anything I can do to help?"

"Just sit down and make yourself comfortable. Bill Ogden will be along any minute."

Tom sat in a small, hard leather chair. Hopkins poured himself a drink and, acting for all the world like an anxious housewife entertaining the rector, fussed about the room, offering Tom first a plate of crackers spread with caviar, and then a porcelain box of cigarettes. (pp. 103–104)

According to Bendix the human relations approach to management arose from the increasing size and complexity of bureaucratic organizations. These led to the necessity for the widespread exercise of discretionary judgment throughout the corporation. Work, therefore, could not be done strictly on the basis of mechanical performance of strictly physical tasks. It needed to have more meaning than that. It needed to have, in other words, a place within a directly experienced emotional nexus.

The impact of this emotionally sophisticated form of management on the subordinate's feeling about work is indicated by Rath's response to Hopkins's criticism of his speech, which differed sharply from the response of Ogden, his immediate superior:

"Wonderful!" Hopkins suddenly boomed.

Tom turned around.

"*Marvelous*," Hopkins said, even louder. His whole face was beaming with satisfaction. "You've really got the feel for it!"

"I'm glad you like it," Tom said modestly.

"This really *sings*," Hopkins said enthusiastically. "It's remarkable that you could do so well the first time around!"

"It's a second draft, actually," Tom said. "Mr. Ogden gave me some suggestions."

"The *heart* of the thing is just right!" Hopkins said. "Now let's just go over it together. Did you bring a copy? . . ."

Sentence by sentence Hopkins took the whole speech apart. When he finished, he had asked for changes in almost every paragraph. "Well" he concluded, "You certainly did a grand job! Just fix up the details we've worked out and let's see it again in a few days. Would Wednesday be too early?"

Tom gulped his drink and excused himself. . . . He was halfway to Grand Central Station before he fully realized that Ogden and Hopkins had simply told him the same thing in two different ways: to rewrite the speech. In spite of this, Hopkins had somehow left him eager to try. Well, he thought admiringly, I always heard he could drive men and make them like it. (Wilson: pp. 114–115)

The important point here is that the traditional differentiation between the roles of the father and mother, based on the separation between engaging indifferent reality on one hand, and emotional expression on the other, could not be maintained in these organizations. The organization had to be reconstituted as a mother, and the manager's job became this process of reconstitution. For this, he had to develop his feminine side.

Mayo understood, however, that the manager could not simply express his emotions. The manager, as part of his job, had to express emotionality in accordance with what was required within the situation. But there would be no reason in the world to expect that the manager's emotional makeup would accord with the organization's necessities. Thus, although his job was to create a world that others took as warm and caring, his own emotions had to be very tightly controlled.

Mayo was emphatic in demanding that the elite control its sentiments, develop logical thinking, and hence master the "human-social facts." . . . Mayo made short shrift of the invidious distinction between the real wants of workers and the ideal qualities of employers. . . . He saw the individuals in both groups as creatures of sentiment and nonlogical thinking. The difference between them consisted simply in the capacity of an administrative elite to engage in logical thinking, to be independent from social routines, to free themselves from emotional involvement in order to "assess and handle the concrete difficulties of human collaboration." (Bendix: pp. 315–316)

Take these together. The job of the manager is to create an atmosphere of warmth and caring, an atmosphere in which employees feel as if others feel warmly toward them and care about them. But this creation is not supposed to reflect the spontaneous feelings of the manager; it is supposed to be part of a drama, a display of feeling that is under conscious control. One could not, returning to the charge of the alienated students, have a better definition of "phony" than that.

Push this a bit further and one can also see how the center of the manager's emotional life may have shifted from the family to the corporation. Consider, in this respect, that the manager was human, too. He needed connection, caring, and warmth as much as any other employee, but the world he lived in was quite the opposite. By virtue of the very fact that he had the function of creating an emotional nexus that did not express his own feelings, he and his feelings were excluded from, forbidden in, the world he created. The richer the world of his creation, the colder his own life. He had to know that he was a phony. Torn in half as he was, how could he live with himself? At the same time, his job was the economic mainstay of his family. He could not simply abandon it.

Under the circumstances it is not surprising that the person would defend himself through a fantasy in which he would be unified with his feelings within the context of the work organization. Within this fantasy, which is an aspect of the psychodynamics of hierarchy that we discussed in Chapter 2, elevation in the hierarchy would permit the individual to find a place in the organization that would permit him to express his spontaneous feelings. It would correspond to setting one's own agenda, rather than receiving one's cues for the appropriate emotional displays from superiors. To be sure, at any level of the organization, this would not happen, but the fantasy could still be maintained by projecting its realization to a higher level. In this way the manager could live with the wound in his identity by conceiving it as temporary, to be healed at some time in the future (Schwartz, 1990).

Tom Rath put the matter this way:

The thing to remember is this, he thought: Hopkins would want me to be honest. But when you come right down to it, why does he hire me? To help him do what he wants to do—obviously that's why any man hires another. And if he finds that I disagree with everything he wants to do, what good am I to him? I should quit if I don't like what he does, but I want to eat, and so, like a half million other guys in gray flannel suits, I'll always pretend to agree, until I get big enough to be honest without being hurt. That's not being crooked, it's just being smart. (p. 183)

Returning to the question of identity, though, notice what this would do to the individual's identity, and to his connections with others. It would result in him abandoning his commitment to who he really was at any given moment, and to the connections with concrete others, replacing them with a commitment to a fantasy identity, and fantasized relationship, which would be realized at a later date. In this way the center of the individual's life, the meaning of his activity, would shift toward what he had to do to climb up the hierarchy and realize this fantasy, and away from the concrete life he lived in the context of his family. He would have abandoned his family in the way that his wife and his alienated son charged. Thus, Ralph Hopkins, the master of the appropriate emotional gesture, the genius at the display of concern, lived a monastic life apart from his family, whose feelings of abandonment were powerful.

Moreover, to the extent that he would be around, he would not be around in a way that would lead his family to admire him. Rath understood very well the abandonment of himself that this would involve and was given a clear inkling of the loss of admiration that would result. He said to his wife, Betsy:

"There's a standard operating procedure for this sort of thing," he said. "It's a little like reading fortunes. You make a lot of highly qualified contradictory statements and keep your eyes on the man's face to see which ones please him. That way you can feel your way along, and if you're clever, you can always end up by telling him exactly what he wants to hear."

"Is that what they do?" Betsy asked. She didn't laugh. . . .

"I think it's a little sickening," Betsy said bluntly.

"Damn it, have a sense of humor. What's the matter with you?"

"Nothing's the matter with me. I'm just interested in knowing the answers to a few questions. What do you really think of that speech?"

"I think it's terrible," Tom said. "My business education, you see, is not complete. In a few years I'll be able to suspend judgment entirely until I learn what Hopkins thinks, and then I'll really and truly feel the way he does. That way I won't have to be dishonest any more." . . .

"You're angry with me," he said. "Can't you take a joke?"

"I don't think you were joking."

"Of course I was. I was knocking myself out with humor."

"What are you going to tell Hopkins tomorrow?"

"I don't know. Why's that so important all of a sudden?"

She put the kettle on the stove and turned toward him suddenly. "I didn't like the look of you sitting there in that big chair talking so damn smugly and cynically!" she said. "You looked disgusting! You looked like just the kind of guy you always used to hate. The guy with all the answers. The guy who has no respect for himself or anyone else."

"What do you want me to do?" he asked quietly. "Do you want me to go in there tomorrow and tell Hopkins I think his speech is a farce?"

"I don't care what you tell him, but I don't like the idea of your becoming a cheap cynical yes-man and being so self-satisfied and analytical about it. You never used to be like that." (pp. 185–186)

In concluding this section, then, it now seems possible to understand the disdain and anger the alienated son and his mother felt toward the corporation man. He was indeed a phony and he had abandoned the family. We can also understand the development of the facets of his character that the family found objectionable. Yet we can see that, whatever his sins, there was nothing specifically male about them. The corporation man was a model of androgyny. He was not the patriarch, and his sins were simply not the Sins of the Father.

THE FEMININE MYSTIQUE AND THE PRIMORDIAL MOTHER

If the sins of the corporation man, serious as they were, were not the Sin of the Father, we are left only with the final element of the charge against him—that he prevented the fulfillment of his wife. The question then becomes, what did this charge mean to his wife, his accuser? What was going on with the suburban housewife of the time that led her to feel unfulfilled and led that feeling to develop into the attack against the patriarch? Staying within the literature of the period, we are fortunate to have the original material that makes that case, the enormously influential book *The Feminine Mystique* by Betty Friedan (1962).

Friedan, following a general recognition of the time, observed that the middle-class American housewives of the period were experiencing a deep and serious unhappiness and discontent. This unhappiness was in sharp contrast with social expectations, according to which the housewife should have been perfectly fulfilled and ecstatic. Instead she suffered from what Friedan called "the problem that has no name." According to Friedan, the "problem that has no name" was occasioned by the housewife being trapped by the "feminine mystique," which Friedan defined this way:

The feminine mystique says that the highest value and the only commitment for women is the fulfillment of their own femininity. It says that the greatest mistake of Western culture, through most of its history, has been the undervaluation of this femininity. It says this femininity is so mysterious and intuitive and close to the creation and origin of life that man-made science may never be able to understand it. But however special and different, it is in no way inferior to the nature of man; it may even in certain respects be superior. The mistake, says the mystique, the root of women's troubles in the past is that women envied men, women tried to be like men, instead of accepting their own nature, which can find fulfillment only in sexual passivity, male domination, and nurturing maternal love. (p. 43)

Now this feminine mystique, pushed off on women by such forces as the male editors of women's magazines, psychoanalysis, functionalist sociology, advertising, sex-directed educators, and even turncoats such as Margaret Mead,

gives to American women . . . the old image: "Occupation: housewife." The new mystique makes the housewife-mothers, who never had a chance to be anything else, the model for all women; it presupposes that history has reached a final and glorious end in the here and now, as far as women are concerned. Beneath the sophisticated trappings, it simply makes certain concrete, finite, domestic aspects of feminine existence—as it was lived by women whose lives were confined, by necessity, to cooking, cleaning, washing, bearing children—into a religion, a pattern by which all women must now live or deny their femininity. (p. 43)

The problem that has no name showed up at this point because these women, educated as well as men, found that the life of the housewife, though perfected in its own terms, sharply curtailed the possibilities for the development of the talents that they had cultivated and the gifts they had to offer. The problem without a name was the feeling of stultification, of an unfulfilled need for growth:

It is my thesis that the core of the problem for women today is not sexual but a problem of identity—a stunting or evasion of growth that is perpetuated by the feminine mystique . . . It is my thesis that as Victorian culture did not permit women to accept or gratify their basic sexual needs, our culture does not permit women to accept or gratify their basic need to grow and fulfill their potentialities as human beings, a need which is not solely defined by their sexual role. (p. 77)

To begin the analysis of Friedan, it is first necessary to observe that her perspective on the situation of the housewife is in perfect concordance with the theory I have sketched so far. Recall that the sexual division of labor discussed earlier had the underlying fantasy that the male would engage external reality, pushing it away, so to speak, so that the free play of emotionality, presided over by the female, could have its safe and unrestrained operation in the home.

What we need to understand is that the external conditions that were supposed to represent the realization of this fantasy had been fulfilled. External reality, for the housewife, had indeed been pushed away.

Reality, as I have said, consists in whatever it is that makes it possible to make a mistake. It is what makes constraint necessary. But there was nothing that she had to do in which a mistake could be made, or at least one in which the consequences would be rapidly visible. There was nothing she had to see as a constraint.

Contrast this with previous times. Not long ago, if she had not arisen before dawn to renew the fire, the family would not have been able to get comfortably dressed. If she had not cooked properly, the family would not have been able to eat. If she had not made clothes, the family would have gone naked. She lived in negative conditions, to be sure, but prevailing against these negative conditions defined a life for her. What would give her a life when all she needed to do was set a thermostat? Or call out for pizza? Or go to Macy's? The problem is that the self, as a construction, is defined by contrast with what is not the self. Take away what is not the self, and the contrast with the not-self is lost. Take away the not-self, therefore, and the self disappears along with it.

This is the condition that Friedan confronts from the other side.

Just what was this problem that has no name? What were the words women used when they tried to express it? Sometimes a woman would say "I feel empty somehow . . . incomplete." Or she would say, "I feel as if I don't exist." (p. 20)

[B]y choosing femininity over the painful growth to full identity, by never achieving the hard core of self that comes not from fantasy but from mastering reality, these girls are doomed to suffer ultimately that bored, diffuse feeling of purposelessness, non-existence, non-involvement with the world that can be called *anomie*, or lack of identity, or merely felt as the problem that has no name. (p. 181)

This was the situation within which the housewife found herself. It was a condition drained of meaningful activity, of sense, of purpose, filled only with activities that had been created to occupy her time. As Friedan says, "When a woman tries to put the problem into words, she often merely describes the daily life she leads" (p. 30).

Indeed the problem was even worse than that, for the self, in Freud's terms the ego, is what provides a framework for the organization of our activity. It structures our experience and gives a direction to our desire. Without it our desire is experienced only as formless excitation. But this is the condition that Freud (1895/1962) originally described as the cause of anxiety! What was sought, what it was thought would be created, was a rich and full self that could express its love. This love would structure life at home; all she had to do was be herself. *But she had no self to be.* Her affective experience consisted not of love, but of anxiety. Her freedom created no structure, but only anomie. They thought they were building paradise. It turned out to be hell.

Friedan's solution for the problem, and one that I endorse, was that women's roles needed to be changed, and with them needed to be changed the sexual division of labor. The idea that men would go out and engage reality, leaving women to express emotionality within the home, had led to an unbearably painful stultification. The solution had to be the creation of the possibility, even the necessity, of growth. The separation of women from reality needed to be undone. Women needed careers that would permit them to engage reality at the limits of their capacities and talents.

Returning to our search for the origins of the attack against the father, we can see that parts of its roots are here. The alienated student and his mother were united in their disdain for the father. He saw his role as going out and engaging reality, attenuating its effects within the family so that emotion could reign there. This meant that she would be excluded from engagement with reality and therefore of the possibility of growth, which left her in exquisite misery. He expected to be appreciated and admired for performing this role, and that appreciation and admiration were the root of meaning for him. But he was not appreciated and admired, and we can see why. He had left her in an absolutely intolerable position. What was she supposed to appreciate him for? If her appreciation was the touchstone of the whole program of meaning for them, in the absence of her appreciation, how could she admire him? If she did not admire him, how could he be emulable? And from this denial of emulability, postmodernism, the un-committed alienated student, as we have seen, would follow. Thus:

strange new problems are being reported in the growing generations of children whose mothers were always there, driving them around, helping them with their homework—an inability to endure pain or discipline or pursue any self-sustained goal of any sort, a devastating boredom with life. Educators are increasingly uneasy about the dependence, the lack of self-reliance, of the boys and girls who are entering college today: "We fight a continual battle to make our students assume manhood," said a Columbia dean. (pp. 29–30)

Returning more fully to the idea of the Sin of the Father, though, we can see that there is a problem with this explanation. For even if we assume that the sexual division of labor deprived the wife of her growth, and even if we assume that the father got the better part of the deal here, there is still no basis for denying the value of his works. It is worthwhile noting that Friedan does not make such a denial. On the contrary she values his achievements. And, in fact, she could not devalue them without undermining her whole program. For her claim was that women have been denied the opportunity to do something constructive with their talents, a point that she makes by contrasting women with men, who have had the opportunity to do something constructive.

Consider, for example, this argument from Maslow (1970):

Even the need for self-respect, for self-esteem and for the esteem of others—"the desire for strength, for achievement, for adequacy, for mastery and competence, for confidence in the face of the world, and for independence and freedom"—is not clearly recognized for women. But certainly the thwarting of the need for self-esteem, which produces feelings of inferiority, of weakness, and of helplessness in man, can have the same effect on woman. *Self-esteem in woman, as well as in man, can only be based on real capacity, competence and achievement; on deserved respect from others rather than unwarranted adulation.* (p. 315; emphasis added)

Thus, deny that men have done something worthwhile and the claim that women have been deprived of the opportunity to do likewise falls apart.

In addition to this problem there is a difficulty that arises within Friedan's analysis itself. It is the apparent passivity of women, their willingness to be swept up by the feminine mystique, to yield to it easily and without resistance. For, as Friedan describes it, it is hard to see the source of its attractiveness. Recall her description:

[S]exual passivity, male domination . . . [the feminine mystique] makes certain concrete, finite, domestic aspects of feminine existence—as it was lived by women whose lives were confined, by necessity, to cooking, cleaning, washing, bearing children—into a religion, a pattern by which all women must now live or deny their femininity. (p. 43)

That doesn't sound so great. How could it appeal to anybody? It is not enough to say that the power of the feminine mystique was overwhelming. Where did it get its power? Advertisers, for example, may have mobilized the full weight of their creativity in constructing it, but advertisers do not generally go against the tide. Nor do university administrators, or magazine editors, or manufacturers. The idea of them throwing their enterprises behind the creation of a product to which no one was attracted is hard to believe. The idea that they would succeed mightily in the process is even more difficult. One could make the claim, of course, that women are, by nature, passive creatures, weak, easily swayed, and dominated, but that is not exactly a claim that Friedan, or I, would support.

The solution I propose provides an answer to both of the problems, disparate as they appear. It is that the image that appealed both to men and to women, which drew women into the suburban nest, was not an image of weakness and triviality, it was in fact the most powerful image in the psyche. It was an image of the Madonna, a person complete unto herself, of infinite love, infinite goodness, and at the same time omnipotent in the sense that her boundless love could provide for the complete fulfillment of all of our needs. *The appeal of the feminine mystique was the power of the primordial mother.*

The constraints imposed by necessity having been removed, nothing stood in the way of her tendency to identify with that powerful figure, the fantasy that had energized the whole configuration. This was supposed to have permitted the free flow of desire and spontaneity. The problem was, as we have seen, that the freedom she had to be herself did not result in bliss; it resulted in torment. Still, the omnipotence inherent in the image was not something that anyone would turn their back on, especially in the absence of a compelling alternative.

The idea of the castrating mother was a staple of Friedan's time. Typically, she notes, it was projected onto those women who abandoned their "feminine" role and competed with men. But, Friedan argues, it was not the women who sought professional careers who were responsible for a lack of masculinity among their sons, it was the ones who stayed at home, those whose occupation was housewife. This is a point that parallels Keniston's account (1960). Keniston's alienated students' mothers were housewives who had *given up* their careers.

Yet the image their alienated sons had of them is far from the image of the weak, passive, dependent creatures that such women were supposed to have become. For these young men, the mother was the dominant person in the household. They were dominant not only over the sons, but especially over the fathers. From what could this strength have been derived?

It can be explained on the grounds of an identification with the primordial mother, whose judgment of worth was the keystone of these men's sense of meaning, and who therefore had the power to render their lives meaningless by withholding that judgment. One cannot imagine a greater power.

Again, Friedan seems perplexed that few of the housewives of her time took the route of professional activity out of their misery. They could engage in amateur activity with no difficulty.

It is the jump from amateur to professional that is often hardest for a woman on her way out of the trap. But even if a woman does not have to work to eat, she can find identity only in work that is of real value to society—work for which, usually, our society pays. Being paid is, of course, more than a reward—it implies a definite commitment. *For fear of that commitment, hundreds of able, educated suburban house-*

wives today fool themselves about the writer or actress they might have been, or dabble at art or music in the dilettante's limbo of "self-enrichment,." . . . These are also ways of evading growth. (p. 346, emphasis added)

Friedan attributes this fear of commitment to the feminine mystique. The assumption that the feminine mystique was the appeal of the primordial mother leads to perfect agreement on this point, but provides a different slant. Commitment means the acceptance of obligations. It means doing what one ought to do, rather than what one wants to do. It means submission and subordination to an external agenda. It means the acceptance of limitation. It necessarily involves a descent from the fantasy of perfection, omnipotence, and freedom that the primitive mother involves. Refusal of commitment is understandable if one understands the fantasy that it is preserving.

Again, if the feminine mystique is the power of the primordial mother, we can understand the denial of the value of men's works. The fantasy of perfection inherent in the primordial mother would cause the value of men's works, limited as they are, to fare badly by comparison. Whatever the status, the prestige of the father, they would be seen as undeserved. Whatever his accomplishments, they would be seen as insufficient. Did he bring home income for the family? He did not bring home enough. And in what depravity does he engage in order to get it?

Under the circumstances, returning to our earlier exploration, we can better understand why he did not spend very much time at home. We find that we are also better able to understand the response of the alienated son. This mother was larger than life, so to speak, and her power to enrich the son's sense of importance was overwhelming. But he could only gain that sense by maintaining and feeding back to his mother her sense of omnipotence. What he was definitively barred from doing was admiring his father, because denying the worth of the father was a part of the very structure of the mother's image of herself and her condition. The postmodern consciousness, as we have seen, would follow.

We are still not at the end of our quest, because there are still two questions we have not answered. We have found again the source of the alienation of the son, and hence of the structure of postmodern consciousness. But we cannot, as yet, understand its strength. Thus the alienated son, while his consciousness reflects postmodernism, was not in a condition to push it. His was, after all, an alienated consciousness: his victory in the oedipal struggle was pyrrhic, as he well knew. He was filled with longing and loss. Postmodernism, on the other hand, as we may see from the dominance it has attained in so many academic disciplines, has been an aggressively active force. There has been tremendous power behind it. Where has this power come from? The second question is still the original one. What was the Sin of the Father? For, again, the image of the father here is weak, and not to be admired, but if there is in this very little capacity for great good, there is also very little capacity for great evil. How could this puny creature commit the Sin of the Father?

THE POWER OF THE DAUGHTER

As before, these two questions may be answered on the basis of the same recognition. This recognition brings to focus the one element of this familial stew that we have not touched on at all. This family not only had sons, but also daughters. And it was, as I argue, the daughters who inherited the power of this configuration and hold it to this day. The daughter in this dysfunctional ménage is the power behind postmodernism, seen as a political force.

The son was weak because he could not develop power through identification with a valued father. Yet his identification with his powerful mother, for the obvious reasons, had to be partial and incomplete. No such strictures applied to the daughter. She did not have to admire the father in order to gain strength. She could identify with the awesome power of the primordial mother. She could adopt the mother's denigration of the father, not losing strength in the bargain, as the son did, but gaining it because it would give her a way of understanding why her mother was both so powerful and so miserable.

This finally gives us an answer to our question of the origin of the Sin of the Father. The primordial mother, in addition to being omnipotent, is also the fount of all goodness. She is, essentially, goodness herself—the original goddess, as some might say (Eisler, 1987). If someone were to identify with her, and yet find limitation and anxiety in her life, an explanation would be required that would do justice to this in moral terms. The imputation of badness would serve very nicely here, and it would have to be commensurate with the magnitude of the goodness it prevailed against. Perfect goodness would draw out, then, an imputation of perfect badness to explain its limitation, and they would be locked in a condition of essential conflict—the sexual holy war.

What we need to see here is that this imputation of badness is itself a psychological process. Badness is whatever is experienced as posing limitations to the power of her absolute goodness. But what presents such limitations is reality itself—her own real limitations and the limitations posed by the existence of an external world. As we saw before, the father is the symbolic representative of reality. His Sin is a projection onto him of the badness of the reality he represents.

His achievements were bad, and his failures were bad. His presence was bad, and his absence was bad. What he did was bad, and what he didn't do was bad. This makes sense if we understand that it did not matter what he did or did not do. The idea that he had sinned came first, and then everything he did was interpreted to exemplify it. He did not even have to consciously take up the role of representing reality. The very existence of reality, of anything that did not fit into the fantasy nexus of Madonna-and-child, would have been enough. If a suitable personification for this role had not existed, one would have been created.

The idea of evil must be created if the idea of perfect goodness is to be preserved, and it must be attributed to a palpable form so that goodness can be capable of realizing its potential by overcoming it. The Father has become the incarnation of perfect evil, the devil. His new role is to fit into a drama, the morality play of the struggle of good versus evil that we have called the sexual holy war. His role in this presentation is to personify evil.

Within this context we can see that a good life, indeed a perfect life can be lived in the service of the destruction of his power. If that happens, according to the script, the power of the primordial mother, as represented now by the daughters, can come into its own, creating a perfect world.

What would arise from all of this would be a tremendous feeling of potency on the part of the daughter. Within this configuration we can also see that the daughter would have power over the son, for whom overdependency on the female was the defining characteristic of the psychological framework. That tells us what we need to know about the power of postmodernism.

WOMEN'S STUDIES AND THE FEMININE MYSTIQUE: THE IDEOLOGY OF THE DAUGHTER

There is an element of this analysis that bears further elaboration. I have argued that the feminine mystique was the power of the primordial mother. I have further argued that the daughter of the suburban housewife identified with her mother's primordial power, and took it as her life's meaning and mission to destroy her father's power, substituting the expression of her self. The implication of this, though, is that the daughter identified with the feminine mystique. Yet, clearly enough, being a suburban housewife is the last thing in the world that these daughters want to do. How do we account for this apparent contradiction?

The contradiction is accounted for by the fact that the daughters brought the feminine mystique with them and maintain it as the fundament of their feminist ideology and practice. We see this most directly in the areas of theory and practice over which they have the most control: feminist pedagogy and, especially, women's studies programs in the university. Feminism, as women's studies programs understand it, is the feminine mystique taken out of the family and turned toward the world. Add the attribution that men are the reason the feminine mystique has not yet made the world perfect and you have the whole program, including the elaboration of the toxic man/Madonna-and-child motif with which we began our investigation.

Recall in this connection Friedan's formulation: "The feminine mystique says that the highest value and the only commitment for women is the fulfillment of their own femininity" (p. 43). Compare it with formulations of how the expression of the female, typically understood as nurturant, caring, and nonhierarchical will be inherently superior to the work that is done by men in a wide range of fields. Thus, in the field of governance, MacKinnon (1988), who defines feminism as "the theory of women's point of view" (p. 120), says:

Its project is to uncover and claim as valid the experience of women. . . . This defines the task of feminism not only because male domination is perhaps the most pervasive and tenacious system of power in history, but because it is metaphysically nearly perfect. Its point of view is the standard for point-of-viewlessness, its particularity the meaning of universality. Its force is exercised as consent, its authority as participation, its supremacy as the paradigm of order, its control as the definition of legitimacy. (pp. 116–117)

Again, in science, we have this from Sandra Harding (1986), approvingly presenting the view of Nancy Hartsock:

A feminist epistemological standpoint is an interested social location ("interested" in the sense of "engaged," not "biased"), the conditions for which bestow upon its occupants scientific and epistemic advantage. The subjugation of women's sensuous, concrete, relational activity permits women to grasp aspects of nature and social life that are not accessible to inquiries grounded in men's characteristic activities. The vision based on men's activities is both partial and perverse—"perverse" because it systematically reverses the proper order of things: it substitutes abstract for concrete reality; for example, it makes death-risking rather than the reproduction of our species form of life the paradigmatically human activity. (p. 148)

One could go on from there to many other fields, such as administration (Ferguson, 1984), music (McClary, 1991), and even logic (Nye, 1990). In all of this, one can see the idealization of the primordial mother. To be sure, in many of these cases, it is maintained that the feminine attributes, so called, are "socially constructed" rather than "essential." Nonetheless it is uniformly assumed that when women gain power the new social arrangements they create will retain the virtues of women, even though an entirely different set of social arrangements would presumably have "socially constructed" gender entirely differently. This suggests that the mythology of the primordial mother goes a great deal deeper than feminist thought about social construction.[2]

Finally one may point to the characteristics of the feminist classroom itself. Patai and Koertge (1994), two disillusioned veterans of the feminist movement, in a devastating critique of Women's Studies programs, observe: "Many feminist classrooms cultivate an insistence on feeling," which, on examination, turns out to be the traditional split between intellect and emotion recycled, with the former still assigned to men and the latter to women" (p. 3).

Compare this with Friedan's description of the "home economics" classroom of the fifties, in which the feminine mystique was pushed: "There is a pseudotherapeutic air, as the professor listens patiently to endless self-conscious student speeches about personal feelings (verbalizing) in the hopes of sparking a 'group insight' " (pp. 169–170).

And it is worthwhile noting that Friedan's objection to this:

But though the functional course is not group therapy, it is certainly an introduction of opinions and values through manipulation of the students' emotions; and in this manipulative disguise, it is no longer subject to the critical thinking demanded in other academic disciplines. (p. 17)

is paralleled precisely by Patai and Koertge's observation that:

In feminist pedagogy, the new valorization of women's modes of communication and interaction has led to the use of sentiment as a tool of coercion. (p. 3)

In this we can see the core of "political correctness," which is the way in which the primordial mother exerts her power, and toward which we will shortly turn our attention. For the time being, though, we do well to note that we have some unfinished business.

THE MISERY OF THE DAUGHTER

If this were a detective story, we could stop here. "The daughter did it," we could say, and that would be the end of the matter. But it is not a detective story. It is an attempt to understand human beings and, therefore, it seems to me, it should not end until it ends with sympathy.

How shall we find sympathy for the daughter? More precisely, and bringing this matter as close to home as I can manage, my question is how can *I* find sympathy for her? I find her narcissism, her self-righteousness, and her rage obnoxious. She claims standing as a victim of oppression, but she is a part of the most privileged large group of human beings the world has ever known. She condemns the selfishness of men, but what is there outside of herself that truly concerns her? As Simpson (1995) has argued, her supposed connectedness is not connection to anything real, not to other concrete human beings, but is abstract and empty. She is a fantasy to herself, and she connects only to fantasy. Her grandiosity condemns all mortals and their works, but I want to know on what basis of achievement she feels the right to have such contempt for men. What good has she brought? What are the benefits that have come from the increase in her power?

In this distressing picture, there is a human being who can be engaged. I can engage with her in her misery, for she is a deeply, desperately unhappy person. I can see this in the very rage that is so repellent to me. For if it is disagreeable to me, I must have an idea how it feels to her. As with all rage, it destroys the inside as it tries to destroy the outside. And if she is deeply unconnected to others, imagine how lonely she is. If the correlate of her grandiosity has to be infinite and uncompromising love, imagine how bitterly she must feel the ineluctable indifference of the world.

Reflecting on this, it seems to me that, of the damaged creatures in the modern family, her wound is the most painful. It is the most painful because she must have the most difficult time healing it. To heal it, she will have to find common ground with mortal, limited creatures capable of sin—creatures like me, for example. Yet she bears from her relationship with her mother the premise of being infinite and divine. If the son has a hard time separating from this overwhelming mother, think how hard it has to be for her.

She must separate, if her misery is not simply to get worse. She must realistically take the measure of her mother if she is going to come to a realistic appreciation of her father. And unless she can value the father and his work, she will not be able to learn what he has to teach, nor be able to emotionally engage herself in the work that she inherits from him. That work, then, will have to seem empty, sterile, and meaningless. Again, missing its meaning and unable to take her predecessor as a model, she is likely to fail at it and not understand why she has failed. Her rage is likely only to increase.

I can have compassion for the difficulty of her journey, whether in any individual case she has begun it or not. She is, after all, my sister.

CONCLUSION

It is time to reiterate that the primordial mother is not a problem because she is a mother, but because she is primordial. She is a product of the psyche at a point before we have gained a firm sense of ourselves, and of the distinction between ourselves and what is not ourselves. Her power is based on our desire to deny the world outside ourselves, and what that world tells us about our own limitations. So it is with postmodernism, which tells us that reality is just one fantasy among others. The fact that they bear the same message is no coincidence.

Again, what we can catch in all of this is an image of larger, deeper forces at work, expressing themselves through this family. The operative force arises from a level of organizational and technological development, largely the result of the work of the organization man, which has rendered us powerful and wealthy beyond anything that our wisdom can direct. We have become so powerful that the very idea of limitation has seemed to lose its meaning; the idea that stupid behavior will have adverse consequences has lost the quality of being obvious.[3] We have become so wealthy that we seem to be able to buy ourselves out of any misfortune, and if we cannot, we feel justified in becoming indignant. So rich and powerful have we become that we can take our dreams and fantasies as the norms for our lives, seeing the reality that conflicts with these dreams as an offense and an insult.

It is critical to see, however, that this is an illusion. Reality has not disappeared. It is simply that we do not relate to it *mano-a-mano* as previous generations did. The result is that we cannot take its measure directly. Reality has been displaced to a level where we must deal with it collectively and symbolically, relying on a collective, symbolic definition of our relationship to it.

The suburban housewife was, in an important sense, designated the role of inheriting the godlike wealth and power that this collective effort brought forth. It was the sense of her omnipotence that went along with this that came increasingly to dominate our collective definition of ourselves and of our relationship to the world. In place of the continual development of a realistic sense of the self that contact with reality made both possible and necessary, a space was opened that could be filled by fantasy.

Repudiating the father and his function established this fantasy as the norm. This norm was based on an illusion, and as such it constituted a deep psychological regression. This regression is what we see working through the culture in the guise of postmodernism and the primitive form of feminism that concerns us. The attack against the patriarch, then, represents and is driven by the rage that infantile narcissism holds for the existence of anything beyond itself.

We turn now to understand the danger of this regression in more detail, in terms of the ways it affects concrete social institutions. That is our purpose in the next two chapters. There we will try to gain an understanding of the transformations undergone by two of our most important institutions for engaging external reality as they come under the rule of the primordial mother. These institutions are our system of higher education, which has the function of engaging external reality by thought, and the military, which engages it by force. We discuss the former in the context of political correctness, and the latter in terms of the issue of women in combat.

NOTES

1. Actually, as we saw in Chapter 1, the real father has not sinned all that much. Our skeptic, here, is making a logical case, not an empirical one.

2. An aspect of this is revealed by Patai and Koertge (1994), here quoting one of their sources:

It constantly happens in class that students argue for social constructionism on the one hand, but revert to essentialist ideas quite opportunistically. It's as if everything they dislike about "women" gets dismissed as social construction, while all the rest is the Real Thing. (p. 144)

And, by contrast,

As for men, most everything about them is not socially constructed, since that would, in some sense, let them off the hook, so men get heavy doses of essentialist attributes while the students imagine they're espousing a straight constructionist line of analysis. (p. 144)

3. In an interesting book that parallels much of what I have described here, Neil Lyndon (1992) discusses the role of the birth control pill and safe and reliable abortion in the evolution of feminism. His point is that they put women in an undefined situation for which they were unprepared. This accords with the theory of anomie I have employed here and, as an aspect of this, the separation of action from adverse consequences.

Chapter Five

Political Correctness and the Revolt of the Primitive

The term "political correctness" made its way into public consciousness through an article by Richard Bernstein in the *New York Times* (1991). It referred to a strain of postmarxist leftist thought in which the struggle be-tween economic classes had been replaced,[1] as a primary ontological framework, with a more differentiated set of oppositions based on such dif-ferences as sex, race, and sexual orientation.[2] Thus, as Bernstein put it:

Central to pc-ness, which has its roots in 1960's radicalism, is the view that West-ern society has for centuries been dominated by what is often called "the white male power structure" or "Patriarchal hegemony." A related belief is that every-body but white heterosexual males has suffered some form of repression and been denied a cultural voice. (Section 4: p. 1)

He added that, to many of those concerned with this phenomenon, the dis-turbing thing about political correctness ("PC") has not been the content of its ideology, but the principle of argumentation that it has employed:

more than an earnest expression of belief, "politically correct" has become a sarcas-tic jibe used by those, conservatives and classical liberals alike, to describe what they see as a growing intolerance, a closing of debate, a pressure to conform to a radical program or risk being accused of a commonly reiterated trio of thought crimes: sexism, racism and homophobia. (Section 4: p. 4)

Anyone familiar with the climate of the universities of our time[3] will recognize these developments, but for others a story may be useful. One that will do as well as any recalls an early experience of my own with PC. This was in 1987, after I had returned from a sabbatical where I had been working on a book on narcissistic processes in organizations. The campus minister was interested in my work and asked me to make a presentation at an institute that he was starting. The presentation required an overview of Freud's concept of the Oedipus complex.

As I was going through this part of the argument, a woman in the audience, who happened to be the chair of the psychology department at the time, had what can only be called a fit. Without addressing herself to anything I was saying in particular, and without any apparent attempt to control her rage, she said that Freud was a sexist and a misogynist, and went on to condemn the entire psychoanalytic enterprise, which she said was "shot through" with sexism and racism. As she talked it became clear to me that she didn't know what she was talking about. She said, for example, that the Oedipus complex did not apply to women, which was why Freud invented the idea of the Electra complex. She was evidently unaware of the fact that it was Jung, not Freud, who used the term "Electra complex."

Despite this woman's evident lack of grounding in her subject matter, her voice seemed to express a feeling of absolute authority. I recall that at the time this struck me as very odd. But what struck me as even more peculiar was that as she engaged in this frenzied performance, the other members of the audience were not looking at her as if she were acting strangely, but were looking at me as if I had done something contemptible and despicable.

For the psychoanalytically oriented social scientist, nothing is more useful than a sense of the bizarre. I was being browbeaten, and the other faculty present for the occasion were looking at me as if I had committed a crime. The atmosphere in that room more resembled a police interrogation than the dispassionate search for truth that traditionally has characterized the academic setting. This was a fact that was at least as well known to the other faculty members in the room as it was to me, yet there they were, passive participants in this assault.

So what was going on here? How did ideas representing such ignorance not only arise in a university setting, but also come to be dominant within it, and to dominate it so powerfully that it has become acceptable to meet alternative ideas with rage and disdain? Certainly it was not through their merits, as demonstrated in the intellectual competition that has heretofore defined the university. Observers will acknowledge that these ideas are rarely defended on their intellectual strengths. Rather they are simply stated, and their critics insulted. At one level the answer to how they have come to monopolize intellectual life is "political correctness." Although that is certainly true, it simply raises the question at another level. For where did political correctness get its power? How did an assemblage of dubious ideas, together with a manner of argumentation foreign to everything the university has traditionally stood for, come to dominate the university? And what is the nature of the university so transformed? Those are the questions toward which our inquiry now turns.

Part of the foundation for our inquiry has already been developed. As we have seen, our times have been marked by an increase in our distance from reality, by a separation of behavior from its consequences. This has given rise to the idea of the uselessness of the father and to a rebellion against him in the name of the primordial mother. Political correctness, as a social movement, is the form that this rebellion takes. At the same time, it has come to be the way our ideas of ourselves are shaped in the absence of a direct engagement with reality. To get a better idea of what this means, we need to explore further the role of the father.

THE ROLE OF THE FATHER IN SOCIALIZATION

The father's function, as we have argued, is to engage the indifferent external world and to make a space in that world that is amenable to the life of the family. His role is to create a distance between the family and external reality so that the maternal world can be realized within the family, giving the children a deep feeling that they are important and loved. His role in bringing up the children is related to this. The role of the father is to represent indifferent external reality within the family so that, by introjecting him, the children can come to see things from that point of view and learn to cope with that reality.[4]

The father's job is to convey to the children the image that indifferent others would have of them. Seeing ourselves from that perspective, we develop the capacity for what I shall call *objective self-consciousness*. By this I do not mean to say that we see ourselves as we really are, but rather that we come to be able to see ourselves as objects, in ways that are not determined by our own feelings, whether positive or negative. We develop the capacity to see ourselves as objects in a world of others who share the same idea of reality and understand themselves as objects in the same ways. This is what

George Herbert Mead (1934) called the "generalized other." In Jacques Lacan's (1977) terms, we learn to place ourselves within the symbolic. It is how children learn the rules of exchange that operate within their culture; what they must do to get along, in a reciprocal way, with others who are indifferent to them as individuals. It gives us a basis for coordinating our activities with others in our culture and mediates our relations with them.

The institutionalization of these rules forms the society's normative structure—the mutual expectations we have of each other and the associated beliefs about appropriate behavior. The normative structure mediates our relations with others and ties us into their lives. This mutual relationship among our lives is what gives the normative structure its moral character. We become socialized members of the society by internalizing the normative structure, turning external demands into obligations. In this way we come to differentiate between legitimate authority and coercion. We learn why we must inhibit our sexuality and aggression, and what a fair day's work is. Indeed it is only through this process that the child comes to make sense of the fact that it has to work in the first place. In general, we come to understand what we previously could not understand: why we must do what we do not want to do.

In performance of this teaching role, the father acts both as the agent of the external world and as our agent in helping us learn how to live in that world. The father is successful in this role when he becomes unnecessary. As the normative structure becomes our own, we develop the capacity to act autonomously and without being dependent on him. This capacity represents a configuration of the mind that Freud called the superego.

One can see the value of the superego by reflecting on the culturally useful activities that it generates. It provides the psychological substrate for the understanding of social order and the experience of obligation. It also preserves society from the distortion of reality and the sense of infinite entitlement that narcissism would otherwise generate. Through the superego people are enabled to give up their infantile narcissism on the promise of being able to earn the ego ideal later through fulfillment of their obligations.

None of this takes away from the value of the ego ideal and the maternal role. Only the ego ideal can give inspiration to what would otherwise be a dry and joyless pattern of responsibilities. The superego structures our understanding of how we are separate from the world around us and therefore how we must engage it on its own terms, but the ego ideal provides a meaning for this engagement by giving us an image of overcoming our separation and becoming one with the world. Under the narcissism of the ego ideal, I experience the external world as part of myself. Under the superego, based as it is on objective self-consciousness, I experience myself as being part of the external world. The superego articulates with the ego ideal to form the basic psychological configuration of the socialized adult.

This understanding can clear up a number of difficulties we may have in reconciling ourselves with society. For example it will be useful for those who are offended by the very idea of seeing themselves as objects. What we need to recall, in this connection, is that this objectivity is only part of the total picture. Far from precluding our subjective understanding of ourselves, it gains its importance by its capacity to enhance our subjective experience by making us richer and more complex human beings. Taken by itself, it is the basis for organizational structure, for universalistic law, and for much else besides. It is never taken just by itself, however, and it is this recognition that enables us to appreciate the benefits of these institutions while, at the same time, remaining aware of their limitations.

The family, as Freud understood it, incorporates both the superego and the ego ideal in the form of paternal and maternal elements, recognizing the difference and the value of each. It encompasses the functions of each and the interplay between them, forming a complex whole. It manifests what I shall call a *biparental* model of child rearing.

If Freud is correct about the function of the family, it means that the image of the sexual holy war that first confronted us represents a profound distortion. Neither society as a whole nor families have been formed by the domination of the male principle over the female. Rather they have been formed by an evolution in which paternal elements are engaged with maternal ones to form a complex, biparental whole. The revolt of the primordial mother, then, is not simply an attempt to overturn a paternal order, but an attempt to unravel the connection between paternal and maternal. It is a regressive attempt to repudiate the father's role within the biparental order, and to bring us back to a world in which the primordial mother, who in the infant's mind did not need the father, prevails. This is the meaning of political correctness.

FROM THE BIPARENTAL TO THE PRIMITIVE MATERNAL IN THE UNIVERSITY

To understand the social meaning of a revolt against the paternal, we need to understand how the superego, the institutionalized paternal, traditionally operates in an institutional context. This is an easy matter, with regard to the university, because the workings of both parental functions are clear, and they come to us as "common sense."

In the biparental model, the meaning of the university is the transmission and development of objective self-consciousness. We transmit our best understanding of ourselves, of our world, and of our place within it; and we further develop that understanding.

The function of the superego in the university is primarily the development, application, and transmission of standards. The superego, by acknowledging the existence of an objective external world that can punish us if we get things wrong, places a premium on getting things right. The meaning of standards is the establishment of the best ways we know of getting things right. The function of research, of course, is to get to know the world better, which means increasing what we rightly know about the world and dismissing what we find out to be wrong. With regard to teaching, the university, in its paternal function, prepares students to achieve something in the world based upon the modeling of good work, work in accordance with the highest standards, and the differential reward of good versus bad work. If the process is successful, the student internalizes this polarity between good work and bad work as part of his superego. The student learns to hold himself to account and goes out into the world where he or she achieves something based upon the standards that are now his or her own.

With regard to decision making in the biparental university, the superego manifests itself as intended rationality. The whole panoply of procedures for making decisions in the university exists for the purpose of taking possibilities for action and subjecting them to the highest standards of rational criticism. It attempts to eliminate subjective distortion, to minimize parochial and narcissistic bias, and to get as close as possible to a course of action that will have the desired concrete result. Surely this is not to say that the university, any more than anyone or anything else, always gets things right. Certainly it does not mean that university professors are less narcissistic than anyone else — a view that only those unfamiliar with the university could uphold. It is simply to say that rational criticism is an accepted and legitimated mode of university discourse, that the distortions that narcissistic bias creates are recognized as distortions, and that the structures created to limit their effects are seen as legitimate.

None of this is to deny that the ego ideal is present in the university in equal measure to the superego. The ego ideal is the source of the university's ideals, without which it would lose the spirit of its existence and the impetus for its development. It is also present, perhaps most importantly, in the nurturing of the individual student, bringing that student to be able to accept his or her own spontaneity, which is the wellspring of creativity. It should never be forgotten, in this connection, that the muse is a female figure. But within the biparental university, creativity and the pursuit of ideals are channeled by the representation of external demand into good work and concrete achievement. Indeed, it is the dialectical relationship between the ego ideal and the superego, between the creative impulse and the demands of rigor, which constitutes the conversation that is the university's most characteristic form of life.

The premise of the superego within the biparental model is that love needs to be earned through good work, through achievement. To be sure, the superego cannot provide us with love, but only with respect. Love attaches to who we are, not what we do; it cannot be earned (Sennett and Cobb, 1972). But the superego can provide the criteria on which people agree that persons *should* be loved, based on the fulfillment of its requirements. This provides the basis for the social dramatization of love that we call status or prestige, and this is what those of low status feel deprived of.

Put the idea of a self-subsistent, objective external world into question, and one undermines objective self-consciousness, the meaning of the father. Take away the idea of an objective world, and you deny the legitimacy of external demand and the superego that represents it. The distinction between legitimate authority and coercion is lost. Demands come to be seen as oppression. Deny the superego and all that is left is narcissism; the only question becomes whose narcissism.

When the idea of an objective external world is lost, the idea of doing good work, of achievement, no longer has meaning. Individuals who have had status in the past, and who legitimated that status by claims of achievement, come to be seen instead as having acquired their status illegitimately. The idea of gaining status through achievement comes to be seen as a smokescreen for theft. Those who have had status are thus redefined as having stolen love from those of low status. They are seen as oppressors who deserve to be hated and attacked, and to have their power destroyed. In this way the idea of achievement, and the distinction between good and bad work, which served to provide the meaning of the university in the biparental model, come to seem self-serving categorizations whose meaning is to be found in the expression of the father's narcissism.

Undermine the idea of an external world and the father is not seen as having contributed anything, but only as having stolen love. He may be expelled with no loss to anyone. No barrier would then remain between the children and the primordial mother. They would be able to live in permanent enjoyment of their closeness with her. Her power would guarantee their happiness. This is the meaning of the PC university. It is an attempt, in the name of the primordial mother, to expel the father, and the external world he represents, and to substitute the unconditional love of the mother.

In what follows, I develop this analysis with regard to various aspects of the university, beginning with the organizational considerations of structure and process.

ORGANIZATIONAL STRUCTURE AND PROCESS IN THE PC UNIVERSITY

In order to understand both the appeal and the danger of organization based on the primitive mother, it is necessary to underscore the fact that the primordial mother is a fantasy. She is not a real mother. She is the image of mother cast in the mold of the infant's desire. The primordial mother is the infantile fantasy of a person who would complete the circle of a loving world centered upon the infant. In other words she is the complement of the infant's narcissism. When individuals identify with her, when they re-form themselves in her image, they give up their own adult character and remake themselves on the basis of the most primitive levels of their psyches.

The appeal of this regression is clear enough. As we know, we all desire to fuse with the primordial mother and again be the center of a loving world. But, as a principle of organization, the rule of the primordial mother falls well short of delivering on its promise.

First notice that the loving world of which the person would be the center would have only one person in it, plus that person's reflection: it would contain no independent others. This is not recognized as a problem by the narcissistic child, who sees no need for independent others, but as a principle of organization in a real world which contains real others, it has a contradiction at its core.

Narcissism, which the connection with the primordial mother enshrines and guarantees, makes it impossible to live peaceably in a world in which there are real others. I demand that you take me as the center of your world, and you demand that I take you as the center of my world. There is no way in which we can make sense out of the otherness of the other. It does not belong in the maternal world, the "good" world which has me as its center, and so therefore must be "bad." It has to be met with total emotional rejection. The gulf between persons is absolute. How can organization be possible at all?

As we can see the love of the primordial mother, which it seems to us would make the world complete, appears to be a perfect principle of organization. In reality, however, it would shatter the world. It is a principle of perfect *disorganization*, of chaos.[5] Within it, we expect to find harmony and meaning. We find instead what Friedan's housewife found in her suburban ghetto: anxiety and anomie.

The problem here is that love is specific. The kind of unconditional love that defines the primordial mother for me means that she (or he) takes my point of view without subjecting it to judgment or to categorization. Love means being accepted because we are exactly who we are. But our own inclusion on the grounds of such specificity defines for us a moral universe which excludes everyone who is not who we are, which is to say everyone else.

At one level this problem is resolved by the psychology of the group. If the person can substitute a group identity for an individual one, social organization becomes possible at the level of the group. An idea of oneself as a member of a group can serve as one's ego ideal. This opens the possibility that others can adopt the same ego ideal. Those who do so may identify with each other based on that fundamental similarity. In this way relations previously characterized by envy and antagonism are transformed into group feeling (Freud, 1921).

This means that the problem of narcissistic disorganization will reappear between groups. Instead of believing that the world should revolve around us as individuals, we come to believe that it should revolve around us by virtue of our group identity. It is those outside the group, those who do not take the group as their own ego ideal, who are now experienced as threats and as not belonging in the world. Thus, for mutually antagonistic individuals, we have simply substituted mutually antagonistic groups. This is the first element of the structure of the PC university.

The second problem of organization based on the primordial mother is the need to provide an affective connection through which the people can make claims on her. In the family, or for that matter in Japanese organizations where the maternal principle is powerful (Doi, 1973), a strong interest on the part of the mother is sought through an appeal based on continual association, but in the university, where people come and go, this is not a viable option.

In the university dominated by the processes of PC,[6] this problem is dealt with through an abstraction. The abstraction is the idea of the child who needs love the most, the one who has been least loved in the past, the victim. It is this abstraction, this specific claim to having been damaged in a certain way and at a certain time, therefore, that provides the basis of the group's identity. This provides the reason why individuals who deviate from the group with regard to the ideology of its victimization are treated as if they do not belong to the group. (See, for example, Carter, 1991.) It is a mistake, therefore, to think of these groups as defined by demographic characteristics. At their root they are defined by an *ideology* about demographic characteristics. My point here is that understanding conflicts among such groups rests less on understanding the claims of the specific groups against each other than on understanding the fundamentally intrapsychic dynamics of the idea of such conflict itself.

The differentiation into groups based on level of victimization determines the logic according to which social structure develops within the PC university. It also gives rise to the basic social process within the PC university, which is, on one hand, to love the victim and to provide for those so designated a maternal world in which their narcissism will be fulfilled. I call this *compensatory narcissistic inflation*. The other side of this is to withdraw love from and to hate those who have previously been loved, who come to be seen as having stolen that love from those who now are in need of it.

The idea of compensatory narcissistic inflation provides the key to understanding a number of the characteristics of the PC university, which our inquiry now undertakes to elaborate. Perhaps the most obvious of these is the fragmentation of the campus into mutually antagonistic groups that is often referred to as *the balkanization of the university*.

THE BALKANIZATION OF THE UNIVERSITY

As we have seen, the shift from biparental psychology to the sole dominion of the ego ideal has the effect of delegitimizing achievement as a ground for appreciation. The concept of respect loses its meaning. The claim that some have earned their status comes to seem an expression of racism, sexism, or classism, depending on who fares badly in the comparison. In a word it becomes politically incorrect. In the place of achievement, as a basis for appreciation, the politically correct substitute perceived deprivation.

From this vantage point, we can understand why the students come to engage in a competition for sympathy and even pity. By arguing that they have been victimized, oppressed, abused, devalued in the past, the students assert their claims to compensatory appreciation, for the love that, in their view, has been stolen from them. The African-Americans have their history of slavery and discrimination. The Jews have the history of anti-Semitism and the holocaust. The women have the history of rape and sexual harassment. The homosexuals have homophobia and gay bashing. The white males have a more difficult project, but it is far from hopeless. They can, for example, condemn their ancestors for depriving them of their purity, and in that way join the anti-oppressor chorus with full fury. It would be absurd to say that such claims do not refer to real histories of oppression. Often they do. My point here only concerns the way they function to express resentments and legitimate competing demands for appreciation.

This emotionally charged conflict, when it takes place in our intendedly multicultural universities, undoubtedly is a source of constant surprise, perplexity, and sadness to the well-meaning individuals who have given rise to it. Certainly they meant nothing of the sort. For them "the point is to join differences in such a way that the integrity of none is destroyed." They had in mind a mosaic, or a quilt in which "differences are sutured together at their edges to form a whole" (Choi and Murphy, 1992). But by establishing narcissism as the norm for university life, PC advocates made it inevitable that the actual university would be the locus of bitterness, envy, and ill will. Resentment and hostility are not just temporary feelings that will be outgrown in the PC university; they are built into its very structure. The fact that each of these groups recognize and are constituted by the difference of the others does not mean, as Choi and Murphy appear to believe, that they appreciate those differences. All it means, within narcissistic psychology, is that they define themselves *against* the others.

It is the superego, and specifically objective self-consciousness, from whose indifferent vantage point each voice is only one among many, that makes it possible for groups to get along with each other. This is the premise of legal-rational authority (Weber, 1947), arguably the greatest achievement of Western civilization. Of course the superego can be changed. It can be changed to better approximate our ideals, and it can be changed in accordance with differing and developing reality. This is implied by the term "rational" in "legal-rational." But objective self-consciousness is *not* just one voice among many. It needs to be located at the top of a hierarchy, not only if it is going to function at all, but also if *other* voices are going to function without engaging each other in a duel to the death. The fact that, with its rules, its reliance on reason, its demand for superordinate status, rational-legal authority is seen by the PC as the very source of oppression (e.g., MacKinnon, 1989) has the most profound impact on the way the university makes its decisions.

THE SUBORDINATION OF RATIONALITY IN DECISION MAKING

The premise of the superego is the indifference of the world. Truth is seen as neutral and is given independent standing. On the other hand, the narcissistic psychology of political correctness rests all consideration on a prior differentiation between good people and bad people, whose ideas contain this goodness or badness within them. The idea of an independent truth is replaced by a notion of relative "truths" which are not presumed to have even the possibility of validity outside of the community that uses them (e.g., Fish, 1992). Strained through the moralism I have described, this approach comes to mean that the expression of the feelings of a good person must be granted validity without any independent measure of the agreement of those feelings with facts being necessary. By contrast it is enough to classify a speaker as a member of a bad group in order to discredit what that person says, with no need for any consideration of the content of what is said. Within the context of PC, that is to say, the criterion of logic is replaced by the *argumentum ad hominem*. Later we explore the psychology of PC and show why such ad hominem arguments are as effective as they are.

For the present it will be useful to note that these considerations provide an answer to those who maintain that what is going on in the PC university is the same thing that has always gone on. The university, these individuals maintain, has always been a contentious place. In response one may acknowledge that the university has always been a contentious place, but its contention has been concerned with what is true and who is right. In current PC times, the question has become who is good.

As a result decision making in the PC university loses even the intention of being rational. Argument about possible courses of action no longer involves consideration of the actual effects policies will have. The process instead turns to the competitive avowal of one's own goodness and the imputation of badness to one's opponents. But that is only the beginning of the matter. The separation of decision making from the consideration of results, together with the a priori establishment of some views as morally good while others are morally bad, has other consequences. It leads to a situation in which the intentions of the actor, and, indeed, often only the purported intentions of the actor, are the only matters of importance, removing the means from moral consideration.

One manifestation of this is *legitimization of coercion*. An example of this occurred recently at the University of California at Berkeley, where on May 7, 1999, Chancellor Berdahl gave in to a list of demands from a group of student demonstrators. Berdahl's capitulation came after an eight-day "hunger strike"[7] by six students, backed up by about a hundred other students. They were also supported by a number of faculty members from the ethnic and women's studies program, who had previously negotiated an arrangement with Berdahl that satisfied most of the student demands.

On the heels of the deal worked out with the faculty, which provided for the appointment of seven full-time professors to their department during the next three years, seed money for a Center for the Study of Race and Gender, a multicultural center, and an ethnic studies community mural, Berdahl had said: "We cannot have anarchy with every student believing they have a right to demand what resources a department ought to have" (Rauch, 1999). And, in an official university statement, dated May 3, posted on the UCB web site: "The allocation of resources within the university is not subject to negotiation in the street. It is and must be a part of a reasoned process. I will not allow coercion, intimidation and threat of violence to replace this reasoned process."

But he did allow coercion, intimidation, and the threat of violence to replace reason. When the students refused to accept the negotiated settlement, Berdahl simply negotiated with them. The final deal bumped faculty hiring to eight, promised no future cuts, a review of department space, and a task force that would review the department's progress every six months, together with a promise that the university would not take serious disciplinary action against protestors (Lee, 1999). The students were jubilant.

"We got everything that you asked us to get," negotiator Sara Kaplan told the hundreds of students gathered outside of California Hall to hear the results of the negotiations. "We got it all. But most importantly, we made them listen to us." (D. Hernandez, 1999)

The Berkeley adminstration appeared to take the matter in stride:

UC Berkeley spokesperson said the chancellor has always been committed to shoring up the ethnic studies program, but the protests over the past month only added "urgency" to the problem. He added that the agreement "pretty much closely parallels the agreement" the chancellor had reached with ethnic studies faculty last weekend, but that the new agreement had some "clarifications" with the students in it.

In a statement, Berdahl said that the agreement only reaffirmed his commitment to the strength of the ethnic studies department.

"We have been working to make sure that university support for this department is understood by the entire campus community," he said. "I am pleased to say that today this support is understood clearly by all." (D. Hernandez, 1999)

Some were not so jubilant. Jack Citrin (1999b), a professor of political science, put the matter in a somewhat different perspective:

The campus administration reportedly has agreed to circumvent normal procedures and add faculty to Ethnic Studies, to create a Center for the Study of Race and Gender and another for the Study of the Americas, and to authorize a celebratory mural in Barrows Hall, the home of Ethnic Studies. This despite the fact that

Afro-American Studies and Ethnic Studies are the only social science departments whose faculty allocation has been increased in the last decade, and when
other academic departments, ranked among the top five nationally, are spurned
when they seek to recruit additional leading scholars. Parenthetically, the number
of students majoring in ethnic studies has been declining while its allocated faculty
has grown.

And he asked:

How did it come to this? How did Berkeley, the jewel in the crown of America's
public universities, come to quake before a small group of protesters disdained by
most students and faculty? The answer: This is just further evidence of the decline
of top academic institutions resulting from their embrace of identity politics, a perspective in which every decision is viewed according to how it allocates benefits
among ethnic groups. "No Enemies on the Left" is now "No Enemies of Color."

From an organizational point of view, perhaps the most disturbing thing
about this subordination of reason was not the coercion itself, but the way
that it was seen as being normal and legitimate by the students: " 'We won,'
said hunger striker Alison Harrington, 23, appearing weak a day after she
was briefly hospitalized for dehydration. 'This is the best class I have ever
taken at Cal!' she yelled, drawing cheers" (Lee, 1999). Shamefully, it was
also seen this way among many of the faculty:

At a press conference yesterday, ethnic studies faculty, including noted Professor
Ronald Takaki, pledged to be arrested if the police attempted to remove the hunger strikers' tent encampment in front of the chancellor's office. In addition, one
faculty member announced she was joining the six hunger strikers' fast.
     Norma Alarcon, the chair of the women's studies department and a Chicano
studies professor, wrote a letter to Berdahl to show her disapproval of the current
situation and to announce her decision to join the hunger strike.
     "I would like to inform you (that) as of this moment, I too, am going on a hunger
strike, with the students," Alarcon wrote in a letter to the chancellor. "It is extremely disrespectful for any of us to continue to enjoy food and sustenance, while
our students put their health and bodies on the line for us."
     The protesters said that the announcement of resumed negotiations and the
pledge of faculty, including Takaki, Alfred Arteaga and Elaine Kim, to be arrested
alongside student demonstrators signals a growing base of support for the ethnic
studies cause.
     Takaki, a nationally-renowned scholar on multiculturalism, said he was hon-
ored to stand in solidarity with the protesting students.
     "If you (Berdahl) decide to arrest the students, then you will also decide to arrest
me and at least nine other faculty members," Takaki said. "Education is about this

reality of students being directly involved with negotiating. We take action to create a history." (Ahmad, 1999)

Another manifestion of the subordination of rationality in decision making is the *manipulation of emotions*. As thought declines in importance, its place is taken by feelings. What else could take its place? Yet feelings have a logic that is quite different from thought, and lends itself easily to manipulation. For one thing, in what has become a standard scenario, individual incidents are used as the material for stories that, in the absence of alternative stories, can easily be taken to represent the whole. In this way events that may be quite unrepresentative come to support and drive the formulation and implementation of policy. I call this *policy making by isolated example*.

A good illustration of this is provided in an article by Romel Hernandez in the *Oregonian* (1999). At Oregon State University, Frederick Harris, a black student in his senior year, passing a fraternity house in the early morning, heard racial epithets and firecrackers. Harris had been the subject of racial harassment as a freshman. That incident had sparked an antiracism demonstration by 2,000 students and a massive institutional effort to promote "diversity":

After the 1996 rally, the university stepped up recruiting minority students. Students successfully pushed to form minority education offices for African Americans, Latinos and Asian Americans to offer students social and academic guidance. In addition, the university incorporates diversity training into orientation and requires undergraduates to take a course called "Difference, Power and Discrimination" to graduate.

The offenders were expelled from school and jailed.

Despite the fact that African Americans, who represented only 1 percent of the student population, had won election victories as both student government president and vice president at OSU, Harris wrote in a letter published in the campus paper: "I'll tell you about the dread and hopelessness I feel every day knowing things are not getting better, they are only getting worse. Things are getting worse, and it is the responsibility of this university to do something about it!" (R. Hernandez, 1999).

University officials were crestfallen:

OSU officials worried the incident was a tough blow to take.

"This will have a huge negative impact on us," said Larry Roper, vice provost for student affairs who has helped to lead OSU's diversity effort. "You can work on this broad effort and then have a couple of people at 3 A.M. on a Saturday morning cause a problem that raises questions about an institution's character."

The university is weighing sanctions against the students.

But President Paul Risser said the alleged actions of a couple of students should-n't undermine the university's recent efforts to improve the campus racial climate. He hoped to use the incident as a moment for the campus to learn about discrimination.

In a written statement, Risser apologized to Harris and promised "that we will become even more diligent in our efforts to promote diversity."

Ironically, the students in the fraternity house did not know that Harris was passing by. " 'They didn't even know he was outside,' [fraternity president] Johnson said. He added that the students—a member and a pledge—were more guilty of 'stupidity than racism.' " Nonetheless, "the fraternity ordered them to write letters to Harris, perform 10 hours of community service and develop a diversity program" (R. Hernandez, 1999).

Policy making by isolated example, of course, thrives in circumstances in which the information media are controlled by a faction that uses it to advance its own views, and which may suppress alternative views. This is far from uncommon. For example, an article by Don Feder in the *Boston Herald* (1999) reports that:

Wellesley College and Brandeis University are almost neighbors. Both are well-regarded, expensive, and prime examples of the academic inclination to crush the larynx of dissenting voices. . . .

Instead of outright censorship, the establishment snubs conservative events and denies funding to alternative publications.

The voice of sanity at Wellesley, Women for Freedom, arranges debates and speakers on issues like racial preferences and academic freedom, presenting ideas students are unlikely to encounter in any other campus forum.

Noting that the organization has sponsored Dinesh D'Souza (author of *Illiberal Education*) and Christina Hoff Sommers, Feder observes that the *Wellesley News*, which is supported by student activity fees, not only refuses to list Women for Freedom's events in its calendar section or cover its programs, but won't even accept paid advertisements. He goes on to say that:

Larisa Vanov, the Wellesley alumnus who started the organization, reports the publicity blackout has had the desired effect.

In terms of reaching the student body, the only alternative to an ad in the official campus paper is flyers, but these are usually torn down within minutes of being posted. When Horace Cooper, press secretary to House Majority Leader Dick Armey, spoke to Ivy Leaguers for Freedom (affiliated with Vanov's group) at

Princeton, he drew an audience of 70. Over 140 attended a debate in which he participated at Boston University. At Wellesley, the minority critic of quotas addressed four students.

The *News* won't admit rejecting the ads. Instead, when the group wants to advertise, there's never space available—though there's plenty for in-house advertising. Could this be stealth censorship?

The college administration is terribly blasé about all of this. Officials say they can't interfere with a student publication, even one that bears the school's name and receives $20,000 in annual subsidies while violating its rules. If this happened to a feminist or gay organization, be sure administrators would read the offenders the riot act.

Feder asks whether, if conservatives can't get coverage in the campus paper, they should consider starting their own. He says that at Brandeis they did, and experienced another aspect of academic repression:

Established two years ago, *Freedom* magazine is irreverent and iconoclastic—everything the left can't stand when it's on the receiving end.

Last October, the conservative periodical ran articles criticizing the student senate for extravagance and self-interest. Thomas Jefferson said that if forced to choose between having a government and having a free press, he'd pick the latter. Brandeis prefers a complacent student government.

Following the exposé, one senator destroyed copies of the publication while another threatened editor Bryan Rudnick with physical violence. The same loose cannons alleged that *Freedom* is, among other stuff, anti-Semitic—a neat trick in that Rudnick and several staffers are Jewish.

After cutting the publication's funding by 50 percent last semester as a punishment for its dissenting views, the senate totally defunded *Freedom* in April.

Marxist, feminist, homosexual and other sanctioned perspectives all are funded from compulsory activity fees. Conservatism is where proponents of diversity draw the line. As at Wellesley, the Brandeis administration tacitly condones this bias. At a school named for the Supreme Court justice known for his expansive view of the First Amendment, this is indeed ironic. Perhaps Brandeis should be renamed Comstock U., to honor the Nineteenth Century book-burner.

Where control of information media is fairly well secure, a further step in the manipulation of emotions can take place through the *fabrication of incidents*. For example, as the power of PC increases, the number of real incidents that can be used, fairly or unfairly, for the manipulation of emotions decreases toward the vanishing point. Yet such incidents may be seen as necessary to drive or maintain policy. As a result there is an incentive to deliberately manufacture incidents that will serve the purpose. What is perhaps even more striking is the way that, given the assumed righteousness of the cause, the fabricated nature of these events may not even be taken to mar their legitimacy. An article by Fisk and Finnerty (1999) on one such incident at Kalamazoo College offers an illustration:[8]

[Acting Capt. Jerome Bryant of the Kalamazoo Department of Public Safety] noted that a segment on ABC's "20/20" regarding black students concocting racial hoaxes aired a week before the Kalamazoo College incident. In recent years, there has been a rash of alleged and proven hate-crime hoaxes on college campuses across the county. At Duke University, shortly after a black baby doll was found hanging by a noose from a tree last fall, two black students confessed to perpetrating the mock-lynching to make a statement about race relations on campus. Two weeks ago, police arrested two black students at Miami University in Ohio on charges of staging a hoax that sparked protests last fall. Fingerprints on racist fliers were traced to the students, who denied committing the crimes but withdrew from the university.

In this instance:

[A] racist letter pinned to the dormitory door of black Kalamazoo College freshman Bryant Lusbourgh and a fire that charred his room shocked the small, private school and thrust it into the national spotlight.

On the night of the fire, Jones called students, faculty and staff together on the college's grassy quadrangle to solemnly detail the previous days' events. He was greeted with silence and stunned looks as he read aloud the hate-filled letter taken from Lusbourgh's door. It said the college had a "no-nigger policy" that was "designed to insure the failure of all non-white people" and threatened to take whatever measures necessary to enforce the policy.

In the days after the incidents, students covered campus sidewalks and stairways with a rainbow of chalk messages denouncing racism and extolling diversity. They held a candlelight vigil and organized a festival dedicated to tolerance.

Professors devoted class time to discuss the incidents and students, faculty, the Board of Trustees and the alumni association all drafted resolutions condemning the racist letter.

But the actual evidence suggests that these condemnations may have been misdirected:

Reports obtained by the *Kalamazoo Gazette* disclosed that police suspected Lusbourgh of authoring the note that sparked a massive outpouring of anti-racist sentiment, from unity marches to sidewalk scrawlings pleading for tolerance.

Although police were unable to prove Lusbourgh's involvement, several factors made detectives highly suspicious, said Acting Capt. Jerome Bryant of the Kalamazoo Department of Public Safety. For one, investigators found it curious that Lusbourgh had retained an attorney.

"There does seem to be something suspicious about why a victim gets an attorney because it's not needed when you're a victim," Bryant said. "The only other victim that I know of who hired an attorney is the parents in the Jon Benet Ramsey case."

Even before he got an attorney, Bryant said, Lusbourgh did not give police "100 percent cooperation" and was caught in a lie by investigators when asked if he'd smoked in his dorm room, which is prohibited by college rules. Lusbourgh had smoked cigars in his room, according to interviews with other dorm residents.

"The black male occupant of the room had been smoking the night before in the room. Originally, he stated he wasn't smoking but, after the box of cigars was shown, he stated he did smoke earlier," reported Marty Myers, Kalamazoo's deputy fire marshal. "(He) refused to have any further interview with the fire marshal's office to confirm any factors concerning the fire or give any statements of the fire."

Although something could obviously have been made of the strong suspicions of the police, especially given the pattern of similar events, that angle was not developed either by the newspaper or by the university administration. In fact Kalamazoo College President James Jones Jr. played the matter this way:

"This, I'm sure, sounds probably strange—but the major thing I've gleaned from this is how stalwart the student body, the alumni, the parents, the people in the community have been in supporting the college, and the student body's sincere outcry scorching ideas of racism and violence and intolerance."

The response against racism helped unite the campus, minority student recruitment is up this year, and efforts to recruit minority faculty at the 165-year-old college are encouraging, Jones said.

"I don't see any adverse long-term consequences of what happened here at all," he said. "In fact, I see the reverse."

Bear in mind that this "sincere outcry scorching ideas of racism and violence and intolerance" that "united the community" was directed against ideas that evidently did not exist within the community, because the community was united in opposition to them. In fact it was directed against something the evidence for which appeared to have been contrived for the purpose. Yet it is apparent that whether the community's response was based on objective reality did not matter to Jones. He appeared to believe that the creation and maintenance of such politically correct sentiments whether they had any real focus was an end in itself, and justified such means as were necessary for its accomplishment.

At any rate the subordination of rational decision making to moralistic sentiment is largely what lies behind what I call the *drive to the extreme.*

THE DRIVE TO THE EXTREME

The psychology of the superego contains a built-in conservatism. This psychology rests on an internalization of external order and places a premium on the maintenance of established structure. In politics the superego presses toward a solution that can be applied universally and then toward the acceptance and maintenance of that system. Narcissistic psychology, because it presses for the attainment of something that cannot be attained, has a built-in radical bias. It is fundamentally opposed to established structure. The psychology of the superego is realized through creation of an organization. The ego ideal attempts to realize itself through creation of a movement. History, it seems to me, embraces both of these dynamics, and recommends a proper balance between them. When the realism of the superego is repudiated, however, the sole operation of the ego ideal creates a politics that manifests what I think of as a drive to the extreme.

There are a number of dimensions of the drive to the extreme. First is what we may see as the insatiability of demand. At the core of the insatiability of demand is the fact that the ego ideal demands something that is impossible. It demands that the world be our mother, which would mean the end of the separation between the individual and the external world. But this means that others are not permitted to be others. They cannot make judgments about us from a perspective that is separated from our own desire. They must love us both spontaneously and unconditionally. Recall again Chasseguet-Smirgel's characterization:

In my view, this fantasy corresponds to the wish to rediscover a smooth universe without obstacles, roughness or difference, identified with a mother's insides to which one can have free access, the representation, at the thinking level, of a form of unfettered mental functioning with the free circulation of psychic energy. (p. 30)

Reflection suggests that there cannot be anything more extreme than this. Yet it is not difficult to find statements that express exactly this objective. For instance, consider a recent study by the Committee on Women at the University of Wisconsin-Madison, which issued a report called "Climate Initiative—A Springboard for Discussion." According to an article in the *Wisconsin State Journal* (Brixey, 2000), it says that contemporary concerns go beyond illegal activities such as sexual harassment and unequal pay:

The Committee on Women report describes these second-order concerns as "a category of communications—verbal and nonverbal—that create a distance between the speaker and the recipient . . . to the extent that he or she feels separated from colleagues or peers.

The committee's report includes dozens of anecdotes from UW-Madison faculty and staff about perfectly legal exchanges among colleagues that were perceived as hurtful and distancing.

Ostensibly, the concern here is with the way such behavior creates a climate in which women feel uncomfortable, and may have a negative impact on their health and productivity. The premise that it is only women who are made unhappy by things that other people say is peculiar, as is the idea that one has the right to be made perfectly comfortable by everyone else, but these may be seen as just the standard follies of political correctness. Over and above that, there does seem to me something interesting in the idea of striking out against behavior that makes one feel as if there is a distance between oneself and others. Our inquiry has led us to see in this the possibility that these women are demanding the opposite of distance, which is to say fusion between themselves and others, and to have this fusion strictly on their own terms.

Taking themselves as entitled to this fusion, in effect they are assuming the right to destroy whatever stands in the way of their experience of the world as their mother. In the way that is by now familiar, they take it to be men who are causing their distress, which lies behind their perception of this as a woman's issue. Of course what stands in the way is not men, but the existence of an external world. So it is the external world, and especially the existence of independent other human beings, that is the ultimate focus of their indignant rage and their attempts at destruction. Having said that, and having recognized the absurdity and impossibility of their attaining their goal, we can easily understand how political practices that would, to anyone with a foothold in reality, seem foolish and absurd, look to them to be practical and righteous. Of such material is the drive to the extreme compounded. And so one must look with concern at the seriousness with which their proposal is being taken: "UW–Madison Provost John Wiley has endorsed the report and will discuss it with university deans this fall. 'I think it's the natural and needed next step,' " he said (Brixey, 2000).

Many universities have already been driven far toward the extreme. A suitable illustrative example is provided in Kors and Silverglate's magisterial study *The Shadow University: The Betrayal of Liberty on America's Campuses* (1998):

In June 1989, the Massachusetts Board of Regents adopted a statewide "Policy Against Racism" for higher education. It "proscribes all conditions and all actions

or omissions including all acts of verbal harassment or abuse which deny or have
the effects of denying to anyone his or her rights to equality, dignity, and security
on the basis of his or her race, color, ethnicity, culture or religion." It mandated
both "appreciation for cultural/racial pluralism" and "a unity and cohesion in the
diversity which we seek to achieve," outlawing "racism in any form, expressed or
implied, intentional or inadvertent, individual or institutional." The regents
pledged "to eradicate racism, ethnic and cultural offenses and religious intolerance," and "required," among other things, programs "to enlighten faculty, administrators, staff, and students with regard to ways in which the dominant society
manifests and perpetuates racism." (p. 150)

What we see illustrated here is the way the university believes it can
mandate one's feelings and even make one responsible for the feelings that
others may have about one's feelings, even without regard to whether they
perceive them accurately or not. But to go further into our exploration of
the drive to the extreme, we must observe the extreme political behavior
that is legitimated by demands of this sort:

At the state's flagship campus, the University of Massachusetts–Amherst, in the
spring and summer of 1992, the student newspaper, the *Collegian*, lost all real protection of the rule of law. At an angry rally on the campus after the acquittal of the
Los Angeles police officers in the Rodney King affair, protesters turned their hatred against the supposed "racism" of the *Collegian*, which had written of the L.A.
"riots," unlike Professor John Bracey, later head of the Faculty Senate, who at the
rally termed the rioters "our warriors." Protestors invaded the offices of the *Collegian*, smashing windows, destroying property, and assaulting staff. Northampton
police arrested one protester for attacking a *Collegian* photographer with a baseball
bat and dragging him to the Student Center (the municipal court sentenced him
to counseling). The *Collegian* appealed to the university for protection, but was refused. Editors and staff got a Northampton police escort to another municipality,
and published a few editions in hiding, but these were stolen and destroyed. Marc
Elliott, editor-in-chief, told the *Boston Globe* that it was "like a Nazi book burn-
ing." Undefended by the university, the editors of the *Collegian* surrendered and
agreed to an editorial structure of separate editors and sections for every "historically oppressed" minority on campus. Managing editor Daniel Wetzel told the
Daily Hampshire Gazette, "There's 100 people running scared right now, and 100
people intimidating them. I'm not going to put a student organization above my
safety." He told the Associated Press, "We gave up our journalistic integrity for the
safety of the students."
    When the *Collegian* appealed for protection, U. Mass's chancellor, Richard
O'Brien, replied that there was a conflict between two values that "the university
holds dear: protection of free expression and the creation of a multicultural community free of harassment and intimidation." (pp. 150–151)

The idea that these storm trooper tactics were defended in the name of creating a climate free of harassment and intimidation was expressed without apparent irony by this university chancellor.

In 1994, in response to an inquiry about the actions taken by the administration in 1992, the new chancellor, David K. Scott, replied, in writing: "*Collegian* takeover of May 1, 1992: charges were not brought; Whitmore occupation of May 1, 1992: no disciplinary action was taken; Theft of copies of *Collegian* May 4, 1992: Individuals who may have taken copies of the *Collegian* were never identified. It is difficult to call the action theft because the paper is distributed to the public free of charge." As for the physical assault and the destruction of the newspapers: "I am not aware of any specific statements by the administration in response to the incident with the *Collegian* photographer or the theft of copies of the *Collegian*."

In 1995, Chancellor Scott proposed a new harassment policy that would outlaw not only "epithets" and "slurs," but, in addition, "negative stereotyping." The policy caught the eye of the media. *New York Times* columnist Anthony Lewis illustrated the gulf between liberal and campus views of freedom. U. Mass's policy, he wrote, would "create a totalitarian atmosphere in which everyone would have to guard his tongue all the time lest he say something that someone finds offensive." Lewis asked: "Do the drafters have no knowledge of history? No understanding that freedom requires 'freedom for the thought that we hate?' And if not, what are they doing at a university?" He concluded that the "elastic concept of a 'hostile environment'" intolerably menaced "freedom of speech, at universities of all places." (p. 151)

"Universities of all places," indeed. For the U.S. federal courts have held uniformly that the university has a very special place in American society, and that the free exchange of ideas is critical to its function (Kors and Silverglate, 1998: p. 56). This is a fact that in previous times was known to everyone. It is stunning to reflect upon how far we have come from this bedrock understanding.

In the absence of a superego that can adjudicate between reasonable and unreasonable claims, the measure of victimization must be the subjective feeling of being victimized. To be sure, the feeling of being victimized may come from real victimization, but the exploration of narcissism shows that this feeling also can come from interpreting the indifference of the world as a personal threat. This, of course, is the mechanism of paranoia. It means that, as real victimization is eliminated, the university's process stands in danger of coming under the control of the community's most easily offended, paranoid, and hysterical elements.

Recent events at Saint Cloud State University in Minnesota provide an illustration of this. In this case, which began in the summer of 1998, two black graduate students in the Applied Psychology program (APSY) issued charges of racism against the department. One of the students, Susan Bullock, objected to the word "nigger" in one of the books being used in her course, *Social Bases of Behavior*—an anthology of readings on disability issues. She confronted the professor, John Hotz, before class. According to a story by William F. Meehan III in the *Minnesota Scholar* (Meehan, 2000), Hotz was stunned by the student's objection, having used the text for ten years without the slightest protest. So when he went into the classroom, he immediately addressed her concern. He told the students that he also found the word offensive and never used it. And he sincerely apologized for the distress that the word may have caused anyone. He stopped short only at saying he would remove the book from the class reading requirements.

Bullock, who stopped attending class but passed the course, persisted in her public charges of racism. Taking up her cause, the chairman of the department, Avelino Mills-Novoa, tried to bring her charges up at a departmental meeting. The faculty refused to consider her charges, saying she would have to bring them through the official channels for student complaints. Mills-Novoa, evidently, made it clear she would not have to proceed through such channels, saying, "I have seen what the process does to students of color" (p. 2).

At about this time, Bullock's grievance came to be associated with another charge by a black graduate student, and one which is, for our purposes, a bit more interesting. In this case, according to Meehan, a black male graduate assistant named Ray Shorter charged that the Counseling Psychology curriculum "was a 'white' (Eurocentric) theoretical perspective, and that 'Black Psychology' and 'Black Psychologists' were excluded" (p. 2). His letter, written September 9 and distributed publicly on the campus e-mail system, led to a meeting of the faculty committee of Graduate Counseling Program, his major. "Many of those on the committee acknowledged that activities to address 'diversity' issues had been ongoing in the department for some time, but they renewed their commitment to educating themselves further in the area of minority differences in counseling practice and agreed to future exploration and training in this area," according to one faculty member (p. 2).

Shorter launched a malicious public attack on APSY, however. In the coming weeks, he sent letters and e-mails to the administration and to all SCSU faculty via the campus e-mail system on 22 September and 16 and 23 October. The gist of the letters was to accuse the APSY faculty of harboring "evil thoughts and practices," of making him experience "a mental and spiritual, torturing death," of even trying to "kill [him]." The following is part of 16 October letter:

Anytime that I enter any area of the department or its classes, I'm in constant fear and danger of my life. White faculty members within the department are trying to murder my mind and spirit. They are continuing to forcefully inject me with the deadly disease called White Supremacy which is viciously attacking every aspect of my life. The more I demand that white faculty members stop trying to lynch me, the more they continue to deny my request; as if they were like starving cannibals, slobbering over the last human remains. (p. 2)

Shorter continued his vicious campaign. However poorly written, Shorter's letters contained ugly references to "Hitler," "genocide," "torture chambers," and "lynching." (p. 3)

One might think from this that Shorter, and perhaps Bullock, had blundered into a department dominated by the Ku Klux Klan, but it appears that this was far from the case. On the contrary, the APSY department appears to have been the very model of multicultural sympathy:

The APSY Department can be considered "diverse," and it can point to a record of commitment to University-mandated, as well as self-initiated, professional development in "diversity training." When the allegations of racism first arose in the fall of 1998, the department was chaired by a minority male faculty member, and its largest graduate program (Counseling Psychology) was chaired by a minority female faculty member. Of twenty full-time faculty in the department at the time, twelve were white males, six were white females, three were minorities (two females, one male) and one white female was designated as partially disabled.

At their own initiative, in 1996, the APSY faculty designed and held an all-day retreat at one faculty member's house where they discussed ways to improve cultural diversity, including development of two new courses in the area. This retreat was a follow-up to two other extensive training sessions in which the department contracted with nationally known multicultural consultants to evaluate their programs and curriculum and suggest improvements. (p. 3)

Notwithstanding their efforts, notwithstanding the fact that independent observers completely exonerated those faculty members subsequently charged with racism, and despite the fact that the students' charges were based on nothing but their feelings, the university administration adopted the students' orientation and subjected the APSY faculty to a campaign of abuse. This included what faculty members called "tongue lashing" and "woodshed whipping," as well as a form of "sensitivity training" that included what one faculty member called "level shifting":

On one level it attempts to get us to agree that we lived in a white-dominated culture, with a history of slavery and oppression of blacks (and, indeed, all minorities), and that we also must have benefited personally from this "white privilege." But when we would agree to this "institutional racism," the level of accusation shifted to a much more serious one of "intentional (personal) racism." That is, we were racists and were therefore guilty of the allegations directed against us. (p. 3)

The end result follows:

By March 1999 the "functional" department was in disarray. Two minority faculty (the Chairman and the Counseling Psychology Graduate Program Director) simply refused to meet with the white faculty under any circumstances, and have yet to do so. Three white female faculty and a minority female faculty aligned themselves with the Chairman and Graduate Director to form the separatist group. Moreover, in a dreadful display of disregard for academic quality, academic standards, and APSY students, the separatists requested APSY become two departments, themselves in one department, the rest of the faculty in another. "The net effect of their 24 March 1999 proposal was to take away the courses (and programs) that some of the senior (white) faculty had developed and taught, in some cases, for thirty years." (p. 4)

As far as the effects on university process are concerned, nothing that has occurred at St. Cloud State is more extreme than the depredations that have been described elsewhere in this chapter. What I particularly want to call attention to in this case is the fact that universities have the purpose of education and, in the case of a department of applied psychology, of training. The fact that the university was dragooned into supporting these students' allegations represents, at the same time, a shift in the Counseling Psychology program in the direction of legitimizing these students' views and attitudes within the context of their profession. Yet a look at the way that Shorter, in particular, distorted what was, in reality, a quite benign and supportive environment, leads us to a very frightening view. It is that the university has given itself over to a process in which extremely unbalanced individuals are loosed upon the world as trained counseling psychologists.

To be certain, Shorter may have been invoking these epithets as a way of gaining an advantage, or calling attention to himself. On the other hand, if he truly felt that "[a]nytime that I enter any area of the department or its classes, I'm in constant fear and danger of my life" and was convinced that these good liberal folks were trying to "forcefully inject me with the deadly disease called White Supremacy which is viciously attacking every aspect of my life" and lynch him, one cannot help but be appalled at the effect he is likely to have upon his clients. And he would gain credibility in his endeavors from the enthusiastic endorsement of St. Cloud State University.

Another factor that operates in the drive to the extreme arises from the psychodynamics of resentment. Resentment, because of its narcissistic premise, is a bottomless pit. This explains the curious phenomenon that, at politically correct universities, the absence of serious racism or sexism, for example, does not appear to diminish the intensity of the struggles concerning them. This is suggested by a report on Oberlin College, written for *The New Republic* by Jacob Weisberg (1991).

To see how obsessed the campus is, one only has to pick up an issue of *The Oberlin Review*. The news, letters, and editorial columns of every issue are full of accusations of racism, sexism, heterosexism, homophobia, "ableism," and a host of other insensitivities abhorrent to the disciples of what might be called Oberlinism.

Oberlin has a long liberal pedigree. The college, which first enrolled blacks in 1835, was a stop on the underground railroad. Today it brags of its achievements in recruiting and retaining minority students and faculty. With the exception of the odd bit of bathroom graffiti, there is little of what anyone outside of a college campus would call racism. But in a perverse equation, perceived racism at Oberlin is inversely proportional to actual racism: the less students see, the harder they look....

Last spring two black women were asked to leave an outdoor table at a local bakery because they were eating food bought at a rival restaurant. They initiated a boycott, vowing to make life hell for the racist establishment. "The ignorance, the audacity, the arrogance, and the racist attitude to do such a thing is what is horrifying to us," one said in the letter to the *Review*. "We have got to realize that it is not just the administration and all of the other top brass practicing bigotry. It's the everyday person perpetuating it." (pp. 22–23)

The point here is that the oppressed's ego ideal, never fulfilled, is defined by the oppression directed against it. It only exists in a state of conflict with whatever it experiences as keeping it from fulfillment. In a way it needs racism, or sexism, or the like in order to survive as an identity. In the absence of real racism, sexism, or other real assaults, it needs to project it. But, ultimately, what keeps our ego ideal from being fulfilled is reality itself. By projecting oppression onto reality itself, narcissism manages to ensure its permanent continuity, for there is always plenty of reality to fulfill that purpose. It means that reasonable steps to deal with real problems are never enough, and are overtaken by unreasonable steps to deal with fantasy problems.

Seeing the world in terms of schemata of victimization has a profound irony associated with it. As Maslow (1970) observed, most of us want a positive conception of our self. We want to see ourselves, and want others to see us, as persons who have done something worthwhile: to have a sense of our self as strong and active. In a word we want respect and self-respect. This is not something we can attain on the basis of having been victimized in the past.

At its best recognition of oneself as having been victimized reflects a sense of the self as comparatively weak and passive. To be sure the circumstances of victimization may have been such that any self would have been overcome. Be that as it may, there is no way of resolving this dilemma. Failure, no matter how inevitable, is still failure. And the pity of others can never help us to get beyond the sense of ourselves as pitiful. At its worst the claim of victimization may fall on deaf ears, and be met with increasing resentment, hostility, and a feeling that one is getting more than one deserves.

In the absence of a superego that could offer a program for the attainment of respect, the perception that others pity or resent them is likely only to raise the level of the victim group's feeling of being victimized. Sadly the logic of narcissism leads victim groups to redouble the efforts that caused them this pain in the first place.

A final reason why PC tends to move the university toward the extreme has to do with the logic of moral debate. As I have said earlier, under the superego, debate centers on the issue of what is true and what course of action is right. Under the rule of the primordial mother, debate becomes a matter of who is good. The aim of the debate is to show that one's opponent is bad (in this case racist, sexist, homophobic, or the like) and that one is good. For some groups being good just means being a member of the group, as defined by its ideology of victimization. For others, and specifically for white males, being good means proving that one is good despite one's group identification. The result of this is that, for white males who make up the university power structure, goodness is always in question and must be demonstrated continually, through a kind of moral one-upmanship that operates by an incremental ratcheting up of the stakes.

For a full understanding of this, one must see the intrapsychic dimension that operates here. The PC individual, especially the white male, not only must operate according to the rules of a game of moral goodness, but also must prove to himself that he is good. Goodness in this case means the absolute love of the oppressed. There is no room here for ambivalence or measure. Yet love is within the domain of the ego ideal. It is irreducibly narcissistic. Even the love of the mother for her child is based on her identification with the child.

The love of the oppressed demands something that is psychologically impossible, the permanent abandonment of one's own separate identity in exchange for enthusiastic subordination to the narcissism of another. Individuals who accept this demand must experience their own spontaneous responses with shame, as a continual indictment and condemnation of themselves. The point is that in a moral universe defined either by being or by loving the oppressed, one's own ego ideal and superego are defined as oppression. This is intolerable to the self, which must be permanently vigilant against this perception of badness, political incorrectness, at the core of its own being.

The problem is that unacceptable thoughts and feelings are naturally going to be produced with some frequency. The mind moves, so to speak. This is the source of human creativity. For the politically correct it would also be the source of feelings of extreme danger.

Consider the question of racial preferences in this regard. A society may have good reasons for giving a preference to some groups or individuals in the distribution of rewards and opportunities. There is no need to dispute that. Yet the choice to give a preference will naturally be a contentious issue, since whenever some are given preference, others will be disadvantaged. Experience tells us that they will have a case to make, and it will be on terms that stress their own worthiness. The interchange among affected parties on these issues of relative worthiness is a central process in a democracy.

Look at what happens in the case of political correctness. Here, the arguments made by those who have been disadvantaged become unthinkable. They cannot be weighed, because they cannot be considered. Considering them would subject oneself to the shameful feeling of being bad for simply having them. Thus, the spontaneous movement of the mind must be truncated and cut off. This will especially be a problem in the case of an individual who is himself a member of the group that is being disadvantaged, and who is therefore likely to naturally feel enhanced by assertions of worthiness on behalf of his group, including statements that assert the values he uses to justify his own position.

In order to have a sense of how radical a departure this is, one needs to recognize how natural and ordinary are the contentious disagreements among competing groups over the distribution of resources, and how extraordinary it is for some of these groups to be deprived of the capacity to assert their own claim and defend themselves. It is surely the moralization of the issue of race and its ideological cognates that has been the cause of this. But in the course of this moralization the most basic understanding of the process has been lost. For the fact is that the politics of identity is still politics. Racial groups, along with any of the other groups defined by the ideology of victimhood, have become political actors. If they are looked at in that way, it would be seen to be the most natural thing in the world for other groups to oppose them in the light of their own interest. But it is this opposition, and even the idea that such an opposition can be legitimate, that is lost under the regime of political correctness. With it goes much of the range of feelings that provide the motivational base of the democratic process. All of these lose their feeling of legitimacy and become phenomena which one is supposed to condemn. All of this shows how much of oneself one must rule out of bounds in this process of political correctness.

Notice again how this process differs from what one would find under the superego. The superego operates with the currency of guilt and attaches goodness and badness to behavior. It permits behavioral acts of reparation as ways of compensating for previous badness. Operating with the currency of shame, narcissism attaches goodness and badness to the self. It does not permit reparative actions as a way of reestablishing one's goodness. Narcissism demands an absolute, perfect goodness, and our own recognition that we fall short of that ideal drives the continual re-creation of a perfect fictional identity and the abandonment of who one is.

There are two ways of responding to the experience of the self and its feelings as shameful. They each further different elements of the drive to the extreme. One way is simply to endorse this viewpoint and condemn oneself. When this happens, one loses connection with one's own ego ideal. One then becomes dependent for one's sense of direction on those who originated one's self-hatred. In this way, one loses the capacity to give resistance to the forces of political correctness, whose natural drive toward the extreme becomes more powerful as a result.

This will be particularly crippling to white males because the persons to whose narcissism they must subordinate themselves hate white males and define their own identities against them. There is no real possibility of identification here without the necessity of the white males taking hatred of white males directly into themselves.[9]

The other way of dealing with the unacceptability of one's impulses is by turning an internal conflict into an external one. One can project one's shameful thoughts and feelings into others and hate them there. One thereby joins the forces of political correctness and in that way enhances its drive toward the extreme.

Psychoanalysis refers to this dynamic as "projective identification" (Klein, 1975). Through projective identification one is enabled to reject the unacceptable element without rejecting oneself. This permits a remarkable trade-off. One loses the pain of finding oneself wanting and gains the feeling of perfect goodness that comes with being a pure and righteous warrior in the struggle against evil. That's quite a role and it's not surprising that so many adopt it. It offers narcissistic benefits, especially in the form of self-righteousness, in excess of anything the real world can provide. All one loses is a realistic sense of who one is.

Projective identification, no doubt, helps to explain some of the vigor and verve with which the campaign for PC is pursued, and the unabashed hatred and contempt that the politically correct hold for those whom they attack. In addition, it gives us cause to reflect that the common explanation for intergroup hatred, that we hate those who are different from ourselves, is fundamentally mistaken. Insofar as projective identification is behind the hatred, we do not hate others who are different from us. Rather, we hate those whom we experience, rightly or wrongly, as being like us with regard to characteristics that we cannot accept in ourselves. Ultimately, then, we do not hate others at all. It is ourselves we hate. Political correctness is a way of defending ourselves against our own self-hatred.

Others who are different from us may make us feel uncomfortable, but the recognition that they exist simply acknowledges that there is an objective external world. Most of us can manage that. Hatred involves a wish to destroy. Yet the desire to destroy the external world cannot ever have been anything but an aberration, otherwise there would be none of us available to tell the tale. It would seem to be our postmodern, politically correct colleagues for whom the existence of an external world is peculiarly a problem, and our inquiry has now offered us further insight into why that is so.

The irony in all of this is that, if PC is to be justified, it must be justified as a way of combating racism. Young (1993) has observed that racism, that is to say *real* racism, is itself a form of projective identification. Seeing PC as a form of projective identification leads us to wonder how effective it possibly can be in this combat. It suggests the alternative possibility of complementary dynamics of projective identification, each helping to convince the other that their enemies are not the products of their own imaginations but are quite real. In this way they reinforce each other, justify each other, and ensure each other's existence. Racism and political correctness are both fantasies of persecution and they need a persecuting object. If the other is not available, it must be invented. Moreover, since the object of one's hatred is inside, no amount of attacking an external representation will reduce its force, but will cause only an amplified antagonism with outside forces as our tactics, increasingly desperate, escalate and as our enemies respond. In this way we see the power behind an additional element of the drive to the extreme.

THE REDEFINITION OF THE PURPOSE OF THE UNIVERSITY

In the biparental model, the university provided a place where ideas were not acted upon, and where they could therefore be separated from their consequences and debated in accordance with their merits as ideas. Time has winnowed out the best and most powerful statements of these ideas and has left the results to us in the form of a canon of great works. These great works have been the fundament of the educational process in the traditional, biparental university. In the postmodern PC university, the distinction between ideas and their consequences is lost, which para- doxically makes it seem as if ideas *are* their consequences. This subordi- nates the discussion of ideas to the university's overall morality play and turns it into just another arena of political activity.

FROM THE STUDY OF GREAT WORKS TO THE PRACTICE OF POLITICS

An indication of how far the university has moved from the study of great works to the practice of politics is provided in a study by Will Morrisey in the journal *Academic Questions* (1992–1993). Morrisey sampled the contents of the *Proceedings of the Modern Language Association*, the preemi- nent journal in the field of literature, over the period 1930 to 1990. Read- ing all of the articles for the years 1930, 1940, 1950, 1960, 1970, 1975, 1980, 1985, and 1990, he classified them as ideological, nonideological, or tendentious. He defined ideology in this way:

[A] systematic or (if vague and incoherent) at least a general view of contemporary society and of large-scale or fundamental respects in which it should or should not be changed. Thus, ideology combines beliefs and moral opinions pertaining to the social, economic, and/or political system.

Typically, an ideology also comprises beliefs about human nature, its malleabil- ity or permanence, and its divine, natural, or historical origin. However, in this study such beliefs were not counted as ideological unless explicitly associated with beliefs and moral opinions about the social, economic and/or political system. (p. 56)*

And he said:

In this study, an article is classified as ideological when (a) there is, assuming his sincerity, no mistaking its author's ideological commitment *and* (b) its argument is either clearly intended to support that ideology or depends for its plausibility on the reader's sharing it. (p. 57)*

Articles in which "political comment is prominent and yet still incidental to the argument of the whole" were not considered ideological in his criteria. "Yet," he said, "they may signal a preoccupation with political or
social issues." He therefore introduced the category of the "tendentious" to
refer to "articles in which incidental political or social comment is so prominent it raises a question about whether the author's true motive in writing
is not at least in part political" (p. 58).*

The results were as follows:

From 1930 through 1960, few articles are ideological (varying from 0 percent to 3
percent), and those few are dominantly centrist; the sole exception, in 1960, was
moderately conservative. . . . The number of tendentious articles was also very low,
but only through 1950. From having made up no more than from 1.5 percent to 4.0
percent of all articles in earlier volumes, tendentious articles leapt to 15.5 percent
in 1960. After 1960, the percentage of tendentious articles remained in the very
low double digits, reaching 19.5 percent in 1990. However, after 1960, the percentage of ideological articles increased markedly in the 1970s and dramatically in
the 1980s, until, in 1990 they made up 52.5 percent of all articles. Only 28.0 percent of articles in 1990 were neither ideological nor tendentious. (p. 59)*

Morrisey classified the overwhelming majority of these articles as leftist,
saying:[10]

The categories of "left" and "right" are deliberately crude, and are chosen because
they are easy to apply and address the major point at issue. However, they hardly do
justice to the specific flavor of the articles in question—a defect subsequently rem-
edied, to a degree, by some representative quotations. (p. 59)*

Morrisey's further specification finds that

one might expect these articles to exhibit great ideological diversity, even if they
are all alike in rejecting American society or Western civilization. And, indeed,
several distinct ideologies—Marxist, feminist, Afrocentrist, and so forth—are represented. . . . [But] in the last decade or so, *PMLA* articles of leftist persuasion, despite what must seem to an orthodox Marxist or a democratic socialist as their
extraordinarily *outré* quality, have had more ideological elements in common than
can be found to distinguish them from one another — to the point where one may
speak of a *PMLA* ideology. (p. 61)*

*Reprinted by permission of Transaction Publishers. "Ideology and Literary Studies: *PMLA*
1930–1990" by Will Morrisey, *Academic Questions*, Winter, 1992–3. Copyright ©
1992–1993 by Transaction Publishers; all rights reserved.

This ideology is radical egalitarian — *PMLA* articles almost uniformly condemn hierarchy and authority of any kind. Even the assumption that something is real—that is, that it exists independently of cultural perspectives—is disdained as implicitly hierarchical. . . . Foremost among suspect realities are (so-called) gender differences, and one of the worst manifestations of hierarchy is to take heterosexuality as a norm. . . . Above all others, the word "subversive" and its variants evidently provides a *frisson* these writers find hard to resist. (p. 62)*

In other words what Morrisey finds in this *PMLA* ideology is the same spirit that motivates political correctness in all of its other manifestations.

The standard response to the charge that the university has become politicized is the idea that "everything is political." This is a view that follows from the denial of an objective external world. It means that ideas are not to be judged on the basis of their objective truth, but rather as attempts by a group to serve its interests. Ideas are accepted as true, then, only because of the power of the group that puts them forward. For example literary criticism that does not address issues of power is still political in that it serves the political interests of those who wish to keep the issue of power out of literary discussion.

Of course one may see this aspect of things, if one wishes, without giving up the idea that such criticism may have independent validity in its own terms. But this is exactly the point that the forces of political correctness want to make. For them literary criticism not only has a political aspect, it has *nothing but* a political aspect.

The absurdity of this view is best revealed in its application to science. Scientific theories are developed within a human community in which power is distributed in certain ways, and they may have consequences that affect the distribution of power, but that does not mean that they are not true or false in their own right.

The classic story illustrating this comes from the dawn of modern society, with the Catholic Church's attempts to force Galileo to deny his view that, contrary to the canonical teachings of Aristotle, the earth moves around the sun. They threatened him with torture and he did, indeed, recant. But, the story goes, under his breath he said "*eppur si muove*" (and yet it moves) (Furedy, 1996). Independent of the correlation of human forces at any given time, it still does.

THE TRANSFORMATION OF TEACHING AND RESEARCH

The university isn't just any institution, it has a specific function or purpose, and that purpose has to do with teaching and research, with the transmission and development of knowledge and ideas. Underlying everything that takes place within the PC university is the dual process of excoriating those seen as oppressors and expressing love for those seen as victims. As a consequence of this, the entire nature of what constitutes knowledge changes in the PC university. Knowledge becomes whatever ideas express hatred of the oppressors and love of the victims. As a consequence of this come changes in the ideas of the transmission of this knowledge, in the form of teaching, and the creation of new knowledge, in the form of research and scholarship.

The meaning of teaching and research changes completely in the PC university, and the result is nothing less than a redefinition of the purpose of the university. The university turns into a setting for a Manichean battle between the forces of goodness, as personified by the victims and their righteous allies, and the forces of evil, personified by the oppressors: those who previously had status, and the whole panoply of social institutions through which they gained that status and have maintained it.[11] Teaching and research are redefined within this context.

Research becomes advocacy research. Rather than the disinterested pursuit of the truth, research becomes the development of weapons for use in the holy war. We have already seen some of the products of this in Chapter 1 where, as we noted, inconvenient facts are buried or ignored, research "findings" are molded to fit conclusions antecedently drawn, and critics are intimidated.[12]

Teaching is no longer the study of intellectual and artistic achievements, characteristic of the superego, but becomes a politicized process in which the forces of goodness are trained and mobilized and the forces of evil are subverted. Everything that is done is legitimated by reference to its function in this battle. The narcissistic premise here is that anything else serves the purpose of oppression. As the well-known slogan of the 1960s put it, "If you're not part of the solution, you're part of the problem."

For example, here are some of the ways the politically correct, writing in academic journals, redefine the teaching of composition: "All teaching supposes ideology; there simply is no value free pedagogy. For these reasons, my paradigm of composition is changing to one of critical literacy, a literacy of political consciousness and social action" (Laditka, 1990: p. 361). And, in an award-winning essay: "[The classroom in composition ought to

be considered] a disruptive form of underlife, a forum which tries to undermine the nature of the institution and posit a different one in its place"
(Brooke, 1987: p. 151).

Take a recent case at Wesleyan University, which, until the *Hartford
Courant* brought the matter to public attention, offered the course COL
289, "Pornography: Writing of Prostitutes." The course was characterized
this way in its own course description:

The pornography we study is an act of transgression which impels human sexuality
toward, against, and beyond the limits which have traditionally defined civil discourses and practices—defined, that is, by regimes of dominance and submission,
inclusion or exclusion, in the domains of organ and emotional pleasure. Our examination accordingly includes the implication of pornography in the so-called perverse practices such as voyeurism, bestiality, sadism, and masochism, and considers
the inflections of the dominant white-heterosexual traditional [sic] by alternative
sexualities and genders, as well as by race, class, age, mental and physical competence. (Weinkopf, 1999)

It had a suitable final project: "Just create your own work of pornography"—video, essay, live performance. "I don't put any restraints on it," Professor Hope Weissman explained.

Wesleyan student Brian Edward-Tiekert told the *Hartford Courant* that
the assignment is not "substantially different from a literature class where
the instructor gave a creative-writing assignment for a final." But Edward-Tiekert may never have had a literature class in the traditional sense.
If he had he would have known that in such a course the final project is intended to demonstrate what the student has learned about how to write,
not how to transgress. It is difficult to imagine what the analogue would
have been for Matthew Smith's final project, which was a video of him
masturbating. To be sure one may give oneself comfort by supposing that
such courses and projects are an aberration at the university, but if one did
that, one would be in disagreement with Smith, who said: "That's what kids
do these days, they make porn at school" (Weinkopf, 1999).

In all this we find a disparagement of the idea of great works that is
closely related to the depreciation of achievement I have already discussed.
The very idea of great works comes to be seen as a technique of oppression
(Searle, 1992). As we have seen, what replaces the study of great works is
overt political activity, itself intended to exemplify the morality play in
which the forces of goodness attack the forces of badness.

It is worthy of mention that the depreciation of greatness also leaves the
way open for the elevation of material that is stunning in its triviality, an
indiscriminate outpouring of material with no serious claim to distinction

based only upon its location in the Manichean order of battle. Thus we have this:

"I couldn't have taught this class 10 years ago," declares Stanford Prof. Kennell Jackson to an overflowing classroom on the first day of the spring quarter. " But people don't look at me like I'm crazy anymore — what history does has broadened considerably." And Prof. Jackson is not exaggerating. "Black Hair as Culture and History," his ambitious new upper-level seminar, addresses how black hair "has interacted with the black presence in this country—how it has played a role in the evolution of black society."

If not for Prof. Jackson's earnestness, one might mistake the class for a parody of multiculturalism. The syllabus, handed out on the first day of class, includes such lectures as "The Rise of the Afro" and "Fade-O-Rama, Braiding and Dreadlocks." According to this course outline, local hair stylists will visit for a week of discussions. Enrolled students will view the 1960's musical "Hair," read Willie L. Morrow's "400 Years Without a Comb," and Dylan Jones's "Haircults," and study the lyrics of Michael Jackson's hit pop single "Man in the Mirror." (Sacks, 1992)

A special element of the faculty's contribution to the transformation of the course of study is worth mentioning in its own right. This is the denial of reality. As we saw before, in the traditional family the father had the function of coping with external reality. This was the meaning of the superego. Thoroughly repudiating the superego and denigrating its works means that the necessity of coping with external reality must be denied and, indeed, with it must go the idea that there is an external reality that has to be coped with.

From this we get the idea that each group may define reality however it sees fit, and that, indeed, groups have done so all along. Thus denial of an objective reality is seen as politically correct because the assertion of an objective reality was merely a power ploy on the part of the politically dominant group to legitimate and make natural its dominance. From this we get the fact that peculiar claims concerning history, for example, are not only asserted but taken seriously. This is perhaps most blatant in "Afrocentric" thought. Thus, for example, a collection of essays called "African-American Baseline Essays," which was adopted by the public school system of Portland, Oregon, maintains, according to C. Vann Woodward, that "Africa is the mother of Western civilization, that Egypt was a black African country and the source of the glory that was Greece and the grandeur that was Rome. Africans also discovered America and named the waters they crossed the Ethiopian Ocean, long before Columbus" (Woodward, 1991: p. 42). When a teacher in Portland, Richard C.

Garrett, questioned such things, he was told, "You have your scholarship, we have ours" (Garrett, 1992).[13]

More important, though, is the denial that the laws of the physical universe are objective. The contrary claim is that they represent, again, only the outlook of the white males. Thus "[d]espite the deeply ingrained Western cultural belief in science's intrinsic progressiveness, science today serves primarily regressive social tendencies. . . . its ways of constructing and conferring meanings are not only sexist but also racist, classist, and culturally coercive" (Harding, 1986: p. 9).

Counterpoised to this is an emerging "feminist" science, based on a feminine communion with the object of study (Harding, 1986). We see in this communion the loss of boundaries between self and other characteristic of the maternal world. What will be left of the technological capacity of the West if the laws of physics, for example, lose their special place among the universe of possible texts is anybody's guess.

RESTRICTIONS ON SPEECH

Most widely publicized among the abuses of PC have been restrictions on speech. These have taken place in the classroom. For example Stephen Thernstrom was pilloried for insensitivity for reading, in his course on race relations at Harvard University, from white plantation owners' journals (D'Souza, 1991). Ian Macneil, a visiting professor, was denounced by the Harvard Women's Law Association, who repeated their denunciations in letters sent to other universities who might have considered hiring him. His crime consisted, in the first instance, of including in his case book, as an example of the legal "battle of the forms," a "sexist" quote from Byron and then for being awkward in his response to the ensuing vilification (D'Souza, 1991: pp. 197–198). The quote follows:

A little she strove, and much repented,
And whispering, "I will ne'er consent" — consented.

More widely publicized have been the proliferation of restrictive speech codes designed to combat "hate speech." Thus the University of Michigan adopted a code that prohibited "any behavior, verbal or physical, that stigmatizes or victimizes an individual on the basis of race, ethnicity, religion, sex, sexual orientation, creed, national origin, ancestry, age, marital status, handicap, or Vietnam-era veteran status" (cited by D'Souza, 1991: p. 142).

Because of the obvious danger that such codes would, as they have been, declared in violation of the First Amendment, a great deal of effort has gone into crafting them so that they would prohibit what is offensive and preserve what is valuable. But such efforts would have to come to nothing. They would have to be based on a formal distinction between types of speech. The real issue for their politically correct authors was never *what kind of* speech is offensive, but *whose* speech is offensive.

A student newspaper funded by Vassar College termed black activist Anthony Grate "hypocrite of the month" for espousing anti-Semitic views while publicly denouncing bigotry on campus. In an acrimonious debate, Grate reportedly referred to "dirty Jews" and added, "I hate Jews." Grate later apologized for his remarks. Meanwhile, outraged that the *Spectator* had dared to criticize a black person, the Vassar Student Association first attempted to ban the issue of the publication, and when that failed it withdrew its $3,800 funding. The newspaper "unnecessarily jeopardizes an educational community based on mutual understanding," the VSA explained. (D'Souza, 1991: p. 10)

The point is, as I have argued, the whole purpose of the politically correct university is to idealize the oppressed and demonize the oppressors. This holds true of speech as well as anything else. Symbolic activity that feeds the narcissism of selected groups not only is protected but also obligatory. Given the totalizing character of narcissism, anything that conflicts with it is forbidden. This is what the discourse of "sensitivity" is all about. Put this baldly it is hard to see how anyone except the most ideological could accept it, and that is the dilemma of those who want to write speech codes.

Finally we may mention among the abuses of PC, programs designed to "fight" racism, sexism, homophobia, and other offenses by "sensitizing" individuals who do not have the right opinions or emotions. A good deal of emotional brutalization may often be seen in these programs. Remember that a failure to idealize the underappreciated groups is seen as a sign of racism or sexism, or whatever the underappreciated group is. These attitudes do not belong in the loving maternal world and cannot be allowed to persist at the university. The subjectivity that underlies them is seen as diseased or evil, and any steps that eradicate it are seen as legitimate and worthwhile. The methodology here most powerfully involves the infliction of shame.

SHAME AND THE EMOTIONAL POWER OF POLITICAL CORRECTNESS

The issue of shame enables us to return to our starting point and to engage more fully some of the dynamics we encountered in explaining the drive to the extreme. How does political correctness get its power over its opposition? The stands taken as politically correct are often quite radical and have a great deal of opposition to them among more traditional elements of the university. These traditional elements are often rapidly and decisively overcome. They often stand quite mute in fact. How does that happen? Much of the answer may be found in an understanding of the way the PC university mobilizes the power of shame through public humiliation.

Consider this case of a student describing his experience at a mandatory "Diversity Seminar," given to incoming students at the University of Michigan.

One activity that particularly angered me was called "Take a Stand." An imaginary line was drawn down the center of the room. One side is the "comfortable" side, the other is the "uncomfortable" side. When the facilitator made a statement, we were to stand on whichever side of the room corresponded to our opinion of the statement. The farther away from the center one stood, the more comfortable or uncomfortable he was.

The first statement was "Dating someone from another race." I walked over to the uncomfortable side, and when I turned around, I found myself alone. I was simultaneously confused and embarrassed.

"You mean all of those people are comfortable with dating people of another race?" I asked the facilitator.

"Yes," he replied. . . .

"Would anyone like to comment on why they're standing where they're standing?" asked the facilitator. Not surprisingly, everybody's eyes were on me.

"Since you asked," I said, "one of the many reasons is that my parents would probably boot me right out of the house." I didn't feel bad about saying this.

One member of the group said, "That's how your parents feel, but how do you feel?"

I feel that I was ostracized from the group because of my beliefs. (Boeskool, 1991: pp. 5, 15)

In this case, students were required to state their beliefs and then be publicly humiliated if they turned out to be politically incorrect. The case is far from being an aberration. In fact, under the aegis of university administrators, such practices have become the norm. For example, remaining with the University of Michigan, Kors and Silverglate (1998) report:

The University of Michigan has an "Office of Orientation," which presented its program, "Commitment to Diversity," to the 1988 National Conference of the National Orientation Directors Association. . . . In October 1988, Michigan set the following primary goal for "future diversity programming": "Establish [a] common base for working definitions and understanding of terms and definitions: societal, institutional and individual discrimination; racism; sexism, homophobia, and heterosexism; religion *[sic]* intolerance; 'ableism' intolerance; understanding [and] appreciation of differences." It instructed "programmers" to instruct students about both discrimination at Michigan and the significant changes achieved "as a result of student activism." The desired result of this was "recognition that University *[sic]* is committed to becoming a leader as a multi-cultural institution and that students are expected to commit to contribute to that goal as new members of the community." It further instructed programmers to "engage students personally in the issues," which included getting undergraduates "to look at personal beliefs, values and behaviors that may discriminate against or harm others," and to "make a personal commitment to change."

Michigan provided programmers with written forms that would lead undergraduates to examine, publicly, their private beliefs and values, and to commit to change. There was "A Personal Exploration," which asked participants, among other things, "What is your earliest remembrance of race? . . . Describe one of the first experiences with race that you had in the classroom . . . Which students do you feel most comfortable with: Black, Chicano, Native American or Asian students? . . . Which students do you feel least comfortable with: Black, Chicano, Native American or Asian students?" What were the goals of such programs? Michigan's Orientation Program Task Force, in its internal documents, stated the "Objectives" of its 1988 Winter Orientation Program for undergraduates: "An understanding of the importance of the issue of diversity, and its applicability to racism and other forms of discrimination, especially sexism and heterosexism; . . . self assessment regarding their own experiences, background, attitudes, and competencies related to these issues; . . . a heightened awareness to the levels of racism, sexism, and heterosexism and their various impacts." (pp. 225–226)

This sort of activity is certainly not limited to the University of Michigan. In fact, perhaps because university personnel must be reliably depended on to participate in this process, it isn't even limited to students. Consider this from the University of Cincinnati:

The University of Cincinnati extended "racial sensitivity training" to staff and faculty. William Daniels, a library employee, described his experience at such a session. Attendance was mandatory, and all participants were ordered to have read Barbara Ehrenreich's essay on "cultural diversity." Vice Provost Mary Ellen Ashley called the group's attention to the silence of the white males among them, saying that she would tolerate this for the moment, but that they would have to participate. The vice provost asked all attendees to write an essay on the topic "What I can do to help our department demonstrate our appreciation for diversity," and explicitly stated that anyone who disagreed with the university's policy on diversity should find work elsewhere. When one librarian denied his need for "cultural diversity training," the vice provost asked the entire group to reflect on the "gall" of such a claim. (Kors and Silverglate, 1998: p. 227)

It is hard to imagine how one could conceivably justify this sort of brutality except through the premise that virulent racism is rampant on university campuses. So it is useful to keep in mind that the term "racism" rarely has any connection with real hatred or prejudice. For example, consider this:

On February 8–9, 1991, the United Ministries in Higher Education, Pennsylvania Commission, held a "seminar" on "Racism on campus" for nine universities in Central and Western Pennsylvania. The goal of the seminar was to send "teams" back to each campus to develop "specific 'nextsteps' in dealing with issues of racism." On several campuses, offices of student life and student services paid participants' travel and registration fees. The seminar provided a packet of materials from universities around the country. These materials lead us to the logical conclusion of current "multiculturalism," group identity, anti-individualism, and intrusive thought reform.

Participants were given a "Glossary of Terms" which asked, "Who is a racist?" and answered, "All white individuals in our society are racists. Even if whites are totally free from all conscious racial prejudices, they remain racists." Another "term" was "White Racism-Power + Prejudice Racism. . . . In the United States at present, only whites can be racists."[14] It defined "Personal Racism" as: "Lack of support for ethnic minorities who take risks to change an organization. . . . Questioning the need for affirmative action goals. . . . 'Color blind' statements that refuse to see race as a part of an individual's identity." It defined "Organizational Racism" as "Premature negotiation to avoid conflict. . . . Absence of a training program that develops staff attitudes, understanding and skills for combating racism." (Kors and Silverglate, 1998: pp. 231–232)

Now let us return to the psychology of the issue. As Goffman (1959, 1967) has shown us, society may be seen as being a very intricate drama, in which participants present claims for deference based upon a definition of themselves and the situation and others transact a drama in which those claims are maintained. Typically, he notes:

Each participant is allowed to establish the tentative official ruling regarding matters which are vital to him but not immediately important to others, e.g., the rationalizations and justifications by which he accounts for his past activity. In exchange for this courtesy he remains silent or non-committal on matters important to others but not immediately important to him. (1959: p. 9)

On the surface, then, we all grant deference to each other. At least we typically give each other sufficient deference to validate each others' characters and keep the drama moving. Underneath the surface, or backstage, so to speak, a vigorous process is at work seeking to ensure that the apparently spontaneous mutual endorsement taking place on the surface comes off. And this backstage activity involves, on all of our parts, a deep understanding of the ways in which we have to play our roles and other people have to play theirs.

Thus we stifle a yawn when a story someone is telling is boring to us, and we try very hard not to show that stifling a yawn is what we are doing. On the other hand, we avoid situations where we know that groups who are deferential to us in public may have reason to be discussing us more critically. In other words we all know that we are playing roles, and we have to know this in order for the roles we are playing to come off. We have this knowledge privately, because the public display is not of the playing of the roles, but of the roles that are being played.

This means that social life is a kind of sleight-of-hand operation, in which we all both know, and don't know, about the performance that we, and others, are putting on. And we maintain this tenuous but necessary balance by asserting our own and accepting each other's privacy.

Political correctness works by denying the right to privacy. In this it simply expresses the premise of the primordial mother whose children have no need, and certainly no right, to have their own minds. PC turns our private awareness of our inner feelings into a source of shame. To have to try to act in a politically correct manner is to be politically incorrect. As George Orwell put it in his book *1984*, "A Party member is required to have not only the right opinions, but the right instincts" (1949: p. 174). Thus love of the oppressed, not the display of love but love itself, is a criterion for one's own moral acceptability.

The alternative to that acceptability is to be the target of rage and scorn. The result of this is that individuals take their own deviation from the public demonstration as indicating that there is something wrong with them. Unable to dispel this impression by admitting their feelings, they each participate in the public ritual of agreement, leaving all the others to believe that there is something wrong with them for their own deviation. It is the apparent unanimity of the consensus so formed that maintains this apparent unanimity.

A classic experiment by Asch (1956) illustrates this dynamic. In that experiment subjects were required to make the simple perceptual judgment of whether lines were the same or different lengths. They were confronted with the question in a group situation in which the other members of the group had already unanimously made their judgments in an erroneous way. Unknown to the subject, the other members of the group were confeder-ates of the experimenter. The question was whether the real subject would contradict the clear evidence of his senses and go along with the group, or whether he would go along with his senses and differ from the group. Strik-ingly, most of the subjects — approximately three-quarters — conformed.

Scheff (1990), analyzing this experiment, argues that the response which occasioned the conformity, a response felt, incidentally, both by those who conformed and those who did not, was shame: "the fear that they were suffering from a defect and that the study would disclose this defect" (p. 90).

Thus he quotes Asch on the subjects who conformed:

They were *dominated* by their exclusion from the group which they took to be a re-flection on themselves. Essentially they were *unable* to face a conflict which threatened, in some undefined way, to expose a deficiency in themselves. They were consequently trying to *merge* in the group in order not to feel peculiar. (Asch, 1956: p. 45; cited by Scheff, 1990: pp. 90–91; emphasis added by Scheff)

The obvious point is that three-quarters of Asch's subjects, in an experi-ment that meant nothing, failed to resist conformity because they feared it would reveal some undefined "deficiency." What could one expect in the tense political atmosphere of a university where the "deficiency" that would be revealed would be, for example, one's "racism," with all the con-notations of slavery, lynchings, and Jim Crow laws that that charge brings with it?

The denigration of the father and his role leaves the individual, espe-cially the male, in the terrible position of being stuck with the sense of un-worthiness that the superego functioned to allow him to turn into guilt and discharge. This unworthiness has to be contrasted with the evident purity claimed by the oppressed. They are idealized and perfect.

In the narcissistic world of political correctness, guilt cannot be seen as being part of the natural limitation of being human. The game has changed. Guilt, which refers to behavior, is no longer the metric of moral-ity. The metric of morality is shame, which attaches to the identity. Thus the white male is stigmatized, not for what he does, but because of who he is—a white male.

We have seen the results of this in the course of our discussion of the drive to the extreme. Within the psychology of shame, as we have seen, the only way people can claim worthiness is to project their unworthiness out-ward and attack it as part of the political correctness project. In that way they become politically correct. Those unwilling to go through this trans-formation typically internalize the rage of the politically correct in the form of depression, and that leaves them without the sense of authority that they need to resist political correctness.

THE MORAL HIGH GROUND

The defenders of PC identify with the primitive maternal, an image of perfect moral purity, utterly without ambiguity. On the basis of this identi-fication, they tend to feel that the moral high ground is theirs by right. The critics of PC, incorporating the paternal, inherit the vision of moral com-plexity that it is the father's business to convey. They understand that within them is the capacity to do wrong as well as right. Psychologically this puts the critics of PC at a disadvantage when up against its defenders.

In assessing their own moral worth, the critics of political correctness should bear in mind that it has not served its purported beneficiaries very well. This is especially so in the case of those whose condition makes the most profound claim for alleviation through race-conscious policies: truly disadvantaged African Americans. PC has prevented robust discussion of serious problems within the lower classes of the African-American com-munity and has guaranteed that their very real problems would remain and even worsen. The classic case here was Moynihan's (1965) observation that the welfare system was destroying the black family, a view that was blasted as being racist. About this, William Julius Wilson said:

[T]he controversy surrounding the Moynihan report had the effect of curtailing se-rious research on minority problems in the inner city for a decade, as liberal schol-ars shied away from researching behavior construed as unflattering or stigmatizing to particular racial minorities. Thus, when liberal scholars returned to study these problems in the early 1980s, they were dumfounded by the magnitude of the changes that had taken place and expressed little optimism about finding an ade-quate explanation. (1987: p. 4)

What needs to be remembered is that the moral stature of PC attaches solely to fantasy. What the paternal offers that the primitive maternal does not is the capacity to assess our actions morally on the basis of their conse-quences. When PC is judged in terms of its consequences, its claims to moral superiority come into serious doubt.

Of course the morality of PC is not a function strictly of its conse-quences. It poses a moral question in its own right. Kors and Silverglate (1998) address this issue directly. They say:

Recognition of the sanctity of conscience is the single most essential respect given to individual autonomy. . . . From the Inquisition to Soviet psychiatry, history has taught us the nightmare of violating the ultimate refuges of self-consciousness, conscience, and private beliefs. In Schiller's *Don Carlos,* Alba proclaims to the mighty Phillip his right to keep his opinion from the king, noting that even "a slave can keep his feelings from a king. It is his only right." The final horror of *1984* was the party's goal of changing Winston's consciousness against his will. The song of the "peat bog soldiers" sent by the Nazis to work until they died was, appropriately, "Die Gedanken sind frei"—"Thoughts are free" for that truly is the final atom of liberty. No moral person would pursue another human being there. Colleges and universities do. (pp. 211–212)

THE ANOMALY OF FEMALE POWER

One further point that needs to be made about the psychodynamics of the PC university relates to the ambiguous position of women. Within the psychology I have outlined here, women are seen both as defenseless victims of male oppression and as exemplars of the omnipotent primordial mother. Thus, we find that the image of the woman as passive, helpless victim is ubiquitous in our society, with whole classes of institutions having been created to protect these victims. On the other hand, and indeed partly through the manipulation of this image, women have manifested enormous power in the transformation of almost every aspect of society. This paradox is particularly interesting in connection with the theory developed here because it is difficult to think of any other way to explain it.

An example of this contrast occured at the University of Michigan in 1992. This case involved a sophomore student in an introductory Political Science course. The student, in a paper criticizing telephone polling, invoked a hypothetical "Dave Stud," who, although "knowledgeable" about a certain area of taxation, refused to answer a pollster's question because he was busy "entertaining three beautiful ladies in his penthouse." This male student's female teaching assistant responded this way in the margin of the paper:

This is ludicrous & inappropriate & OFFENSIVE. This is completely inappropriate for a serious political science paper. It completely violates the standard of non-sexist writing. Professor Rosenstone has encouraged me to interpret this comment as an example of sexual harassment and to take the appropriate formal steps. I have chosen not to do so in this instance. However, any future comments, in a paper, in a class or in any dealings w/me will be interpreted as sexual harassment and formal steps will be taken. Professor Rosenstone is aware of these comments—& is prepared to intervene. You are forewarned! (*Michigan Review,* 1993)

The disparity here between the frail, vulnerable woman, grievously damaged by the merest mention of male sexuality, and the powerful woman, capable of mobilizing the full weight of the University of Michigan against a hapless sophomore, is breathtaking. As we shall see in the next chapter, it reaches its apotheosis in the politics of the issue of women in combat.

CONCLUSION

Having maintained that PC represents psychological regression, it is important to reiterate that regression is not necessarily bad. On the contrary, as psychoanalytic thinkers such as Kris (1952) have observed, regression is a necessary element of creativity. Again it might be argued that times of continuous change such as those we live in call for the enhancement of creativity in all areas of life. This may be, putting the best light on it, the deeper social function of postmodernism and the rise of the primitive maternal. Kris's point was that, in order to contribute to creativity, regression has to be in the service of the ego. What we see being played out in PC, however, and in the revolt of the primitive maternal against the paternal generally, is not regression in the service of the ego. It is regression against the ego. This regression against the ego now forms the core of our educational system. It increasingly controls our image of who we are, of what the world is, and of how we fit within it.

Before leaving this issue, it is important to point out the likely consequences of this regression. As I have said, in contemporary society the individual is protected from the consequences of his actions and shielded, as never before, from direct contact with indifferent objective reality. This does not mean that reality may be ignored. It means, instead, that reality must be dealt with symbolically and by rigorous analytic thought. This makes it absolutely essential that the modalities of free thought and open discussion, by which we seek objectivity by guarding against our biases and limitations, must be maintained with ruthless diligence. It is precisely these modalities that are thrown out by political correctness. In this way society has set itself up to be blindsided by forces that it will not be able to comprehend. These forces will grow in power as the results of our self-inflicted ignorance accumulate.

NOTES

1. This replacement itself is a matter of interest. Defenders of political correctness often note that the related furor did not begin until the Cold War was

over. They take this to mean that the "right" had to find something to oppose after communism collapsed. This fails to recognize that opposition to PC came, not
from the right, which has never been heavily represented within the university,
but primarily from the center. My own view is that it was the left that was put
into crisis by the end of the Cold War.

2. The marxist origins of political correctness suggest an irony that, were it
not for political correctness, might provoke reflection amongst the corporate ex-
ecutives who, through their support for some forms of "diversity training," are attempting to promote it within their own corporations (Lynch, 1997). They
might wish to consider that when a corporation promotes the ideas that all "cultures" are equally valid, they undermine the special character of their own culture and, hence, the motivational structure that energizes their own
organizations. Of special concern would be the cultural premise that the organization needs to maintain economic viability, a premise that is not frequently encountered among the nostrums of the politically correct.

3. From its origins in the university, political correctness has, of course,
spread widely throughout the culture. However, largely due to the effects of political correctness itself, information about its workings elsewhere has generally not
been publicly available. Because the method of our inquiry involves the detailed
analysis of process, this chapter is primarily focused on the dynamics of political
correctness as they have played out within a university setting. Much of what is
said here will easily be seen to apply to other organizational and social settings.

4. It is critical to note that this happens to girls as well as boys, even if not
entirely in the same measure. Thus, consider this from the columnist Anna
Quindlen:

My relationship with my father was more man to man. He required of a fully developed hu-
man being that she have exhaustively studied both Max Shulman and Machiavelli, Django
Reinhardt and Louis Armstrong. . . . His motto was "winners need not explain." He treated
B's as if they were F's. . . . If you couldn't keep up, you got left.

I kept up. . . .

My father exercised only the tyranny of his expectations, but it was tyranny enough.
And then, not so many years ago, I realized that, like a heart transplant after the rejection
phase, his expectations for me had become my own. And I stopped valuing myself by how
my father valued me. I know from literature and life that is perhaps the greatest passage that
human beings ever make. (1993: p. E17)

5. Hobbes (1939) put it this way:

Again, men have no pleasure, but on the contrary a great deal of grief, in keeping company,
where there is no power able to overawe them all. *For every man looketh that his companion
should value him at the same rate he sets upon himself*; and upon all signs of contempt, or under-
valuing, naturally endeavors, as far as he dares (which amongst them that have no common
power to keep them in quiet, is far enough to make them destroy each other), to extort a
greater value from his contemners by damage, and from others by the example. (p. 160; emphasis added)

This contributes strongly to:

In such condition there is no place for industry, because the fruit thereof is uncertain: and consequently no culture of the earth; no navigation, nor use of the commodities that may be imported by sea; no commodious building; no instruments of moving, and removing, such things as require much force; no knowledge of the face of the earth; no account of time; no arts; no letters; no society; and which is worst of all, continual fear, and danger of violent death.

6. Universities clearly differ in their degree of PC. Moreover, it inevitably generates resistance to itself. It is therefore unlikely that any university can be said to be entirely PC. Nonetheless, it is possible to think about the PC university as an ideal case, which is what I am doing here.

7. According to U.C. political scientist Jack Citrin (1999a), the hunger strike consisted in limiting their diet to Jamba Juice and Ensure. Jamba Juice is proclaimed on the web site of its manufacturer to offer: "An extraordinary health experience unlike any you've ever tasted. Jamba is enticing fruit and vegetable flavors, vital nutrients and total convenience: everything you need to live an active, healthy life." See http://www.jambajuice.com/what/index.html. Ensure, a product of Abbott Laboratories, is advertised on their web site as a "complete adult nutritional beverage available in a variety of flavors" (http://www.abbott.com/products/nutritionals.htm). The concept of a hunger strike brings with it a sense that the striker is putting himself in danger through his actions. These students were not putting themselves in danger. In that sense they were not so much on a hunger strike as on a diet.

8. As with all the articles cited in this chapter, the quoted material consists of excerpts, not the entire article.

9. The behavior of white male university faculty and administrators is often quite craven. In understanding it, we do well to reflect upon the extraordinary difficulty of the psychological situation in which they find themselves. Their moral weakness is not without powerful cause.

10. Morrisey's results in tabular form (p. 60):

Percentages of Politically Biased Articles

Year	Ideological	Tendentious	Total
1930	0.0	4.0	4.0
1940	1.5	1.5	3.0
1950	3.0	1.5	4.5
1960	1.5	15.5	17.0
1970	10.0	10.0	20.0
1975	5.5	11.0	16.5
1980	41.5	12.5	54.0
1985	50.0	12.5	62.5
1990	52.5	19.5	72.0

Left, Right, Center

1930	No ideological articles.
1940	1 ideological article, centrist.
1950	2 ideological articles, centrist.

1960	1 ideological article, rightist.
1970	5 ideological articles, leftist.
1975	2 ideological articles, leftist.
1980	10 ideological articles, leftist.
1985	12 ideological articles, leftist.
1990	19 ideological articles, 3 centrist, 16 leftist.

11. There is, of course, such a thing as real oppression, but oppressors are not a mythic force of the sort that the psychology of the ego ideal projects. They are simply human beings who have let their narcissism run away with them.

12. It is worthwhile noting that the prestige given to academic research by society is based on people's capacity to depend on research findings. But that was based on work that was accomplished under a more objective regimen. As time goes by, and as the constraints imposed by ideology increasingly limit the reliability of knowledge so produced, the prestige of academic research will disappear. At that point the academy will have squandered the reserve of trustworthiness that our predecessors, over the course of hundreds of years, devoted their lives to accumulating.

13. For a discussion of Afrocentric "scholarship" see Lefkowitz (1992). This is from her account:

[S]everal years ago I had a student who seemed to regard virtually everything I said about Socrates with hostility. . . . [H]er instructor in another course had told her that Socrates (as suggested by the flat nose in some portrait sculptures) was black. The instructor had also taught that classicists universally refuse to mention the African origins of Socrates because they do not want their students to know that the so-called legacy of ancient Greece was stolen from Egypt.

But,

Because Socrates was an Athenian citizen, he must have had Athenian parents; and since foreigners couldn't become naturalized Athenian citizens, he must have come from the same ethnic background as every other Athenian. . . . It was as simple as that. (pp. 29–30)

14. The idea that blacks cannot be racist, because racism requires power and only whites have power in our society, is a staple at the PC university. But it is absurd. For one thing it implies that the Nazis were not racist until they gained power in 1933. For another, in the face of the fact that white people are overwhelmingly opposed to racial preferences (e.g., Thernstrom and Thernstrom, 1999), and that such preferences remain in place after thirty years, the idea that black people do not have power is ridiculous. It is a measure of the corruption PC has wrought within the university that such preposterous statements go largely unchallenged.

Chapter Six

The March of the Virgin: Psychodynamics of Sexual Politics and the Issue of Women in Combat

The notion of placing women in combat roles[1] has the appearance of an idea whose time has come, but it is difficult to understand why. Assessed in terms of our usual ideas of the bases of political power, it should not have much strength behind it. A presidential commission recommended against it.[2] Military men don't want it.[3] More interesting, the women in the military who would be most intimately involved don't want it either, at least for themselves.[4,5] The countries that have tried it abandoned it shortly thereafter.[6] The consequences of making a mistake in adopting it are incalculable, yet it keeps gaining ground like an inexorable and unstoppable force. Thus, in a study of military personnel, sociologist Laura Miller (1997) reported: "When I asked men who opposed women in combat roles what they thought would happen in the future, they all asserted that integration was inevitable. They concluded that women eventually would have their way despite any reasonable objections" (p. 48).

The question, then, is why? What power lies behind this apparently inexorable force? And if this power is of a different sort than we customarily encounter in political decision making, what are the consequences one may expect from its emergence? These are the questions toward which this chapter is directed.

Miller's research provides a number of different approaches to answering the question. To begin with, her female research subjects have no doubt about who is pushing the issue. They think it is the feminists, a group they see as different from themselves, especially with regard to class and race, and as illegitimately claiming the right to speak for them:

Army women in my survey . . . hardly agree on the issue of women in combat. Enlisted women and women of color particularly are likely to *oppose* assigning women to combat military occupational specialties (MOSs). Many express resentment toward officers and civilian activists who are attempting to open combat roles to women. They argue that the activists do not realize the hardships associated with those roles on the enlisted level. Some, like one white NCO [i.e., noncommissioned officer] with Desert Storm experience, were obviously frustrated: "Who does that Pat Schroeder think she is? Has she ever talked to me? To her? To any of us? If she came here, I'd sure give her a piece of my mind." (Miller, 1995: p. 14)

Although Miller's subjects may be correct, the question of who is pushing the issue does not entirely resolve it. For the source of the feminists' power itself is an issue. If Miller's subjects are representative of the fact that feminists are often detached from the lives of most women (also see Sommers, 1995), and if they therefore would have a hard time mobilizing the power of most women within the conventional political sphere, how is it that they are able to effect such drastic change in the area of military policy? Surely most of the holders of politically powerful roles within the government are still men. How do the feminists get their way among them? Why do men fall down in front of them?

In a more recent paper (1997), Miller provides another way of approaching the question by offering insight into the tactics of the feminists. Discussing what she calls "gender harassment," which she defines as "interactional, indirect forms of protest" engaged in by men who "object to women's increased participation in the military," she says:

Gender harassment is an attempt to push women back into their more "natural" roles, restore the meritocratic order of the organization, and ensure that all soldiers on the battlefield can do their jobs and assist the wounded in times of battle. Certainly these views are considered sexist by many, and potentially could cause problems for any soldier who expresses them openly in mixed company. (p. 42)

This gives us another piece of the puzzle. The idea of women in combat gets power from the fact that the arguments against it, even when they are based on such obviously relevant considerations as restoring the meritocracy and ensuring that soldiers can do their jobs and assist the wounded, are "sexist" and, therefore, "politically incorrect" and unmentionable.

Yet saying that does not so much answer the question as it shifts it to another level. For where does political correctness (PC) get its power? We know that political correctness has power in a university, but what is there about calling an opinion "sexist" that stops the expression of that opinion in its tracks even when that opinion points to consequences that should be considered in making an important decision? The idea that it could have a major impact on policy in a matter that affects life and death, and that it could do so in an institution whose concern for the lives of its members is legendary, seems almost fanciful. But there it is.

My concern in this chapter is not so much with the substantive issue of women in combat, but rather with the way PC, as wielded by certain feminists, affects the determination of whether they will be in combat. In earlier chapters I have tried to gain an understanding of the primitive, unconscious forces underlying the power of certain forms of feminism and PC. These forces are very much at work in the issue of women in combat. Indeed I shall argue that, in the end, the real danger of women in combat comes less from their presence there, which may very well never amount to much, than it does from the damage done to the military through the operation of these primitive forces. My point will be that these forces are directed against male sexuality and masculinity. I also argue, from a related perspective, that if masculinity is undermined, military organization will be emasculated. If that happens it will not be able to fulfill its mission, no matter what the sexual composition of those who occupy its ranks happens to be.

The power of feminism, as it operates within the issue of women in combat, is due to the most primitive forces operating in unintegrated form. In the course of this chapter, I elaborate the framework of this analysis. First, however, it will be useful to get a feeling for the way feminism has operated in this connection. For this purpose there is no better place to start than with the Tailhook scandal.

TAILHOOK

The drive to place women in combat roles gained much of its momentum from the scandal over the Tailhook convention of 1991. Tailhook, a convention of naval aviators with Navy support, had been an annual event since 1956. Valued by the Navy because it afforded the opportunity for frank communication among ranks (Vistica, 1995: p. 234), it was also well known for its raucousness. Following its origination in the northern Mexican town of Rosarita, it moved to San Diego, where it was thrown out of most of the local hotels. Finally, in 1963, it settled in Las Vegas where, according to Vistica (1995),[7] "nobody seemed to mind the men launching couches and other items from hotel windows" (p. 233). The 1991 convention, which followed the U.S. triumph over Iraq, billed itself as the Mother of all Hooks, after Saddam Hussein's boast. By all accounts it left nothing to previous conventions in the way of drunkenness, sexual debauchery, or other sorts of wildness.

The difference between the 1991 Tailhook and previous ones was largely due to a charge by a Naval lieutenant named Paula Coughlin that she had been sexually assaulted by a group of Naval aviators, who had arranged themselves in a "gauntlet," and that her superiors had not responded promptly to her complaint. Out of this emerged a series of charges and investigations that shook the entire institution of the Navy. Taking place in an election year, and following the lurid charges of sexual harassment in Clarence Thomas's nomination hearings, the scandal gave overwhelming momentum to one side in what had previously been a fairly balanced debate over women in combat. As Vistica (1995) put it:

If there were two issues that every candidate either feared or was talking about, they were sexual harassment and lifting the ban that restricted women from combat. Tailhook had combined those two into one extremely powerful mega-issue. Advocates for lifting the ban claimed that until the Navy—indeed all of the services—gave women the same jobs as men had, the sexual harassment and abuse so prevalent at Tailhook would continue. (p. 348)

With regard to Tailhook, it may be stipulated that some men behaved in a disgraceful fashion that was unacceptable under any reasonable standard of behavior and certainly worthy of punishment.[8] This was a fact that was recognized by naval personnel in their own sobriety, and it is represented in a letter whose disclosure was a major starting point in the controversy. Written to all aviation squadron commanders by Captain Frederick "Wigs" Ludwig, a Navy fighter pilot who was president of the Tailhook Association, the letter said, in part:

[J]ust a few specifics to show how far across the line of responsible behavior we went . . . definitely the most serious was "the Gauntlet" on the third floor. I have five separate reports of young ladies, several of whom had nothing to do with Tailhook, who were verbally abused, had drinks thrown on them, were physically abused, and were sexually molested. Most distressing was the fact that an underage young lady was severely intoxicated and had her clothing removed by members of the Gauntlet.

Tailhook cannot and will not condone the blatant and total disregard of individual rights and public/private property! . . . We in Naval Aviation and the Tailhook Association are bigger than this. (Cited by Vistica, 1995: pp. 333–334)

Seen in this way the misconduct at Tailhook may simply be seen as a breakdown of discipline, and although such breakdowns are regrettable, ordinarily they are understood to be within the purview of military organizations' disciplinary apparatus and dealt with there. The enforcement of discipline, after all, is the core process in a military organization. Enforcing discipline would have been an *affirmation* of military culture. But the events at Tailhook gained their significance because they were not seen as a disciplinary problem within the culture; rather they were seen as a problem of the culture itself.

This consideration also applies to the scandalous behavior on the part of the naval command, who, as Vistica shows, attempted to deflect criticism from themselves by blaming the breakdown of discipline on younger officers, rather than acknowledging their own very real contributions. Here again, if they had accepted real responsibility for real infractions, this would not have been in violation of naval culture, but in support of it.

Former Naval Secretary James Webb (1966) drew this distinction very clearly in a speech at his alma mater, the U.S. Naval Academy. In that speech Webb lauded the traditional virtues of the Navy and the role of the Academy in preparing officers to embody them:

And so I resolved to prepare myself so that when the time came I could honor this heritage by showing the same physical and moral courage, the identical dedication to my country and to the people whose lives were being entrusted to me. I wanted more than anything to have the courage to do my duty, to take care of my people, to speak the truth no matter how it hurt, and indeed no matter what the consequences. And I was not alone. In the messhall, on the parade field, walking to class, I could look around me and see thousands who felt the same way I did.

He contrasted the maintenance of the Navy's traditional ideals with the corruption and demoralization that has developed in recent times, largely due, in his view, to the aftermath of Tailhook, and held the Navy's highest officials accountable:

The aftermath of Tailhook was never about inappropriate conduct so much as it was about the lack of wisdom among the Navy's senior leadership. . . . those who were to blame for outrageous conduct should have been disciplined, and those who were not to blame should have been vigorously defended, along with the culture and the mores of the naval service.

The important point here is that this speech differentiated sharply between the culture of the Navy and its leadership. In fact it excoriated the leadership precisely for its failure to uphold the culture of the Navy. Yet it received a standing ovation at the U.S. Naval Academy.

TAILHOOK AS A "CULTURAL PROBLEM"

Largely through the direct involvement of Assistant Secretary of the Navy Barbara Pope, the problem at Tailhook came to be seen as the naval culture itself (Vistica, 1995). In that context attitudes toward women in combat were seen as part of the problem, and placing women in combat roles was seen as part of the solution.[9]

The problems of Tailhook were seen as a cultural problem. This means that they were not a problem *within* the culture, but rather, were a problem as seen from a vantage point *outside* the culture. But what was the point from which the culture of the Navy was seen as problematic?

I think it would be using the term too broadly to say that this vantage point must be another culture. The idea of a culture brings with it connotations that are far wider than a specific interpretation of Tailhook would support. Looking for a term that is narrower, it seems to me that the idea of a "perspective" is about right. It implies a partial view of a circumstance, a view that is partial because it is from a certain location. The implication is that the characteristics of the location must be understood if what the perspective reveals, and what it leaves out, are to be understood.

Having said that, it must also be said that there are only locations. We always see from a point of view, and cannot do otherwise. Some locations may afford us a broader perspective than others, but breadth is not necessarily the same thing as truth, and at any rate what appears to be breadth from one perspective may not seem to be breadth from another. If, in the end, certain ideas and ways of seeing things prove more adequate than others, that determination is one that can only be made at the end. Up until that time, it is best to do the best one can, and to hold one's views with some humility.

But if one should hold one's views with humility, that does not mean that one should not hold them, or that one should not express them boldly and forthrightly. Boldness and forthrightness do not necessarily mean that one is saying, "Finally, this is the way things are." It may mean, "This is the way things look to me and I want to express myself as clearly and strongly as I can." That is want I intend to do here.

My purpose is to try to understand the power of feminism. I try to understand it by looking at the feminists' perspective, and by trying to understand what it tells us about where feminists are, about what is the location from which the perspective of the feminists makes sense. In doing this I am doing no more or less than the feminists have done in trying to understand Tailhook as a "cultural problem."

Trying to get at the feminist perspective, I need to be able to register the difference between those of their observations that are unproblematic and those that are odd and therefore need to be explained. In order to do this, I have to take my own perspective as the measure of oddness. I do this openly and directly, because I think that is the obligation of the thinker and writer. The reader may be assured, however, that my ultimate confidence is not in the specifics of my case, but in the capacity of thought, in the end, to take what it needs and leave the rest. Perhaps that will make do for humility.

My purpose, then, is to try to understand the force of the idea of women in combat by trying to understand feminism, the agent that is pushing the idea. For this purpose, it will be useful to reexamine the question of Tailhook, trying to ferret out the dynamics of feminism by understanding its perspective on the Tailhook incidents.

Thus, in order to see what was involved in the idea that the events at Tailhook represented a "cultural problem," what we need to look at are these questions: First, over and above the acts of sexual molestation engaged in by the participants, what were seen as the sins of Tailhook for which the Navy needed to undergo a cultural change? Second, what does the response to the Tailhook events tell us about the feminist vantage point from which the traditional military culture is being criticized, a vantage point that is evidently intended as a replacement for that military culture, and whose power is represented by the apparently inexorable force of the idea of women in combat.

THE CRIME OF MALE SEXUALITY

Trying to understand the feminist response to the events of Tailhook, what stands out to me above all else is that although attention focused on the relatively rare instances in which women were handled against their will, by all accounts most of the sexual activity that took place at Tailhook was consensual. This was true even for the famous Gauntlet. Thus Vistica reports: "for every woman who resisted, there were many more who couldn't wait to walk down the Gauntlet and be manhandled" (p. 335).

The consensual nature of some of the activities was apparent in their very nature. For example, one of the events was "leg shaving," in which there was not even a hint of coercion or force:

According to the witnesses and the officers involved, the leg shaving was a rather elaborate ritual that included the use of hot towels and baby oil, as well as the [sic] massaging the woman's legs and feet. The entire process took between 30 and 45 minutes per shave. (Vander Schaaf, 1993: p. VII: 1)

and which ran to great general approval:

the Barber of Seville, Lieutenant Rolando "Ghandi" Diaz, had set up his leg and pubic hair shaving chair in room 303. Outside, a fifteen-foot-long banner proclaiming "Free Leg Shaves" hung on the pool patio of the suite, and women had lined up to have Diaz "make them see God." (p. 327)

What is interesting from the standpoint of analysis, though, is the way the acts in which women participated enthusiastically were responded to with the same outrage as the acts of patent abuse, as if the two were equivalent to one another. Thus, Leg Shaving gets a chapter in the Inspector General's report on the horrors of Tailhook (Vander Schaaf, 1993), as do Streaking, Mooning, and Belly/Navel Shots. From this it appears that the apparent crime at Tailhook was not so much sexual abuse, but sexuality.

Now the obvious response is that such public displays of sexual behavior by its officials tend to bring discredit upon the institution and, in that respect, represent "conduct unbecoming an officer."[10] Certainly such behavior constitutes "indecent exposure." These are, of course, offenses in their own right. In fact the rationale for the Department of Defense Inspector General's investigation was that earlier investigations "should have been expanded beyond the assaults to encompass other violations of law and regulation as they became apparent" (Vander Schaaf, 1992: p. 1)

But putting aside the question of whether sexual assault and leg shaving should be regarded with equal opprobrium, this point brings into focus another aspect of the matter, which is close to its heart. It is that even though sexuality was seen as being criminal when it was engaged in by men, the women who engaged in it were seen as blameless. Thus, Vistica (1995) observes:

It was an easy story for the press to trumpet: drunken military men sexually assaulting innocent female victims. The networks, CNN, and the major newspaper dailies easily latched on to that theme and avoided the more complex issues of women as aggressors and men as victims. There were several cases of women grabbing men's crotches in a "package check" or other male officers having their pants pulled down by women. (p. 347)

In one suite, a female Navy lawyer, who is now a naval judge, was serving drinks in a suite while topless. (p. 234)

Perhaps the most ironic example of this was the fact that Paula Coughlin, whose complaint brought the whole investigation into being, had her own legs publicly shaved (Donnelly, 1994).

The crime of Tailhook, it thus appears, was male sexuality. But if that is the case, it puts an entirely different slant on the matter. For if what was exceptionable about Tailhook was sexual behavior that passed a certain point on a line between permissible and impermissible, one could imagine stamping it out, as I have said, by a simple tightening of discipline. But if the crime was male sexuality itself, that would mean that the problem arose not from behavior that passed a point on a line, but from the line itself. That, arguably, might go to fundamental considerations of motivation and meaning that would, indeed, put the whole "culture" of the military into question, with potential consequences of the utmost seriousness.[11]

That the seriousness of these consequences should not be underestimated is revealed by what it seems to me is the second most striking feature of the Tailhook scandal, which was the disproportionality of the response to the events that caused it, and the extraordinary degree to which the lens of sexual abuse was used to examine the entire range of military affairs.

DISPROPORTIONALITY IN THE RESPONSE TO TAILHOOK

As I have said, there is no denying that some of the activities at Tailhook were disgraceful, but it should also be said that the very worst of them were not felonious. No one was hurt, let alone raped, yet the level of outrage in the response was extremely high pitched. There is no way that, without a failure of proportion, these incidents by themselves could have resulted in what has been called "[t]he Navy's worst disaster since Pearl Harbor" (Vistica, 1995: p. 355).

The lack of proportion is shown in the very prominence of the Tailhook scandal itself, and certainly in its consequences. As James Webb put it in his 1996 speech: "Tailhook should have been a three or maybe a five-day story. . . . Instead, we are now at four years and counting, and its casualty list reads like a who's who of naval aviation."

Trying to understand this lack of proportion, what is especially interesting from my perspective, was that much of the opprobrium, and the official punishment, was directed against individuals whose actions were quite tame. Thus, by all accounts, only a relatively few men were accused of assault, but the careers of all of the men at Tailhook were put in jeopardy simply on the basis of their presence.

Perhaps the most egregious case here was that of Commander Robert E. Stumpf, an F-18 pilot who was a former commanding officer of the Navy's prestigious Blue Angels. He was at Tailhook to receive an award, on behalf of the squadron he commanded, as "best in the Navy" during the Gulf War, yet his promotion to captain was blocked because it was rumored, though never proved, and despite his denial, that he was in a room at the same time a stripper was performing. As a direct consequence of his treatment, Stumpf left the Navy (Vistica, 1995).

Perhaps most central to the disproportionality in the response to Tailhook was the loss of recognition that nonsexual matters should have a bearing upon the formulation of naval policy. The entire institution of the Navy was seen through the prism of a few acts of sexual abuse, and a readiness to subordinate every aspect of the Navy's activity in the attempt to eliminate sexual abuse was demonstrated. The most obvious instance of this was the rampant disregard for the fact that naval aviators, among the most rigorously selected and highly trained combatants in the history of the world, were allowed to have their careers jeopardized, en masse, with no apparent regard for the consequences it would have for the Navy's capacity to carry out its mission. [12,13]

Vistica relates an incident concerning Barbara Pope, who was at the time dissatisfied with the results of the Navy's investigation, that illustrates this disregard:

Pope wanted the investigators to go back and interview the several dozen commanding officers whose squadrons had taken part in organizing the hospitality suites. They were commanders and captains and, in the case of one suite, a rear admiral. Something had to be done to make them cooperate, she said, and she threw out ideas like grounding them or docking their flight pay. Hold a board of inquiry or a blue ribbon panel. If necessary, use your secretarial right, she said to [Navy Secretary] Garrett, to remove them from their jobs. "I'm not saying you fire them, I'm saying you remove them for lack of confidence. I don't know about you, but I don't have confidence in these people's leadership abilities." (1995: p. 345)

A particularly striking example of this sort of lack of proportionality is present in the case of Lieutenant Rebecca Hansen. Hansen, who had joined the Navy in response to an ad for women who wanted to become pilots, had a history of marginal performance. She also had a history of believing, rightly or wrongly, that she was a victim of sexual harassment (*Frontline*, 1996). During the course of her flight training, in which again her performance was marginal, she formally charged her flight instructor, Lieutenant Larry Meyer, with sexual harassment. Meyer was investigated and found guilty of "inappropriate remarks." He left the Navy a year later, but, before he did, he made threats that he would see to it that his friends would cause her to wash out of helicopter training.

In the event, when she went up for helicopter training, her performance was found substandard and she was indeed washed out of the program. Believing that it was Meyer's vendetta, rather than her inadequacy, which had caused her downfall, she enlisted the power of her senator, David Durenberger, who took an interest in the matter and brought it up with the Navy.

The Navy assured Durenberger that Hansen was, indeed, incompetent as a pilot, but he was not convinced and wanted to see the actual investigative report. The Navy, however, would give it only to the Armed Services Committee, who maintained that the report contained confidential information and would not give it to Durenberger. The Navy did, however, offer to have the matter reviewed by Admiral Stanley Arthur (Vistica, 1995, p. 390).

Arthur, vice chief of Naval Operations, veteran of 500 combat missions in Vietnam, winner of eleven Distinguished Flying Crosses, commanding officer of U.S. Air Forces in the Gulf War, and soon to be nominated by President Clinton to be CINCPAC, commander of all U.S. forces in the Pacific, was widely regarded in the armed forces as a fair and honest man. He called in Hansen, then an ensign, to hear her side of the story. Later interviewed for Public Broadcasting System's *Frontline* (1996), she made it clear that she was not impressed by him:

REBECCA HANSEN: He was likable, in a . . . in a . . . I guess, a meeting sort of way. Was he wanting to get down to facts and business? No. He had his mind made up. He was patronizing to me.

In any case, Admiral Arthur, when he had investigated, found that he could not recommend her. This again is from *Frontline*, here narrated by Peter Boyer:

PETER J. BOYER: Admiral Arthur looked at these documents . . . her failing grades, her marginal performance evaluations. He says what he saw frightened him.

ADM. STANLEY ARTHUR: No, she was not going to be a Navy pilot and I knew this was an accident waiting to happen, that at some point in time there would be a failure and the failure could well be tragic.

Again, Ensign Hansen was not impressed:

REBECCA HANSEN: When you have someone of the . . . that has the rank and the respect of Admiral Stanley Arthur declare that you're an unsafe pilot, it doesn't matter that he doesn't have anything to back it up with. Just the fact that he has 11 Distinguished Flying Crosses . . . that's all anybody needs to . . . he's a war hero and he's a known quantity and I'm . . . nobody knows. I'm just some . . . some junior officer and on top of that . . . not just some junior officer. I'm a woman. I'm a woman who filed sexual harassment charges. I must be a bad pilot. Why else would I do such a thing?

Of course, Arthur did feel that he had something to "back it up with":

ADM. STANLEY ARTHUR: If you had to explain it, you could take 10 years to try to explain it, but you get this feel. You've had the feeling before. I've watched people die when I had that feeling, saying, "Maybe this individual shouldn't have been here. Why were they here? This is an accident waiting to happen." And then the next thing you know, it's an accident that happened and you say, "Should I . . . am I responsible because I didn't say anything?" You know. And I know today that that was the right call, in my mind.

These sort of considerations did not register with Senator Durenberger, who put a hold on Arthur's nomination. This began a process that culminated in Arthur's being called in by Chief of Naval Operations Jeremy Boorda, who made it clear that Arthur would not have his backing in a sexual harassment scandal, leading to Arthur's retirement. Here, returning to our subject of disproportion, was Hansen's response:

REBECCA HANSEN: I had no agenda to take him down, but if he can't deal with the facts, then maybe it is time for him to move on and maybe we're better off not having him in charge of a very heated area in North Korea if he is not able to deal with things in a balanced way.

Another form of disproportion consisted in a failure to distinguish between behavior and attitudes. The fact is that many of the "crimes" at Tailhook did not involve behavior, as such, but rather what the behavior was thought to indicate about the attitudes of those who engaged in the behavior. Thus, for example, wearing T-shirts with slogans, making jokes or even standing for their making,[14] even asking questions at a public meeting, were greeted with the same horror as overt sexual abuse. The crimes, that is to say, were not behavioral crimes, but *attitudinal crimes*. It was a belief in the widespread character of these criminal attitudes that constituted the belief that the problem revealed by Tailhook was a "cultural" problem.

So what were these criminal attitudes? To the extent that these attitudes were limited to the belief that sexual abuse was justified, one could grant credence to the feminists' belief that there was a cultural problem in the Navy. But, as we have seen, naval authorities understood perfectly well that disgraceful actions had taken place. James Webb, for example, in the speech referred to earlier, observed that "[t]hose who were to blame for outrageous conduct should have been disciplined," yet his speech was given a standing ovation.

The fact that there was something deeper going on is exemplified, for example, by a speech made by Dan Howard, a former spokesman for the National Security Council who had been appointed acting secretary of the Navy. This is from Vistica's (1995) account:

On July 1, four days after he took over the helm of the Navy, Howard sat some three hundred senior officers down in the Pentagon's auditorium and held what he called a "Come to Jesus" truth meeting. "I think it's important to underline the fact that what happened at Tailhook was not just a problem with the integration of men and women in our ranks," he told the admirals and generals, who felt as if they were being lectured. "It was just as much a problem with the toleration of stone age attitudes about warriors returning from the sea, about Navy and Marine Corps people who think the rules of civility and common decency can be suspended at will, and most of all about alcohol as an excuse for disgraceful behavior." (p. 356)

Now, as has been said, to the extent that Howard had confined his remarks to the suspension of discipline and the abuse of alcohol, there would not have been anything exceptionable in his remarks on this occasion. But "toleration of stone age attitudes about warriors returning from the sea?" How does that fit in?

A memorandum written by Garrett (Vander Schaaf, 1992) before he resigned may help us focus on the shift in attitudes that the Navy had in mind. Addressed to the chief of naval operations and the commandant of the Marine Corps, entitled "Behavior and Attitudes Towards Women," it says, in part:

We cannot—and will not—tolerate the demeaning and insensitive behavior and attitudes of the past. Our goal in the Department of the Navy must be to cultivate through education and environment where actions demeaning to women are as a matter of course considered unacceptable—and, even more, where behavior and attitudes reflect respect for women and the valuable contribution they make as an integral part of the Navy/Marine Corps team. How do we get there?

Referrals for Appropriate Action

First, all individuals within the Department of the Navy must understand that we indeed take very seriously our "zero-tolerance" policy; appropriate action will be taken on any incident of sexual harassment by anyone in the Department of the Navy.

Garrett's message seems to be clear enough. The problem, in his view, arises from attitudes and behavior that "demean women" and reflect a lack of respect for them and their contributions. It also seems that he associates these demeaning and disrespectful attitudes and behaviors with sexual harassment.

The problem is, of course, that though the severe sanctions for sexual harassment are associated with these attitudes and behaviors, the terms "demeaning" and "disrespectful" are left undefined. This leaves the way open for them to be defined in practice by political forces. If these forces were moved by the dynamics of the mature personality, there would be no problem, but if they reflected irrational and primitive forces, the consequences would be horrible. Considerable evidence suggests that they have, in many cases, reflected such irrational forces. Here again, we look for the strange. It is not hard to find.

Evidence is readily available to show that the attitudes that have been found demeaning and disrespectful, together with their various cognates such as "sexist" and "antiwoman," have run across a broad range and included affirmations of the traditional male role, positive valuations of male sexuality, the belief that men should protect women, and, along with that, the belief that women did not belong in combat roles. These have been lumped together and conflated with acts of sexual harassment and overt physical abuse.[15]

THE DEFINITION OF DEMEANING ATTITUDES AND SEXUAL HARASSMENT

A good example of the strangeness in the way sexual harassment has been defined is given in a study on sexual harassment at the military academies, conducted by the General Accounting Office, and published at about the same time as the inspector general's report on Tailhook. The study, as discussed in an editorial in the *Washington Times* (1992), revealed "significant" sexual harassment at the academies. But looking at the categories of "sexual harassment," what we find, in decreasing order of frequency, are: (1) remarks that standards have been lowered,[16] (2) derogatory comments or jokes; (3) offensive posters, signs, graffiti, or T-shirts; (4) remarks that women don't belong there; (5) mocking gestures, (6) unwanted horseplay or high jinks; (7) exclusion from social activities; (8) unwanted sexual advances; (9) derogatory letters or messages; and (10) unwanted pressure for dates. Clearly only when one comes to the eighth of ten categories[17] does one arrive at something that involves ordinary notions of sexuality, and even here it is difficult to distinguish how it differs from the sort of trial-and-error in courtship that people of this age characteristically go through.[18]

Within the service itself Vistica (1995) observes this in the context of Navy aviators' response to the climate of criticism that arose out of Tailhook:

The daily drumbeat of negative news, and the brass's implementation of new rules to help end a culture grounded in sexism, only increased the anxiety among men at Miramar and at other bases around the nation. Many of the men held strong, conservative views about duty, honor, country—and embraced moral values instilled in them to protect women and children. Now, even to discuss their fundamental beliefs could cost them their jobs if they were construed as antiwoman. (p. 361)

Defining the belief that men should protect women as "sexism" may be strange enough, but it does not help us with our investigation because we do not know what "sexism" means, or why it is a crime. More interesting, and the point upon which we shall focus, is the idea that it was defined as "antiwoman." How did that happen?[19] What is the idea of "woman" that this is "anti?" That question clearly goes to the heart of our investigation.

Other examples of the strange results of this process of definition may be observed in the case of Colonel James Hallums, as described in a front-page article by Thomas E. Ricks in the March 13, 1997, issue of the *Wall Street Journal*. This article describes the controversy surrounding the dismissal of Colonel Hallums from his position as chair of the Department of Behavioral Sciences and Leadership at West Point.

According to the *Journal*, Colonel Hallums, described as a "soldier of the old school," was brought to the Academy because of concerns that the academy had lost its military and disciplinary edge. While there, although he was revered by many, he ran afoul of a number of the members of the faculty, especially some of his female subordinates. He was accused of, among other things, sexism; found guilty of sexual harassment; and ultimately fired for "abusive leadership."

One incident that got Hallums into trouble involved a line of cadets waiting to file course change slips. He asked one what branch he was going into. The cadet replied that he was going into the infantry. Col. Hallums responded: "Go to the head of the line."

Out of this, and I presume other incidents, came the charge that Hallums "showed a gender bias because he was so gung-ho about combat forces, and under Army rules, women are excluded from ground combat roles." As an investigative report put it, "[m]any in the department perceive that he disdains the non-combat arms, and by implication, female officers."

Now, from the standpoint of organization theory, I can see some validity in this. Arguably, in future conflicts, the effectiveness of the Army as a whole will increasingly depend on the effectiveness of its noncombat arms. To this extent, one might say, as some said of Hallums, that he was a man out of his times.

On the other hand, that was not the charge that was made. Hallums's views were not repudiated as inconsistent with contemporary military requirements as such, but were criticized because they could be seen as belittling roles played by women. In other words Hallums's attitude was judged heretical, not because it was out of keeping with military necessity, but because women were offended by the subordination of their role that it implied. In the terms used here, it appears, Hallums's crime was that his attitude toward women was demeaning and disrespectful toward their contribution.

As further evidence of his demeaning attitudes toward women, his gender bias, and sexism, Ricks reported that he called in the department's civilian female teachers and asked them whether they had any romantic entanglements that he should know about. One of them, Barbara Hunter, later recalled that he told her she was expected to serve at West Point "for the long haul and that I couldn't be expected to get married and move." A married man with three daughters, Hallums was evidently unaware that she was divorced and, according to her, told her he thought people who divorce lack commitment.

Material like this formed the basis of formal charges, filed by two of the department's three civilian female professors, accusing Col. Hallums of "sexism." Hunter identified his denunciation of those who divorce as "gender discrimination." The other teacher said that in a conversation with her he had "implied that as a woman, my career shouldn't come first. This is sexism." (The third female civilian professor differentiated herself from the charge. She filed a statement saying that she had found Col. Hallums to be supportive.)

If we are interested in the truly strange, we need to look at the material that supported the charge of sexual harassment. It was based on two charges. One was that he made women feel uncomfortable by walking through the department in his exercise clothes: a sleeveless shirt and Spandex shorts. The other, made by a Capt. Sharon Bowers, was that he showed off his biceps and invited her to touch them. "In retrospect, I believe this was sexual harassment," she said. On the basis of these charges, Col. Dennis Hunt, the head of West Point's law department, found Col. Hallums guilty of sexual harassment, not for seeking sexual favors, but for creating "an intimidating, hostile or offensive environment."

We need to ask, what was there in Hallums's actions that created "an intimidating, hostile or offensive environment?" Where was the threat, the hostility, the offense? The man didn't *do* anything. He was just walking around in his exercise shorts. And he didn't threaten to fire Bowers if she refused to touch his biceps, nor was there any other threat reported. The threat, the hostility, the offense must have been felt to be in his attitude. But what was the attitude he was felt to have that was experienced as offensive? There is only one conclusion that I think can be drawn from this. Hallums appeared to them to experience and affirm himself in his masculinity. That must have been the attitude crime with which he was charged. It appears that these women felt his experience and self-affirmation of his sexuality as a hostile attack against them. It seems that the crime with which he was charged was masculine sexuality itself.[20]

MORRIS

The criminalization of male sexuality, and the related idea that male sexuality is directed against women, is surely the strangest aspect of the sexual contestation in the military, beginning with the response to Tailhook. It is therefore the one that is most interesting from the standpoint of psychoanalysis. A development of this idea is in an article that grew out of Tailhook, though it was not part of the scandal directly. Written by Morris (1996), a professor of law and a high-level consultant to Secretary of the Army Togo West, this article attempts to explain why, although military personnel commit less rape than civilians do, the decline in the incidence of rape is not as substantial as the decline in other crimes. Morris rules out the idea that this may have to do with sexual deprivation, although she is receptive to it at another point in the article. She argues instead that this is due to a "masculinist" culture within the military. Part of this masculinist culture is a portrayal of "women as sexual targets and men as sexual consumers." As an example of this, she cites *Playboy* magazine, which is more likely to be read on military bases than in civilian life (p. 715). What is of interest to us is her use of the term "sexual target," as if a combat were being described. This impression is borne out on the next page, when the expression becomes "sexual targets or adversaries" (p. 716). The point is that she could have chosen other words. She could have differentiated between an active and a passive role, or between assertiveness and responsiveness; she could have talked about *yang* and *yin*; she could have spoken in any of a number of ways which would have seen both the male and female roles as being constitutive and vital elements of the same sexual act. But she chose to describe them in the language of assault. Trying to explain rape, she assumes it in the words she uses. For her, evidently, the active role in sexuality, the male role, is already rape.

Taking it for granted that there is no biological basis for sex role differentiation and acknowledging the importance of the soldierly virtues of dominance, aggressiveness, and toughness as long as they can be purged of masculinity, Morris envisions a new military in which the hierarchy has precise control over the norms of the group, even to the point of being able to eliminate sexual desire among the members of a unit, while allowing it to express itself among soldiers of different units.[21] On the basis of this stack of speculations, for the sake of a marginal decrease in the incidence of rape, she is ready to bet the capacity of the nation to defend itself. She thus gives us a picture of the condemnation of male sexuality, lack of proportion, and the criminalization of attitude wrapped up in one small package.

Let us stay with Morris for a moment and consider the underpinnings of her case. Her view, in accordance with the current fashion, is that sexuality is "socially constructed." It has no roots in biology, and even its roots in deep levels of the personality are constructed by changeable social arrangements. For her the attitudes of military men toward women are created by the necessity to define themselves against a female other, a relationship obviously fraught with the potential for antagonism. Integrate women fully into the military and such problems will be solved.

But will they? Is there nothing deeper than norms lying underneath sexuality? Is the difference between the sexes simply a matter of the differing circumstances of social groups constituted by anatomy? Thousands of years of history, as well as the evidence of biology, suggest that there is something deeper, but thousands of years of history may have simply served to transmit bias from time to time, and, after all, biology isn't over yet.

Up until this point, I have been concerned to show that there was something strange, something odd, about the response to Tailhook and its sequelae. My purpose in doing so has been to legitimate the use of psychoanalysis, a mode of analysis that takes the strange as its focus of investigation. If the response to Tailhook had been balanced, reasonable, and proportionate, there would have been nothing for psychoanalysis to explain. It could have been explained in terms of rational, conscious thought. But its weirdness requires that we go beneath the surface and look for unconscious forces that may have been at play. That is the domain of psychoanalysis.

From a psychoanalytic point of view, the strange characteristics of the response to Tailhook and what has followed have a familiar unity. The key to their unity is the lack of proportion, which suggests the presence of a transference, a response to present circumstances as if they represented the circumstances of an earlier stage of our development. This is the approach I take here. I try to develop a theory of the feminists' response to Tailhook which will help to explain the features we have discussed. It also helps to explain the power of feminism, why a view deeply rooted in primitive dynamics has had the power to become the dominant view, and why, especially, men have been powerless to resist it.

THE PSYCHODYNAMICS AND POWER OF FEMINISM

As we have seen, male activity is ultimately directed at the construction of an identity that can regain fusion with the female on terms that are no longer threatening. Men construct in order to present their product to women. Their wish is that her approval of it will mean acceptance of them as men, a recognition and appreciation of their separate identities, so that they can emotionally come together with them without the fear of being swallowed up, abandoned, and destroyed.

Typically this motivation is unconscious. To acknowledge it would be to admit the dependency whose threatening nature drives the whole process. But to say that it is unconscious is not to say that it is any less real. Its reality shows up in its effects, and chief among these effects are the compulsive, anxiety-driven, partiality of male striving. "A man's got to do what he's got to do," men say in explaining their behavior. In this way they make it plain that they cannot provide any better answer for why they do what they do. On the conscious level, they simply do not know.

Even though unconscious, however, this constructive activity has the function of keeping alive the image of the omnipotent, loving female and, indeed, of bringing this fantasy into realization. The meaning of positive male activity, that is to say, is to remove the blockages that limit the power of the female, to expand the sphere of the female's love and its effects.

We have seen that the meaning of economic activity, for men, has been to create material circumstances that would remove the limitations that necessity places on the efficacy of the mother's love. Its purpose is to increase the distance between indifferent reality and the home, so that the home can be a perfect seat of warmth, love, and connection. What I wish to argue in the present chapter is that this is also the meaning of war.

It is easy enough to see destructiveness in war. As Koenigsberg (1996, 1999) has pointed out, however, it is not the image of destructiveness that has colored the picture of war that we have given to ourselves, and that therefore must be seen to represent our real motivation. That image, instead, has been the image of service, and sometimes sacrifice in the name of something higher. As Koenigsberg (1999) puts it, "War is a sacrificial ritual, the way in which members of a nation prove their devotion to the object they worship, their country. Death and mutilation on the field of battle demonstrate sincerity." The soldier will beat back and vanquish the enemies of the group—the tribe, the nation, and, most powerfully, the combat unit (e.g., Manchester, 1987). The enemies are seen as responsible for the soldier's separation from the group's goodness. In that way he will find acceptance in the body of the group. If he is killed, his death will realize this connection, marking the end of the separation of his individual existence. What we see here, then, is that war has always been in the name of the primitive, omnipotent mother, represented as the group. Its destructiveness is the destruction only of what is other to her. It dies so that she may be enhanced.

At the level of the personal, the mythology here is of the soldier who battles the enemy, making the world safe for his woman and children, and then comes home again to their love. Of course all this is mythology. Yet in an activity that has as few rewards for the individual as war has, the importance of mythology cannot be overstated. We now may note that we have arrived at the explanation of the "stone age attitudes about warriors returning from the sea" toward which Secretary Howard devoted such scorn. This indicates that we are almost ready to begin our explanation of what we need to explain, but first we need to consider the way in which sex fits into all of this.

SEX

For classic psychoanalysis, sex is part of the given, a basic drive (*trieb*), not subject to further psychoanalytic explanation. Nonetheless, drives have "vicissitudes," and are subject to being transformed in various ways by culture and conditioning. To ask where one draws the line between what is biologically determined and what is culturally configured is, of course, to enter into a great dispute. It may be, however, to try to answer a fundamentally wrong-headed question (Foucault, 1980). One never sees sex without cultural configuration, any more than one sees content without form. Our concern here is primarily with these cultural configurations. It is, in other words, not so much with sex as such, as with the *meaning of* sex.

For Freud the primary sexual object, both for men and for women, is the primordial mother, and the fantasy of fusion with her underlies all sexual desire. As we have seen, however, Chasseguet-Smirgel (1986) sees the difference between the sexes as rooted in their relations to the mother, with whom the child will or will not be able to identify. This difference is represented in the fantasy of fusion with this primordial figure, which for the male and the female take on quite different meanings. For the female this fantasy is much more self-contained. Her capacity to identify with the primitive mother means that she can imagine this fusion in the image of being herself, with her child, who is part of herself, and through whom she incorporates the male as part of herself. For Chasseguet-Smirgel this conditions the meaning of her sexuality:

Motherhood is consubstantial with female psychosexuality whether or not it results in the birth of a child . . . . It seems to me, then, that her *capacity for motherhood* enables the woman to realize in fantasy her dual incestuous wish: to recover the state of primary fusion with the mother by means of the union established with the fetus during pregnancy, and to keep the love object, the father or his penis, inside herself. Thanks to the fusion with the fetus inside her, the woman has the possibility of recovering access to the mother's body in a more complete, more profound and more lasting way than the man. (pp. 30–31)

For the man the matter is not so straightforward. As we have seen, the mother is the focus of male desire, but the idea of satisfying that desire is the source of a terrible fear, because it brings with it the threat of dissolution. So he must achieve something and in that way create a self that is substantial and valued, in order that sex with this loved but terrifying figure can be managed with safety. In the classic case, he will identify with and learn from his father, his model of valued achievement, and then, achieving something based on that model, be able to start his own family.

Having said that we see that to the contemporary ear this seems like strange material. The idea of the female as prize for his labor, does this not devalue her, the feminist might say. And rooting female sexuality in relation to men, our feminist would continue, is that not seeing her as tied to a social role within an oppressive structure? Have we not, our feminist continues, simply reasserted sexism? Is there not sex beyond that?

Well, yes, Chasseguet-Smirgel (1985, 1986) observes, there certainly is. Sex as it has been described here is genital, oedipal. But, for psychoanalysis, there is sex before the Oedipus complex, before the place of the traditional heterosexual sexual relations has been established. That is where we now turn. It turns out to be the very heart of our understanding.

Before we go to that, a bit of terminology may be useful. In Freudian terms the sexuality we now discuss is called "preoedipal" or "pregenital."

But, our feminist critic will observe, this has the effect of normalizing and legitimating the oedipal process, heterosexuality, and the role of the father. She will tell us that these are all matters that should be challenged, because they inevitably lead to patriarchy and its system of domination. For the purpose of our argument, I adopt terminology that will avoid her objection. Rather than referring to this alternative sexuality as preoedipal, I will call it nonoedipal, meaning here that the internalization of the father, characteristic of the oedipal phase, has not happened, rather then saying that it has not happened *yet*. This terminology contains no judgment about what sort of sexuality should be normative. My business now is to explore, rather than evaluate.

NONOEDIPAL SEXUALITY

Chasseguet-Smirgel's interest in sexuality grew out of her study of perversions. Whether one wants to call such practices "perverse" is, perhaps, a matter of judgment. Let us put it aside for the moment, however, and attempt to be purely descriptive.

Characteristic of the male perverts she studied was that they were under the control of a fantasy she called the *denial of difference* (1985, 1986). This is a fantasy that the mother has a penis, and is therefore sexually complete. The meaning of this fantasy, for the little boy, is that it means that he is, even with his immature sexual apparatus, a suitable partner for his mother. He thus avoids the inferiority that would come from comparing himself with his father and can maintain the fantasy that he can supplant his father in her life. Reinforced in this view by his mother, who typically does prefer him to his father, he thus denies the difference in the generations. As well, he denies the difference between true adult endeavor and the kind of pretended endeavor that a child can manage, which then comes to be the specific perversion. In this way he can maintain his narcissism.

I have discussed the consequences of this male development in earlier chapters. For the present what is more important is the course of nonoedipal sexuality in the girl. For Chasseguet-Smirgel this again represents a fusion with the primordial mother. But there is a difference. For the boy the fantasy of fusion involves taking the place of the father. For the girl the controlling fantasy is not of a partnership with the primordial mother, but of establishment as the primordial mother herself. The omnipotence, then, which is the defining characteristic of the primordial mother, will be hers, but omnipotence has the corollary that the father is a usurper who may be gotten rid of. In her fantasy, then, she can have children, with which she also identifies, by herself, and without male participation:

The companion to the boy's perverse deception regarding the difference between the sexes and between the generations, which installs him as mother's partner, would be, in the girl's case, the denial that the child needs to have a father. (Chasseguet-Smirgel: 1985: p. 35)

And she continues:

Indeed, the bearing of children without the male playing any role is written into the S.C.U.M. (Society for Cutting Up Men) Manifesto: "Reproduction of the species is technically possible without any need for a man. Women could henceforth reproduce only women" (Valerie Solanas, *S.C.U.M Manifesto*). (Chasseguet-Smirgel: 1985: p. 35)

What does that tell us about her sexuality? If she identifies with the omnipotent, primordial mother, and if the aim in sexuality is fusion with the primordial mother, whom does she have sex with? The answer can only be that she has sex with herself. To the extent that she can make sense of having sex with others, they will have to be those with whom she identifies completely. These may be other women, into whom she has projected herself completely and without reservation; or they may be men, if she can strip them of their masculine difference and identify them with herself. Alternatively she can have sex with men but not make sense of it. She may experience this sex as an act of abuse by a person whom she resents and despises, but whom she continues seeing as a result of a part of her personality for which she assumes no responsibility. In either case the basic psychodynamic fact remains. The central figure in her psyche is herself, identified with the primordial mother. Under this identification there is no one else that it would possibly make sense to have sex with. Perfect is perfect, and who could ask for anything more? In fact, to the extent that sex implies a connection with an other, she does not have sex at all. She is not sexual, but erotic. More precisely she is autoerotic. This is an important key to our puzzle.

The idea that she is having sex with herself, that she is autoerotic, and that this underlies her basic approach to the world, may seem strange, but it is in fact a mainstay of feminist writing. It reaches, perhaps, its most explicit formulation in the work of Luce Irigaray.

IRIGARAY

Irigaray (1985) takes sexuality as the core of all human relations, and takes autoeroticism as the model of sexuality. She looks there for the difference between male and female sexuality. She maintains that the phallic sexuality of the male, which has until this point dominated Western culture, has given woman only a subordinate, instrumental function, replacing the hand in male masturbation:

Female sexuality has always been conceptualized on the basis of male parameters . . . For the clitoris is conceived as a little penis pleasant to masturbate so long as castration anxiety does not exist (for the boy child), and the vagina is valued for the "lodging" it offers the male organ when the forbidden hand has to find a replacement for pleasure-giving.
    In these terms, woman's erogenous zones never amount to anything but a clitoris-sex that is not comparable to the noble phallic organ, or a hole-envelope that serves to sheathe and massage the penis in intercourse: a non-sex, or a masculine organ turned back upon itself, self-embracing. (p. 23)

Woman, in this sexual imaginary, is only a more or less obliging prop for the enactment of man's fantasies. That she may find pleasure in that role, by proxy, is possible, even certain. But such pleasure is above all a masochistic prostitution of her body to a desire that is not her own, and it leaves her in a familiar state of dependency upon man. (p. 25)

The loathsomeness of this phallic sexuality, as Irigaray experiences it, is apparent in the way it plays out in culture.

The more or less exclusive—and highly anxious—attention paid to erection in Western sexuality proves to what extent the imaginary that governs it is foreign to the feminine. For the most part, this sexuality offers nothing but imperatives dictated by male rivalry: the "strongest" being the one who has the best "hard-on," the longest, the biggest, the stiffest penis, or even the one who "pees the farthest" (as in little boys' contests). Or else one finds imperatives dictated by the enactment of sadomasochistic fantasies, these in turn governed by man's relation to his mother: the desire to force entry, to penetrate, to appropriate for himself the mystery of this womb where he has been conceived, the secret of his begetting, of his "origin." (pp. 24–25)

She contrasts this contemptible stuff with female sexuality, evidently a higher type:

[W]oman's autoeroticism is very different from man's. In order to touch himself, man needs an instrument: his hand, a woman's body, language. . . . And this self-caressing requires at least a minimum of activity. As for woman, she touches herself in and of herself without any need for mediation, and before there is any way to distinguish activity from passivity. Woman "touches herself" all the time, and moreover no one can forbid her to do so, for her genitals are formed of two lips in continuous contact. Thus, within herself, she is already two—but not divisible into one(s)—that caress each other. (p. 24)

Her model of relationships follows along with this. Male relationships, characterized by possessiveness and modeled on property ownership, are based on the singularity of the penis. Woman, however, understood in her own right, resists objectification. She is diffuse, fluid, several.

Woman always remains several, but she is kept from dispersion because the other is already within her and is autoerotically familiar to her. Which is not to say that she appropriates the other for herself, that she reduces it to her own property. Ownership and property are doubtless quite foreign to the feminine. At least sexually. But not *nearness*. Nearness is so pronounced that it makes all discrimination of identity, and thus all forms of property, impossible. Woman derives pleasure from what is *so near that she cannot have it, nor have herself*. She herself enters into a ceaseless exchange of herself with the other without any possibility of identifying either. (p. 31)

But what can it be with which she can be so near, with which she can be autoerotically bound, which is within her, but which is not her, and with which her whole world, consisting of her and her relationships, can be made? What can this student of Lacan[22] be referring to other than her reflection? We have here the story of Narcissus, the story of the way in which one's self and one's own self-admiration can constitute the whole world for oneself. This, according to Irigaray, is the pure feminine perspective. It is the perspective of the virgin. And how does male sexuality look from this virginal perspective?

This autoeroticism is disrupted by a violent break-in: the brutal separation of the two lips by a violating penis, an intrusion that distracts and deflects the woman from this "self-caressing" she needs if she is not to incur the disappearance of her own pleasure in sexual relations. (p. 24)

Now we are ready to return to Tailhook.

TAILHOOK REVISITED: THE POWER OF THE VIRGIN

I want to look at the response to Tailhook with the benefit of the perspective we have uncovered. My claim is that the feminist perspective, which informed and determined the way the events of Tailhook were interpreted and which carry forward in the issue of women in combat, resulted from an identification with the primordial mother. This was an identification made, more or less completely, by some feminists. If we are to fully understand its effects, we need to understand that that identification was accepted by men as well as women. Looking for the reason why men are so helpless before the power of feminism, in other words, we have to see that the power this identification brings is one that affects men as much as it does women, and that is, ultimately, the reason why the idea of women in combat seems as inexorable as it seems.

Reflecting on this matter, we can easily see why this image is experienced as so powerful by men. *It is experienced in this way because it is not a woman's image of the female; it is an infant's image of the female.* We all have mothers, whether we are male or female, and she is experienced as omnipotent and self-sufficient by all of us. Indeed her diffuse autoeroticism, in which as infants we are included, is the perfect complement of the unfocused polymorphous perversity of the infant. None of these matters were discovered by women because they have some secret access to a female essence, located somewhere inside of them that men don't have. Rather women are simply bringing to consciousness the idea that all of us had toward our mother when we were totally dependent on her and not differentiated from her.

The difference is, as we have seen, that because the mother is a woman and because the girl child is a woman, she can identify with her; for the boy she is far more terrifying and he has to have a project which will make him safe if he is to fuse with her. In the absence of that project, should that project be undermined, her power reduces the male to infantile dependence and helplessness. No longer capable of uniting as an adult with an adult female, he is, for all intents and purposes, castrated. The female, by contrast, is made powerful through it, and powerful, especially, over the dependent, helpless, castrated male. There you have the power of feminism. It is the power of the virgin.

For the explanation of Tailhook, it is easy enough to start at the point where we left Irigaray, with the image of the "violent break-in: the brutal separation of the two lips by a violating penis." *What we can see here, without any difficulty, is the way in which male sexuality itself, and not just the physical abusiveness that no one denies, became a crime.* For, continuing with Irigaray, not only is it violent, it is also "an intrusion that distracts and deflects the woman from this 'self-caressing' she needs if she is not to incur the disappearance of her own pleasure in sexual relations" (p. 24).

The point here is that the autoeroticism of this virginal, primordial mother is sufficient for all the purposes of life. It is perfect in its own right and lacks nothing. Male sexuality is an intrusion into it, an interference with it, a disruption of it. It subordinates the sublime to the base, the sacred to the profane. It cannot be anything but defilement, rape (e.g., MacKinnon, 1989; Dworkin, 1993).[23]

As I have said, tied to this image themselves, requiring its approval for the very integrity of their personality, men must be very sensitive to such feelings. Around their sexuality must cluster, consciously or unconsciously, a sense of shame and guilt. Toward it they must have a sensitivity and sense of vulnerability that will keep them in motion all their lives. Out of this may easily arise a compulsive zealousness in the defense of the sexual purity of the virginal primordial mother, a defense that psychoanalysis calls a *reaction formation:* an affirmation of the opposite of these base impulses for the purpose of denying their presence in oneself. This zealousness, which permeates and provides much of the meaning of the response to Tailhook, is likely to be strongest among men whose sexuality is strongest, and therefore hardest for them to deny.

Vistica (1995) provides a nice enough image of this. In this case Senator John McCain, who was leading an attack on Naval Secretary Lawrence Garrett for not responding more quickly to the incidents at Tailhook, was seen as something of a puzzle by some:

Some officers on Garrett's staff . . . were surprised by McCain's ambush and stricken by the irony that he would have the nerve to speak out on Tailhook. Several of the old aviators were aware of McCain's past reputation. "He would fuck a pile of rocks if he thought a snake was in it," said one former Vietnam POW who had served in the Navy with McCain. (p. 337)

What comes into focus as well, given this line of reasoning, is the lack of proportion in the response to Tailhook. This is so with regard to a number of perspectives. For one thing we can understand the extraordinary fact that the feminist critics of the Navy were ready to subordinate all other considerations to the matter of sexual harassment. The point is that if you take the perspective of the primordial mother, no other considerations are important.

She is, to begin with, sexual, even if that sexuality is autoerotic, and the world in which she operates is suffused with that sexuality. Moreover that sexuality is sufficient. Nothing else is required in that perfect world, whose very perfection is expressed through that sexuality. Given that world, and her place in it, the activities that navies, and navy men, engage in are second-rate and inferior, the expressions of a debased nature. They are, as Irigaray puts it, "nothing but imperatives dictated by male rivalry: the strongest being the one who has the best hard-on, the longest, the biggest, the stiffest penis, or even the one who pees the farthest (as in little boys' contests)" (pp. 24–25).

What we can see happening here, and this is the root of all of the disproportion that we saw, is that the identification with the omnipotent, virginal, primordial mother has rendered, for the feminists, a disdain for the
male activity that would otherwise have allowed Tailhook to be kept in
perspective. If she is omnipotent, her simple existence and the expression
of its sexual essence is all that is necessary for anything. Violation of her
autoeroticism is not a crime among others. Rupturing the perfect circle in
which her omnipotence guarantees perfection is the root of all criminality,
the very meaning of criminality. Nothing else can approach it in importance.

Here it may be worthwhile to pause for a second and reflect upon what
may seem to be the exaggerated role of sexuality that we have brought with
us from Irigaray. Irigaray tends to be a bit sensationalistic, but on the whole,
here, she is following Freud in identifying Eros and sexuality. What may
seem strange here may seem more familiar if one substitutes the idea of love
for the idea of sexuality. Then, with the female as the caring, nurturing
mother, who but for the influence of men, could make everything well by
her simple loving presence, one finds oneself in the precise center of feminist theory.

This observation is of no small importance, because it casts light on another aspect of our material that might otherwise seem peculiar. It is the extreme reaction, the rage, that some women have felt in the face of attitudes
that they considered to be demeaning, and the way they interpret these
"demeaning" attitudes as offenses against them. The point here again is
that the image of the world in which the primordial mother is the central
figure is one that is suffused with love for her, with adoration. "Demeaning"
attitudes toward her, which may involve no more than seeing her as a human being, are experienced as a violation of the very depths of meaning.

We do well to see, in fact, that what is at issue here is essentially a matter
of religion. The primordial mother is the deepest god whom we can know.
Having identified herself with this divinity, our feminist naturally responds
to criticism of herself as if it were blasphemy. We gain insight into the bitterness of our current sexual conflicts if we realize that they are, in a sense,
religious wars.

At any rate, from all of these considerations, we can also understand why
her feelings, insofar as they arise from this primitive identification, have
such power over men. Under identification with the omnipotent primordial mother, she denies the place of chivalric behavior in the relationship
between the sexes. Recall that the meaning of male activity is to make himself suitable for the female. He understands her as omnipotent. Indeed, the
meaning of his deeds is that he is her agent in realizing her omnipotence.

He will vanquish the foe, kill the dragon, and then, having proven himself to her, she will accept him as her lover. Notice that she has to go along with this bargain, and in order to go along with it, she has to acknowledge that it is important that he vanquish the foe or kill the dragon. She must know, in other words, that there are limits to her omnipotence, that the fantasy of her omnipotence is a fantasy.

What we see in this case, however, is that she is not accepting this. She stands by her omnipotence, and therefore she doesn't need him. Vanquishing the enemy, killing the dragon, she sees behind these and understands that these are merely strategies he is using to get into her bed. But this holds no value for her. She does not need him sexually any more than she needs his deeds. She is perfect sexually all by herself. All that he can do is impose himself.

Now look at what this must do for the man. His activities made sense to him because they made sense to her. They were indeed ways to get into her bed, a project that not only provided the foundation of his behavioral agenda, but also of his very feeling of existence. Have that withdrawn and his life falls apart; the meaning of all that he does evaporates. If his activities do not make sense to her, they cannot make sense to him. He is left only with infantile dependence. He understands that he can only be with her under her sufferance, and that he is subject to abandonment at her whim. Being a man having been made impossible, he must content himself with being a little boy. He understands that he must do what his mother tells him to do.

The alternative, of course, is to respond to this dependence with counterdependent hatred and violence. As Irigaray puts it:

Or else one finds imperatives dictated by the enactment of sadomasochistic fantasies, these in turn governed by man's relation to his mother: the desire to force entry, to penetrate, to appropriate for himself the mystery of this womb where he has been conceived, the secret of his begetting, of his "origin." (p. 25)

In this, ironically, he moves the very agenda that the feminist program, ostensibly, was intended to prevent.

There is another point about the response to Tailhook that I wish to get at from this perspective. A form of lack of proportion, it deserves mention in its own right. It is the fact, as we saw in the case of Colonel Hallums, that the positive valuation of male sexuality and of the male role that goes along with it were seen as criminal, even in the absence of concrete acts of sexual abuse. It was as if the very idea of male sexual activity was seen in the same way as a physical sexual attack. How could that be?

The answer may be revealed if we invert the terms. The idea that male sexuality was felt as a physical attack is not what we need for our explanation. Rather what we need to understand is that physical attack, at least in the extremely mild instances that concern us here, was seen as significant because it was an attack on the idea of female sexuality. It was felt as an attack, not so much because there was physical brutalization involved, but because it threatened the idea of the omnipotence and completeness of female sexuality.

This suggests that what took place at Tailhook was not a physical clash between men and women. It was a clash between ideas of sexuality. What was felt to be under attack was itself an idea, the idea of the power of the virgin, and it could be felt to be attacked by another idea. This is no small thing, of course. We live by our ideas, and the violence of an attack upon our ideas of ourselves is very real.

At the same time, we can now see what the feminists had in mind when they said that the problem in the Navy was a cultural problem, and that the solution would have to be a cultural change. Looking at the matter at this point shows us that when we are thinking about cultural change, when we are thinking about substituting one fundamental idea for another, we need to look directly at the meaning of these ideas, and keep in mind the full train of consequences that may ensue.

Previously the two "cultures," the two ideas of sexuality, could be kept apart because the sexes were not integrated in the military. It is also true that they did not need to be kept apart so much, because both men and women, in the course of their development, have been able to integrate the two. In the present case, however, a regressive identification among females was able to establish a drunken, childish, regressive identification among males as being definitive of the Navy, and set itself up as an exclusionary alternative.

At this point, though, we can see some of the implications of what the feminists have in mind when they speak about a cultural change within the Navy. The culture of sexuality traditional to the Navy was one that supported the activity of the Navy. By holding up the idea of fusion, the ego ideal of men having earned the right to express their sexuality, men could experience their military activities with pride, and could accomplish them with courage and élan. The culture that the feminists seek to replace this with is one that undermines the activity of the Navy. It reduces it to imposture, to a peeing contest, to a subterfuge for rape. It deprives military activity of the meaning it has in the heterosexual matrix and leaves men with the shame and guilt that surrounds their sexuality in the absence of the possibility of its legitimation.

Men cannot do their military work under this premise. In defense of the value of this work, it would be optimal if they could fight it, but on the basis of these considerations, we can understand why they have such difficulty in doing so. It is because the whole premise upon which men fight is the omnipotence of the female. It is up to women to see through this fantasy of their omnipotence. Men cannot do it without the greatest degree of upheaval, but if women will not do it, men will find it very difficult to oppose them.

This leaves open the possibility of mischievous activity, through the manipulation of the image of the virgin, that can have the most far-reaching consequences. Interestingly it is a possibility that this is what happened in the scandal of Tailhook and especially concerning the story of Paula Coughlin.

THE WILD RIDE OF LIEUTENANT COUGHLIN

According to the standard view, Coughlin wandered into the Tailhook gauntlet as an innocent, and there met with sexual assault for which she was entirely unprepared. As Vistica (1995) put it:

Shortly before midnight, Coughlin entered the third-floor hallway at the Hilton and began searching through the fighter bubbas, looking for Trusty Steed. She made one lap around the floor but couldn't find him. She was now standing at the beginning of the hallway, looking down the dark tunnel at the men lining both sides. They were the clean-cut aviators she had been with since she herself became a naval aviator years ago. Although the hallway reeked of booze and sweat, Coughlin stepped forward. (p. 329)

Whereupon, in the standard account, followed the defilement of the virgin.

But, on close inspection, even on the basis of Vistica's sympathetic account, the image of Coughlin as a wide-eyed naif simply doesn't hold up. The fact is that Coughlin was a pretty tough cookie:

As a sophomore at Old Dominion University, Coughlin enrolled in the ROTC program, graduating in 1984 and entering the Navy as a commissioned officer. By this time she had developed a hard edge and was determined not to take any guff from anybody. During her summer months home from college, she got a job as the first female lifeguard ever hired in Virginia Beach. When her supervisor said it would cost her a blow job if she wanted to break for lunch, Coughlin shot back: "Sorry, pal, I'm on a diet." And when another lifeguard called her a slut, "I clocked him." (p. 323)

Nor was she a sexual innocent:

Naval aviators took out their anger by spreading rumors about her promiscuity, about her being a second-rate naval officer, and about her willingly taking part in the activities at Tailhook. Coughlin did not run from the attacks. And she told her media handlers, who at first tried to persuade her from going public, not to paint her as a lily-white Virgin, which she said she was not. If there were doubters, a member of Frank Kelso's public affairs staff had passed on a report from her boyfriend, who flew helicopters with Coughlin. According to the report, she had showed up at a Navy dining-in party wearing black fishnet panty hose, high heels, a short black miniskirt, and a black tuxedo jacket and carrying a large rubber dildo. (p. 356)

Now, of course, as Vistica points out: "What kind of personal life Coughlin enjoyed, whether she was a party girl or not, did not justify the criminal sexual assault on her or the other victims (p. 356).

But there is one point about this that Vistica simply does not get, despite the fact that the evidence for it, which he himself adduces, is overwhelming. It is that Paula Coughlin must have known exactly what would happen to her if she walked into the gauntlet. Certainly Tailhook was not new to her. In fact she had been to Tailhooks before, including the 1987 affair, which was widely known within the Navy to have been the most raucous ever. More important than that, the gauntlet was a hallowed tradition. It was known, including its precise location and its schedule, throughout the entire aviation wing of the Navy. The only way an experienced naval aviation officer could have not known about it would have been if she were incredibly innocent and naïve, but Coughlin was neither. She was a savvy political operator who made a point of knowing everything that was going on and didn't shrink from any of it.

Let me make it plain that I don't see anything wrong with that. It only becomes a problem in this case because it contrasts with the image of innocence that Coughlin, whom Vistica shows to have been a masterful and fully purposeful manipulator of the press, put on. It was that image that drove the entire purge of the Navy. Within it Coughlin simply wandered into the gauntlet, unaware of what would happen to her. But that image is impossible to maintain. The only reasonable alternative is that she was aware of what would happen to her, and that was why she did it.

Why would she do it? There is no doubt that she was shaken by the experience. Why would she consciously and deliberately put herself in this position? An answer is not difficult to come by. Coughlin, Vistica tells us, was a person of considerable ambition, and one not to be satisfied by the ordinary career progression of the helicopter pilot:

[S]he was ambitious and wanted more out of the Navy. She yearned to put her career on a fast track, to be close to the movers and shakers in Washington. So she applied to be an aide to Donald Boecker, the rear admiral in charge of Pax River, Maryland. After getting the job, she became close to Boecker, an attack pilot "who without a doubt was the finest officer and gentleman I have ever met in my life," she later said. "I worked my ass off for the admiral twelve hours a day, writing his schedule, getting him wherever he was going on time, making him look good, watching the nuances that count." (p. 323)

For a while this worked perfectly:

The most distinguishing mark of an aide was the gold loop aiguillette, which signaled that the wearer had a place of importance in the Navy. Coughlin wore hers like a badge of honor. It was prestigious. And she was now a cut above her peers. More important, she was in close proximity to senior people, admirals and the like, who would notice her abilities to get the job done. A good flag aide could ride an admiral's coattails a long way in the Navy. And one who performed "properly," always showing sincerity and deference to the admiral, would be remembered when the best jobs came around. Access was always granted to the aide, even after the admiral moved up the chain of command to some other post. (pp. 323–324)

But then there came a problem:

[N]ine months after becoming Boecker's aide, Coughlin sensed that her career had hit a setback. Boecker, her ticket to advancement, the man she nearly gave up dating for so she could give him 110 percent of her time and effort, was now leaving. His replacement was Jack Snyder, the former head of Tailhook who had recently been selected for promotion to the rank of rear admiral. Coughlin was beside herself. She told her mother and other close confidants that she was troubled about Snyder. He was a fighter jock, a new admiral, and not a man to rely on a woman to be his aide.
   Coughlin described Snyder as a man who "came from an environment where you did everything yourself. The concept of having a staff to do things for him, along with a hard-charging female telling him what to do, challenged our relationship." After a month working with Snyder, Coughlin, a young lieutenant with less than seven years' experience, told her mother that she found it difficult "breaking him in as an admiral." (p. 324)

Her apprehension turned out to be justified. Snyder did not rely on her and did not involve her in his professional activities. Her career, which had been flying so high, appeared to have come to a dead-end. Coughlin did not like Snyder (p. 340).

I have no access to Coughlin's mind and cannot say what was going on in it. I can say that whatever else it did, walking the gauntlet gave Coughlin the means to get rid of Snyder. On the basis of a string of allegations that, as Vistica shows, are not supported by the facts, she accused him of not responding quickly enough to her complaints. He was demoted and fired from his command as a result. But that was, perhaps, only the least of it:

> And that Friday night Bush and his wife, Barbara, had tea with Paula Coughlin in the White House. He assured her that justice would be done and the culprits who assaulted her and the other women at Tailhook would be punished. With her appearance on ABC and her visit to the White House, Coughlin was now the poster girl for ending sexual harassment and abuse of women in the military. (p. 355)

As I have said, I have no access to what was going on in Coughlin's mind. All I can do is speculate and infer. But, if my inferences are correct, one has to say, with even a bit of admiration, not bad for a night's work.

Still one cannot leave the consideration of Coughlin without reflecting on the irony that it was a move to protect the frail and helpless Coughlin that gave the critical impetus to the move to place women among the warriors whose courage and indomitability would protect the nation.

THE ISSUE OF WOMEN IN COMBAT

In most of this chapter, we have not directly engaged the issue with which we began, the issue of women in combat, and specifically the question of what forces are pushing that issue. The implications of our reasoning are clear enough in this regard, however. Male chivalry and the deeds it inspires represent men's weakness before the image of female omnipotence. Serving female omnipotence, after all, is what chivalry is all about. But this observation illuminates a stunning paradox. It is that chivalry, which has as its aim the expansion of the sphere of the maternal, the project of making the world a safer place for the maternal expression of love, makes it impossible for men to resist the idea of putting women in combat. War is hell, as General Sherman observed, and the power that the virgin wields in fantasy may well result in the slaughter of women in reality. Even if there were no other considerations involved, men's understanding of their impotence in this regard would be felt as castration.

The consequences for the nation of having a castrated military, a military that looks like a military but no longer sees meaning in the fight, can only be guessed at. The fact is that it is precisely a castrated military, a military in which male sexuality is experienced with shame and guilt, that is the aim of the idea of women in combat. If the women who were pushing this idea were the women who it would apply to, and who understood what it would involve, that would be one thing. If the women in the armed forces wanted to, or felt that they ought to, assume the burden of combat, there would be nothing castrative about the idea. It might not be a good idea, but it would not put the motivational underpinning of the military at serious risk. This would be because it would be based on a sober assumption of risk that understood that it was risk, that represented an appreciation of the risks men have traditionally taken, and that valued the victories that they have won. It would have represented a validation of the male role and a desire to make themselves more whole by expanding their masculinity. Among such women, the question of lowering standards so that they could "succeed" would not arise, since they would understand the reason for high standards. The same would be true of other serious questions that would arise, which would then be subject to rational resolution on their merits. Men would, I believe, respect the motivation of such women because implicit in it is respect for the task that they have themselves respected. But Miller's research has shown that these women do not want to be in combat.

The women who want women to be in combat do not understand what combat means, nor do they value it. Their view is not one that recognizes the seriousness of combat. This is shown in their willingness to subordinate all military considerations to the issue of female participation, and in their disdain for the men who have distinguished themselves in these terms. In the absence of a sense of its seriousness, their vision of what combat involves is empty of the basis upon which respect is given. But if they do not value military efforts, why do they want women to participate? My reasoning leads to the view that it is because, unless women do it also, and on their own terms, it will be a way that men consolidate their identity as men, earn the right to express their sexuality, and demonstrate the limits of the power of the virgin.

If the analysis developed here is sound, the prognosis for the U.S. military is exceedingly grim. The psychodynamic forces pressing for women in combat roles are aimed at undermining the mission of the military. If that happens the capacity of the military to fight the enemies of the nation will be lost. In order to see this, it is only necessary to realize that, as I have argued, the feminists who are pushing this issue are not concerned with making the nation safe from enemies outside of the nation. For them, the enemy is men. Their effect will be to create a fault line, not at the nation's boundaries, but within the military itself. This will make mobilizing against a common enemy impossible.

It is easy to miss this conclusion if one supposes that the conflict we see today is only a temporary one that will resolve itself into a new, stable framework to which everyone will adhere. But, if my analysis is correct, a proper understanding of the dynamics involved will reveal that there cannot be any such stable framework.

The problem is that the image of the omnipotent maternal figure is a fantasy. No woman can be omnipotent any more than any man can. We all have our limits. The fantasy cannot be realized. But commitment to the fantasy, total identification with it, must take the fact of limitation as an enemy and subject it to attack. Because this fantasy is an idea of the perfection of women, it necessarily follows, even without any other considerations, that the enemy will be seen as those who are not women, which is to say those who are men. Antagonism toward men, therefore, is built into this feminist psychodynamic as a permanent feature, not subject to alleviation by any transformation of roles. Whatever changes are made will be seen as insufficient and will simply constitute a new state of affairs that needs to be overcome.

This is a manifestation of what I have referred to in Chapter 5 as the drive to the extreme, and it is a characteristic of all politics at this primitive level. The sexual component in this case, however, gives this situation an aspect that is interesting in its own right. Let us glance at this through another look at the case of Colonel Hallums.

Hallums, as we saw, was charged with sexual harassment for, among other things, walking across the room in his exercise shorts. In analyzing this at the time, we assumed that there was something that he had done that was experienced as offensive. Because there was no behavior, we assumed that what was problematic was his mental state, and the only mental state that would fit was his experience of his own masculinity.

Looking back over this matter, it appears that we have assumed too much. The point was that it was Hallums's masculinity that was the problem, but this did not necessarily have to have a representation in Hallums's mind. It could have served just as well if it were only in the minds of the women who saw him walk across the room. The idea of Hallums's masculinity would have been present in the mind of anyone who experienced Hallums as masculine, whether there was any corresponding representation in Hallums's mind. The experience of Hallums's masculinity is just the experience of him as a sexy guy. Anyone who was sexually attracted to Hallums would experience his masculinity. And anyone committed to the idea of female sexual sufficiency would be disturbed, and hence offended by it.

Now we can see where the problem is. Taking the experience of masculinity as offensive turns female sexual desire for men into a crime. Because
the whole premise here is the perfection of the female, it cannot be a female
crime, but must be committed by a male. In this we can see the possible
scope of male activity that could be considered criminal in this way. It does
not require that they do anything, or say anything, or think anything at all.
It does not even require that they be physically present. Their presence in
the past would suffice, as we see in countless cases of "recovered memories"
of sexual abuse. In fact we can push the matter even further than that.
Their offensiveness is in the idea that women have of them, and women
can have that idea entirely by themselves. His presence in the idea, his spiritual presence, would be presence enough. What we see here is the generation of the idea of the devil, and this devil could take the form of any man at
any time. I leave it as an exercise for the reader to imagine putting together
an effective mixed gender military force with that as the underlying
psychodynamic.

CONCLUSION: THE END OF THE U.S. MILITARY

Diamond (1993) has introduced the useful concept of *organizational
identity*, which represents the sameness and continuity of the organization
in the face of change. Organizational identity, says Diamond:

is a product of organizational culture and history, member psychology, and the psychology of past and present leaders and followers. It consists of repetitive structures
of intersubjectivity found in relationships between superiors and subordinates,
which are primarily driven by unconscious assumptions and expectations that influence organizational decisions and actions. (p. 79)

And he quoted Erikson to the effect that "strange as it may seem, it takes
a well-established identity to tolerate radical change, for the well-established identity has arranged itself around basic values which cultures have
in common"(cited in Diamond, 1993: p. 79).

Given Diamond's point that the roots of organizational identity are unconscious, and given the fact that the changes we have described are attempts at replacing precisely these unconscious underpinnings, the
question must arise whether the U.S. military that comes out of this process
of transformation will recognize itself as the same organization that went
into it. Given the radical nature of this change, it seems to me that there is
every reason to believe that it will not. In that case the organization that
emerges will be something, but it will not, in some very important sense, be

the U.S. military. If that is so, what possible reason will there be for the United States to be able to depend on it to fight the enemies of the country?

For the fact is that the virgin does not march against the enemies of the country. She marches against men and what men represent.

NOTES

1. This issue attains its sharpest focus with ground combat roles.
2.

Recommendation: The sense of the Commission is that women should be excluded from direct land combat units and positions. Further, the Commission recommends that the existing service policies concerning direct land combat exclusions be codified. (Presidential Commission, 1993: p. 24)

The vote on this issue was 10 Yes, 0 against, 2 abstentions. For a thorough discussion of the issues, the report of this bipartisan group is to be recommended.

3. In her survey of attitudes, Miller found that among white military men, from 42 percent (enlisted) to 68 percent (officers) endorsed the statement "I am satisfied with the present Army regulations that exclude women from direct combat roles." From 19 percent (enlisted) to 14 percent (officers) chose instead to endorse the statement "I think that women should be treated exactly like men and serve in the combat arms just like men." However, she added:

Interview data . . . reveal that most of the men who favor opening combat roles to women on the same terms as men do so only because they are confident that women will fail in those roles . . . I term this group "hostile proponents" of women in combat. Such hostile proponents reason that the issue of women in the combat arms will not be put to rest until women have been given the opportunity to prove their incompetence . . . . virtually the entire 20 percent of the men who selected the "same as men" combat option for women fell into this category. (pp. 43–44)

For men of other races, only 34 percent were satisfied with the current policy, but 18 percent chose the "same as men" option.

Note that almost 20 percent of military men favor adopting a policy that, if they are correct, might put their lives in danger, because its demonstrated failure is the only way they see to have the issue "put to rest." The desperation this represents is worthy of remark. It is also important to add that the idea that these men object to women in combat because they believe women are "incompetent" is Miller's interpretation and does not adequately represent the much more complex picture that her own data suggest.

4. The women in Miller's survey are not satisfied with the regulations that exclude women from combat roles. From 70 percent (officers) to 78 percent (enlisted), they prefer the option "I think that women who want to volunteer for the combat arms should be allowed to do so." They generally reject the idea that men and women should be treated the same. When asked, in an earlier phase of the research (Miller, 1995), whether they would volunteer for the combat arms,

however, only 11 percent (enlisted) to 14 percent (officers) said they would do so. In fact, in one wave of the survey, Miller eliminated the voluntary response category, and asked her female respondents to choose between the status quo and the compulsory options. Sixty-five percent chose the status quo, and only 24 percent chose the compulsory option, the rest indicating that it did not matter to them.

It is important to note that the Presidential Commission (1993) rejected the voluntary option for women.

Men can be involuntarily assigned to any position in the Service, and women can be involuntarily assigned to any position open to them based on the needs of the Services. The Armed Forces have never had a "voluntary assignment policy." Such a concept would hinder combat readiness and effectiveness, especially in an era which necessitates a readily deployable force . . . Commissioners believed that if women were assigned to positions on a voluntary basis and men were assigned involuntarily, animosity between the genders would occur and cohesion could suffer as a result. (p. 3)

5. Support for this comes from an interesting source:

B[rigadier] G[eneral] Pat Foote has long been one of Washington D.C.'s most outspoken advocates of women in combat. When she testified before the Presidential Commission on the Assignment of Women in the Armed Forces on June 25, 1992, Foote said that *"the services should move now to strike down every gender barrier to service which remains in place."* BG Sam Cockerman, USA (Ret.) a member of the Commission, asked Gen. Foote whether she thought her views on combat were representative of enlisted women. Foote replied, *"In all honesty, Commissioner, I cannot think of a single occasion when an enlisted woman assigned to any unit that I commanded or at Fort Belvoir brought this issue out as a major concern . . . It is an issue which has never been a concern to the enlisted women I know."* (Center for Military Readiness: February 1997)

6.

The Soviet Union, Germany and Israel have each, to a different degree, utilized women in close combat situations, but did so only when a serious threat to their national survival existed. After the crisis passed, each of the nations adopted policies which excluded women from combat. (Presidential Commission, 1993: C-211)

7. My account here will draw heavily on the book *Fall from Glory* by military reporter Gregory Vistica. Vistica evidently had been working on this book for some time before the Tailhook scandal developed. Its original focus was the deterioration in the Navy brought about Reagan's Navy Secretary John Lehman. In large part Vistica appears to support the feminist perspective on Tailhook. Nonetheless he is first and foremost a reporter, and lets his material speak for itself. It is his material that I use, though often I differ from his interpretation of it.

8. The Executive Summary of the Department of Defense's Inspector General's Report noted that "[M]any attendees viewed the annual conference as a type of free fire zone wherein they could act indiscriminately and without fear of censure or retribution in matters of sexual conduct and drunkenness." The Report substantiates these charges beyond the possibility of doubt. Specifically they

substantiate charges of (1) indecent assault, (2) indecent exposure, (3) conduct unbecoming an officer, (4) dereliction of duty, as well as failure to act in a proper leadership capacity (Vander Schaaf, 1993: II-1) as well as alcohol abuse (V-3).

9. Here again, Laura Miller's (1995) research indicates that this is not a view widely held by Army women:

> When activists discuss sexual harassment and the combat exclusion policy, they usually argue that harassment would decrease if women had the same policy as men because women would then be viewed as equal contributors. Because I detected that women rejected this reasoning, I added a question to a later wave of surveys asking: "How would opening combat roles to women affect the amount of sexual harassment in the military?" Of the 472 responses from women, 61 percent said sexual harassment would *increase*, 28 percent said it would make little difference, 2 percent said sexual harassment would decrease, and 9 percent were unsure. (Men's responses were virtually identical.) (Miller, 1995:31; emphasis in the original)

10. There is an aspect of this that is worthy of mention. U.S. military pilots are officers, but they follow a different career path than other officers. Although other officers command units from the outset and progress through their careers by commanding larger units, pilots generally do not have command responsibility for the first ten years of their careers (Vander Schaff, 1993: p. X: 1). The necessity to act as figures of authority is therefore reduced in their case. This may somewhat serve to mitigate the severity of the charge of "conduct unbecoming an officer."

11. With regard to the connection between sexuality and the motivation of naval aviators, with specific reference to a ribald songbook, Vistica said this:

> The songbook may not have been issued as part of every sailor's ditty bag, but it made its way through the officers corps and became something of a collector's item four years later at the height of the Tailhook scandal. Naval aviators thought the title, *Bull's Brigade*, was fitting. They believed Bull truly understood what made them tick and why they had such an attraction to heavy drinking and unusual sexual fantasies. They felt that each time they went aloft they were cheating death. And they were proud of the fact that they lived dangerously. It was the glue of their camaraderie and the main reason for their lust. Bull was one of them and understood how real their fears could be and how difficult it was for male aviators to express them. Navy psychiatrists had even tried to explain the emotional makeup of a flier in an internal study titled "Sex and the Naval Aviator." It was so provocative that the Navy decided not to release it. (p. 266)

12. It is interesting in this regard to contrast their case with the more recent case of Lieutenant Kelly Flinn, accused of adultery and disobeying an order. One of the main features in the discussion of Flinn's case was the investment the Air Force had made in her training. This was in noticeable contrast to the lack of discussion of the Navy's investment in the training of the individuals condemned at Tailhook, a group made up not only of low-ranking officers, but of personnel up to the very top of the uniformed hierarchy.

13. There is reason to believe that Tailhook and its aftermath have, indeed, damaged the capacity of the Navy to fulfill its mission. For example, in the afore-mentioned speech, James Webb said that

I was recently shown a most disturbing statistic. Last year, 53 percent of the post-command Commanders in naval aviation left the Navy rather than continue their careers. In no other year, ever, has that number reached even 25 percent. These were the cream, the very future of the Navy, officers who had performed for two decades in a manner that marked them as potential admirals. They took their commands, they saw how the Navy is being led, and they walked.

Again this is Vistica reporting on the state of morale after Tailhook:

As the events of that summer rocked the Navy's boat, Commander David Tyler, a squadron commander at Miramar [Naval Air Station] whose reputation for honesty and integrity did indeed epitomize the words "officer and a gentleman," said, "We were willing to fly into combat against insurmountable odds. Even if the pilots knew there was no helicopter to res-cue them when they were shot down, they would do it with a cheery 'Aye, aye, yes sir.' Right now, if their admiral asks them to do the same mission, they would say, 'Why? You lead the way, Admiral.' " (p. 361)

14. That day he [Sean O'Keefe, "the Pentagon's thirty-eight-year-old bean counter" and Secretary of the Navy after Howard] pulled back the promotions of two popular admirals: Jerry Tuttle, who was nominated to be the Navy's top avia-tor, and Joe Prueher, who was slated to get three stars and command of the Third Fleet in San Diego. Tuttle had signed off on a newsletter that his staff put out on electronic warfare that contained an innocuous joke comparing beer and women. He apologized for this insensitivity, but it was too late. A short while later, the man who had been the brains behind some of the most unorthodox naval opera-tions during the Lehman era retired (p. 357).

15. This is from the testimony of U.S. Air Force Maj. Gen. (ret.) Jeanne M. Holm before a congressional committee investigating sexual harassment in the military:

As gross as the conduct of the men in the third floor [Tailhook convention] gauntlet was, the behavior of the admiral on the symposium panel was even more egregious. When asked by a female pilot when women would be allowed to fly combat missions, the male fliers jeered. Instead of taking the situation in hand and giving her the answer she deserved, the admiral apparently ducked his responsibilities by ducking under the table, treating the ques-tion as a joke. (Holm, 1992)

16. In fact they have been lowered throughout the armed services, especially in the area of physical conditioning. For example, to meet the Army minimum requirement for the two-mile run, a man aged 17–21 has to finish in 15 minutes, 54 seconds. To get a perfect score of 100, he has to finish in 11:54. To meet the minimum, a woman that age has to finish in only 18:54. For a perfect score, she only has to finish in 14:54. In other words her "perfect" score is only one minute less than the bare minimum for men. The only physical conditioning standard which is the same for men and women is sit-ups (*USA Today*: September 26, 1997).

Lowering physical conditioning standards is an inevitable consequences of bringing women in large numbers into the military. They simply are not as strong as men. This is from testimony before the Presidential Commission: "Robertson and Trent reported the overlap in dynamic strength scores between Navy men and women was seven percent (i.e., 17 of 239 women had higher strength scores than the lowest scoring men)" (C-4).

Perhaps more important these differences are not amenable to reduction by training and conditioning, because the capacity to build muscle is dependent on the level of androgens, which are much lower among women (C-5). Requiring women to meet the high physical demands of the Academy would have reduced their numbers to extremely low levels.

17. Frequencies of "unwanted sexual advances" were 4 percent at the Naval Academy, 5 percent at the Air Force Academy, and 14 percent at West Point. These are frequencies of women indicating such events at least a couple of times a month.

18. This is from the web site of the American Psychological Association (*http://www.apa.org/pubinfo/harass.html*):

According to the United States Equal Employment Opportunity Commission: Harassment on the basis of sex is a violation of Title VII of the Civil Rights Act and Title IX of the Education Amendment. Unwelcome sexual advances, requests for sexual favors, and other verbal or physical conduct of a sexual nature constitute sexual harassment when:

> Submission to such conduct is made either explicitly or implicitly a term or condition of an individual's employment;
>
> submission to or rejection of such conduct by an individual is used as the basis for employment decisions affecting such individual; or
>
> such conduct has the purpose or effect of substantial interfering with an individual's work performance or creating an intimidating, hostile or offensive work environment.

(American Psychological Association: 1997)

19. To be sure, the idea that women do not belong in combat was not entirely due to the idea that men should protect women. Vistica's account leaves little doubt that it was also due to such ideas as that women were seen as threatening the male possession of jobs. These are not necessarily exclusive. These jobs were not emotionally neutral sources of income. They were deeply tied in with these men's conceptions of their worth, as I show, and their sense of their worth was intimately connected with their need to protect women. The fact that men thought they could do this work better than women and that the presence of women was causing a deterioration in standards and effectiveness were serious issues. The fact that they were blended together as "antiwoman," and seen as the equivalent of sexual assault, is a phenomenon that stands in sore need of explanation.

20. For a similar view, see Patai (1998).

21. Doing justice to Morris's involved and complex argument will have to wait for another occasion. I cannot let this one go by without noting, however, that this powerful adviser on military matters holds up the Peruvian Shining Path Communist Party as a model of gender integration in the military, noting a report that these guerrillas commit less rape among civilians than the Peruvian military. Whether there is any connection between gender integration and the notorious capacity of this group to commit murder is not a matter that she addresses, though her argument that a fighting group may be energized by seeing itself as a force of good against evil may be related.

22. See Lacan's (1977) essay "The Mirror Stage As Formative of the Function of the I As Revealed in Psychoanalytic Experience" where he argues that the child's experience of seeing itself in a mirror creates a fundamental element of the structure of its personality.

23. The idea that male sexuality is the equivalent of rape takes perhaps its purest form in the work of Andrea Dworkin. For example, she says, "The fact is that the process of killing—both rape and battery are steps in that process—is the prime sexual act for men in reality and/or in imagination" (Dworkin, 1993: p. 22).

It would be easy to think of writers like Dworkin as aberrations, but in fact she is not far from the main stream, as was indicated by a review essay in *The New Republic*, in which University of Chicago philosophy Professor Martha Nussbaum (1997) hailed her as a prophet. To be sure the view that male sexuality is rape is often embedded in the idea that under "patriarchy" women are so subjugated that they cannot give meaningful consent. This is an idea, of course, that the whole argument of this book is directed against. The premise of the argument, moreover, is that women get so little from sex with men that they do it only because of coercion. This by itself is tantamount to the idea that male sexuality borders on rape.

Chapter Seven

Conclusion: Littleton and Beyond

In the wake of the massacre in Littleton, Colorado, in which two high school students shot dozens of their fellow students and then killed themselves, the word "tragedy" came easily to commentators' lips. But was this event a tragedy? Everything bad that happens, even every disaster, is not a tragedy. An earthquake is not a tragedy. And if a citizen guns down strangers as the result of a brain tumor, that is not a tragedy either.

The idea of tragedy contains more than that of misfortune. It also contains an understanding of why what happened happened, and locates the root within ourselves. Within the commentary on Littleton there was very little understanding of its causes, and even less that represented self-insight.

To be sure there was much noise, and it began instantly. The very fact of its immediacy suggested that little thought had been engaged. It was, so to speak, commentary off the rack. Those who hated guns said it was guns, those who hated the entertainment media said it was the entertainment media, those who hated men said, well. . . . In any case it was not long before the usual suspects had been rounded up.

Of the reflections on the event one is of particular interest to us because it enables us to go back to our own beginning. Not an immediate response, but one as near to the event as the schedule of the American Psychological Association would allow, the APA specialists on boys expressed their predictable view. This is from an Associate Press article in the online edition *Chicago Tribune* of August 21, 1999:

BOSTON (AP)—Raising boys to be strong and silent is promoting the outbreak of mass school shootings and a broader, smoldering climate of despair among male teen-agers, experts suggest.

"I think we have a national crisis of boys in America," said William Pollack, a psychologist at Harvard Medical School.

He and several other researchers on Friday discussed violent boys at the annual meeting of the American Psychological Association. They were responding partly to public concern over recent mass killings at schools.

The psychologists said American boys are still reared largely in keeping with the traditional code of male toughness, which encourages boys to take action but squelches expressions of feeling and gestures of physical affection by and toward boys.

"You can punch one another, but you can't really have an affectionate touch," said Dan Kindlon, a psychologist at Harvard School of Public Health.

"For some boys who are not allowed tears, they will cry with their fists or they will cry with bullets," added Pollack.

The psychologists said such rearing makes it hard for boys to handle adversity and lays the foundation for a spectrum of depression and violence among teen-agers ranging from male bullying to murder.

The psychologists pressed for big changes in how parents and educators treat boys.

They said parents should give physical affection freely to boys, allow them to show their feelings and reject the widespread belief that boys are inherently more violent than girls.

The psychologists urged educators to foster friendlier schools, provide more counseling and—despite worries about false accusations of sex abuse—not shirk from physically comforting a hurt child.

Our inquiry has brought us to the point where we are entitled to feel skeptical about such claims. For one thing the Littleton shooters cannot have had any problems arising from keeping their feelings bottled up, because they were perfectly open about their emotions. Certainly none of their school companions had any doubts about what they felt and, in fact, one of the shooters had a web site on which he vented his emotions to the whole world. Nor can it be said that they had no one who had any sympathy for their plight. The obvious truth is that they had each other, and out of their mutual sympathy they built and acted upon their plan to create carnage.

We are looking at the matter incorrectly, it will surely be said. These kids did not need anyone to share their hatred. Their hatred was itself the result of abused vulnerability. They needed someone to acknowledge their pain and provide an empathetic response. When what they got instead was a message to hide their pain, that was when the process began that led to the massacre. In Pollack's (1998) view, we should recall, what is at play in boys' violence is not necessarily a desire to dominate or injure. Rather it may be the expression of the needs that they have been told are unmasculine, but which have been painfully repressed. It is this pain that drives the violence. So a boy who is angry or displays a lot of aggression may be indirectly asking for help, and Pollack recommends that you create a situation where he will feel comfortable talking with you and ask him about his feelings.

Yet the examples Pollack offers of such communication are uniformly remarkable for the apparent self-insight and openness of his subjects. If their voices have not been heavily edited for the occasion,[1] they are at least a highly selected group, or perhaps a group heavily practiced in telling Pollack what he wants and expects to hear. At the very least, even if Pollack's theory is true, we would have to admit that most teenagers, indeed most adults, would not be able to muster the degree of self-understanding that they appear to have. It is difficult to imagine that youngsters with their capacity for self-analysis would be in much danger of committing mass murder as the result of uncontrolled rage. Rather, for most teenagers, it seems fair to say, the tendency for insult to transform into rage would be automatic and, if not absolutely immediate, then at least as rapid as anything else in the psyche. Under the circumstances what is likely to be the result of such empathy?

"Not much," will say the parents of most teenage boys, for whom the adjective "sullen" is almost a redundancy. In fact, when Pollack comes to the consideration of real cases, his reliance on the empathy solution is considerably diluted. Has the child been subject to the demands of the Boy Code at school? Empathy will serve to get the information out, but here it is not assumed that parental empathy will be enough. Here a bit of action is not out of line.

For example Pollack tells the story of a mother who intervened in the ultimate male preserve of sports. When a coach verbally abused her son after he fell and injured himself, she called the athletic director. She reported that for a year afterward parents came up to her and told her what a courageous and risky thing she had done: "'*That was* quite courageous,' I agreed" (p. 93).

If even Pollack backs off when the discussion turns to real cases, where can the empathy solution apply?

That is the question that needs to be asked, and one to which our inquiry has given us an answer. Pollack is not talking about the capacity for empathy possessed by real parents in response to real children. He is not talking about something real at all. He has in mind a being whose love really will be all that a teenager, or anyone else, requires for happiness. He has in mind the primordial mother. But the primordial mother, as we know, is a fantasy. She exists in the imagination, not in the world.

Yet she is a nice fantasy, for all that, and if her image leads us to give empathy, what's wrong with that? Before responding to that, I want to consider one other bit of commentary on Littleton, this one a bit more thoughtful.

Writing in the *New York Times* of April 25, 1999, Goode considers the views of a number of specialists on adolescent psychology, who say the shootings raise important questions about how adults need to help adolescents deal with the issues of their developmental stage. Critical here is the role adults play in offering reality testing.

Psychologist Donald Cohen, director of Yale University's Child Studies Center, observed that ordinarily the process of learning to distinguish between reality and fantasy begins early in life, and proceeds through a myriad of interactions between adult and child. Through such exchanges the parent lets the child know both that it is okay to have and speak about angry thoughts and fantasies, and that it is not necessary to act on them. "At 17 and 18, the Littleton gunmen were clearly old enough to have a firm grasp of death's permanence. 'These were big kids,' Cohen said. Yet the two students, he said, 'obviously had fundamental failures in the development of their sense of reality and fantasy' " (Goode, 1999).

Now we can answer our question as to what's wrong with the image of the primordial mother and the empathy it encourages. The answer is that there is nothing wrong with her and nothing wrong with empathy. But in our times, as we have seen, the ideology surrounding the primordial mother is that she is self-sufficient, that the idea of reality, the traditional role of the father, is an agency of oppression. That all we need, so to speak, is love.

Here we come back to Littleton. For by deconstructing the role of the father, undermining the idea of reality, of constraint, of limitation, we have given rise to the idea that narcissism is the norm of life, that if the world does not lovingly revolve around us, there must be something wrong. The result is that the sense of proportion, the capacity to compare ourselves with others and put our feelings into perspective, is lost. We are everything or we are nothing. Under the circumstances there should be no surprise when revenge against an insult, a slight, a slur, becomes a leitmotiv.

In all the talk about how the culture of violence led to Littleton, one fact tends to be overlooked. It is that when Harris and Klebold ended their rampage, their final act was to kill themselves. A look at the commercial fantasies of violence that were supposed to have led to this catastrophe will easily reveal that they never, ever, end in suicide. How is this peculiarity to be explained?

My hypothesis is that the suicide of Harris and Klebold was an act in which they displayed the depths of their suffering and, in that way, legitimated what they had done. In their minds, I suggest, their victims had hurt them. One kid was a better athlete and won the admiration of the other kids at school. It made Harris and Klebold feel diminished. Bang. Another kid was better looking. The girls loved him. It made Harris and Klebold feel diminished. Bang. Another kid was black, and got attention on that score. It made Harris and Klebold feel diminished. Bang. A girl was a Christian, and this gave her a feeling of security. It made Harris and Klebold feel diminished. Bang. And put against these crimes, the suffering Harris and Klebold caused was as nothing. It was over in an instant, after all, and how could it make up for the years in which they had caused Harris and Klebold to feel diminished? How could it even begin to weigh against the perfidy of having, year after year, unlike Harris and Klebold, enjoyed their lives. You could see that they had enjoyed their lives: they were sure of themselves, and what real sufferer is sure of himself? Hell, the real sufferers, in the minds of Harris and Klebold, were Harris and Klebold. They proved this by committing an act of moral triumph, one that trumped everyone else's claims to sympathy: Bang, and one more bang. "See what you made us do?"

If this idea is correct, it generates a strategy that is opposite to that of Pollack. It disagrees that the appropriate response to Harris and Klebold would have been to try and get close to them, to listen to their pain, to empathize and take their side against the world that had made them feel diminished. A bit of empathy is not such a bad thing, but our argument suggests that they did not need further support in their campaign against an uncaring world. They needed help in reconciling themselves to it.

This suggests, in turn, that another reply might have been more appropriate on the occasions, numerous by all accounts, when they would recite the litany of their grievances. "Shut up and stop whining!" seems a bit harsh, but the fact is that any impingement upon their narcissism would have felt harsh. What it fails to do, however, is to provide a context within which the impingement on their narcissism would have made sense and enabled them to view it with a sense of proportion. What they needed in order to stay not only innocent but alive was that sense of proportion.

Given that it would seem that the response they needed to hear, which would have provided such a context and begun to give them a way of channeling the aggression that the impingement on narcissism always evokes, is the time-honored one: "Grow up and act like a man!" Instead, as we have seen, that injunction has been systematically undermined. Indeed, as we saw at the very beginning of our inquiry, the assault upon masculinity has had crippling effects on young men. Among its consequences the Littleton massacre finds a natural home. Yet the alienation of young men does not exhaust the connection between the revolt of the primitive and Littleton. Something more, and even more destructive, may be upon us.

We saw before that political correctness creates the apotheosis of victimization. Within PC itself, of course, the effects are limited to socially defined categories of oppressor and oppressed. This limitation arises only from the necessity of preserving some modicum of social structure. What the events at Littleton, and the pattern of social responses to those events, suggest is that this limitation may itself give way before something perhaps even darker. They suggest that the social order defined by political correctness, and determined by the revolt of the primitive, may be only a way station on the road to pure chaos, to the Hobbesian "state of nature."

This is not hyperbole and is not to be taken lightly. I referred earlier to the tremendous wealth and power that postwar civilization has developed. These have seemed to make the very idea of reality obsolete, but it is not obsolete, it is only distant.

Reality, as I have said, is whatever it is that makes it possible to make a mistake. The corporation man managed to take the boundary with indifferent reality and place it beyond the realm of our day-to-day affairs, but he did not do away with it entirely. He set the stage for individual lives to be largely free of danger, free of the consequences of making wrong choices, but danger still exists and wrong choices can still be made. As I have suggested, the difference is that the primary locus of danger has changed. We face danger less on an individual basis, where we would need to resolve it by individual understanding, than at the collective level, where it must be resolved by collective self-understanding. But how will society come to a realistic understanding of itself if its capacity for seeing itself objectively has been distorted and corrupted?

The problems that the revolt of the primitive has brought—a generation of confused and helpless male children, of women intoxicated by self-worship and victimized by their own grandiosity, decomposition of the family, destruction of the educational system, castration of the military, and many that we have not even mentioned—are monumental. Yet the worst of these is the undermining of self-criticism. The social forces that have created these problems have rendered them beyond discussion and precluded the possibility of solution. What they need are rigorous, robust, frank, and fearless discussion. They need intense commitment to the intellectual process itself, to the ideal of objectivity, to the pursuit of truth for its own sake, to the belief that the truth will make us free. More than that they need common sense. They need the capacity to see things, especially the simplest things, simply as they are. They need the touchstone whose loss we remarked at the outset of our inquiry—the capacity that the child possessed to see that the emperor had no clothes.

In the absence of these, thought itself is cut free from its moorings, and turns against itself. The problems created by the revolt of the primitive become incapable of correction and harden into social structure. The social system goes out of control.

What is there in the cultural offerings of deconstruction, of post-modernism, that can stand in the way of this decomposition? The virgin emerged from the suburban home, the place of anomie, and undertook to visit this anomie on the whole world. Where in her domain can any of us be safe?

How did we get to this? How did it happen that Western civilization, at the height of its greatest achievements, would give its best minds over to the task of taking itself apart? The answer is, of course, an old one. And if there ever was any question about whether Littleton was a tragedy, there can certainly not be one now. For this turns out to be the classic material of tragedy. It is *hubris*. We pushed reality back so far that its existence became only a rumor. Then we suppressed the rumor. We said it was politically incorrect. It interfered with our grandiosity, and we chose our grandiosity.

Of course reality will have its day. For if we have managed to make it so that the consequences of individual mistakes are mitigated, are buffered by the system, there still remains the possibility of making a mistake. All we have done is to ensure that if we make a mistake, and we will make a mistake, it will be a mistake of the whole system—a big, big, big mistake.

At any rate, all of this is part of the same old story. And we cannot say we have not been warned.

> [Chorus] Haughtiness and the high hand of disdain
> Tempt and outrage God's holy law;
> And any mortal who dares hold
> No immortal Power in awe
> Will be caught up in a net of pain:
> The price for which his levity is sold.
> Let each man take due earnings, then,
> And keep his hands from holy things,
> And from blasphemy stand apart—
> Else the crackling blast of heaven
> Blows on his head, and on his desperate heart. . . .
>
> [Creon] Think no longer
> That you are in command here, but rather think
> How, when you were, you served your own destruction.

Sophocles, *Oedipus Rex*

NOTE

1. In his *Author's Note*, Pollack acknowledges altering "names, places, and other details" in the materials he uses and says that the stories and "voices" are "derived from" his clinical experience and research. Of course it is impossible for me to say how closely his text resembles the actual conversations from which they were "derived." It may be worthwhile, however, to note that his disclaimer "any similarity between the . . . stories of individuals described in this book and those of individuals known to readers is inadvertent and purely coincidental" is of the sort one usually associates with works of fiction.

References

Adelson, Joseph. (1996) "Down with Self-Esteem." *Commentary*, February: 34–39.

Adler, A. (1951) *The Practice and Theory of Individual Psychology*. New York: Humanities Press.

Ahmad, Nadia. (1999) "Professors Join Protestors." *Daily Californian*, May 7:1.

Anderson, R. N., K.D. Kochanek, and S. L. Murphy. (1997) "Report of Final Mortality Statistics, 1995." *Monthly Vital Statistics Report*, vol. 45 no. 11, supp. 2, table 7, pp. 23–33. Hyattsville, Md.: National Center for Health Statistics.

Asch, Solomon. (1956) "Studies of Independence and Conformity: I. A Minority of One against a Unanimous Majority." *Psychological Monographs*, 70: 1–70.

Associated Press. (1999) "Researchers: Boys Fashioned for Violence." Online edition of *Chicago Tribune*, August 21, *http://cnews.tribune.com/news/tribune/story/0,1235,tribune-nation-40018,00.html*.

Bendix, Reinhardt. (1956) *Work and Authority in Industry: Ideologies of Management in the Course of Industrialization*. Berkeley: University of California.

Benjamin, Jessica. (1988) *The Bonds of Love: Psychoanalysis, Feminism, and the Problem of Domination*. New York: Pantheon.

Bernstein, Richard. (1991) "The Rising Hegemony of the Politically Correct." *New York Times*, October, 28, section 4: 1, 4.

Best, Steven, and Douglas Kellner. (1991) *Postmodern Theory: Critical Interrogations*. New York: Guilford.

Blee, Kathleen M. (1992) *Women of the Klan—Racism and Gender in the 1920's*. Berkeley: University of California Press.

Boeskool, Ryan. (1991) "Student Speaks Out on Seminar." *The Michigan Review*, 10(1), September 5: pp. 5, 15.

Braver, Sanford L. (1998) *Divorced Dads: Shattering the Myths*. New York: Tarcher/Putnam.

British Home Office. (1998) *Domestic Violence: Home Office Research Study 191*; HMSO.

Brixey, Elizabeth. (2000) "UW Women's Group Turns to Subtle Issues: It Aims at Verbal and Nonverbal Communication that Demoralizes Female Faculty and Staff Members." *Wisconsin State Journal*, August 20: A1.

Broad, William J. (1999) "Scientist Faked Data Linking Cancer to Electromagnetic Fields, Probe Finds." *New York Times*, July 24: 1.

Brooke, Robert. (1987) "Underlife and Writing Instruction," *College Composition and Communication*, 38, May.

Calás, M. B., and L. Smircich. (1991) "Voicing Seduction to Silence Leadership." *Organization Studies*, 12: 567–601.

Carter, Stephen A. (1991) *Reflections of an Affirmative Action Baby*. New York: Basic Books.

Center for Military Readiness. (1997) "Scandal at Aberdeen—Part II: Feminists Control Army Panel Investigating Sex Abuse." *V.I.P. Notes*, Issue no. 26, February.

Chasseguet-Smirgel, Janine. (1985) *The Ego Ideal: A Psychoanalytic Essay on the Malady of the Ideal*. New York: Norton.

———. (1986) *Sexuality and Mind: The Role of the Father and the Mother in the Psyche*. New York: New York University Press.

Cheng, Cliff (ed.). (1996) *Masculinities in Organizations. Research on Men and Masculinities*. Series Vol. 9. Walnut Creek, Calf.: AltaMira Press.

Chodorow, Nancy. (1978) *The Reproduction of Mothering*. Berkeley: University of California Press.

Choi, J. M., and J. W. Murphy. (1992) *The Politics and Philosophy of Political Correctness*. Westport, Conn: Praeger.

Chute, Eleanor. (1999) "SAT Results Show Race, Gender Gaps Still Exist in Schools." *Pittsburgh Post-Gazette*, August 31.

Citrin, Jack. (1999a) "Ethnic Studies in Our Time." *Heterodoxy*, July–August http://www.frontpagemag.com/het/citrin8–12–99.htm.

———. (1999b) "Hunger for Ethnic Studies: University Feeding an Entity Whose Purpose Is Obscure." *San Francisco Chronicle*, May 7: A23.

Cook, Philip W. (1997) *Abused Men: The Hidden Side of Domestic Violence*. Westport, Conn.: Praeger.

Crews, Frederick C. (ed.). (1998) *Unauthorized Freud: Doubters Confront a Legend*. New York: Viking Press.

Csikszentmihalyi, Mihaly. (1997) *Finding Flow: The Psychology of Everyday Life*, New York: Basic Books.

Denfeld, Rene. (1995) *The New Victorians: A Young Woman's Challenge to the Old Feminist Order*. New York: Warner Books.

Department of Defense, Assistant Secretary of Defense, Office of Force Management Policy. (1997) "Population in the Military Services: Fiscal Year 1996." December: 2–1.

Department of Defense, Office of Public Affairs. (1998) "Fiscal Year 1998 Recruiting Achieves 97 Percent of Goal for Quantity while Exceeding Quality Benchmarks." News Release No. 559–98, October 28.

Department of Health and Human Services. (1995) "National Data Show Drop in Homicide and Increase in Youth Suicide," *HHS News*, October 23.

Department of Justice, Bureau of Justice Statistics. (1994) *Special Report: Murder in Families*, July.

Diamond, Michael A. (1993) *The Unconscious Life of Organizations: Interpreting Organizational Identity.* Westport, Conn.: Quorum.

Dinnerstein, Dorothy. (1976) *The Mermaid and the Minotaur.* New York: Harper and Row.

Doi, Takeo. (1973) *The Anatomy of Dependence.* New York: Kodansha.

Donnelly, Elaine. (1994) "Sea Change: Navy Yields to Gender Politics." *San Diego Union-Tribune*, Insight section, May 29: G1, 4.

Drucker, Peter F. (1993) *Post-Capitalist Society.* New York: Harperbusiness.

D'Souza, Dinesh. (1991) *Illiberal Education: The Politics of Race and Sex on Campus.* New York: Free Press.

Dworkin, Andrea. (1993) *Letters from a War Zone.* New York: Lawrence Hill and Co.

Eisler, Riane. (1987) *The Chalice and the Blade: Our History, Our Future.* San Francisco: Harper and Row.

Emerson, Richard M. (1962) "Power-Dependence Relations." *American Sociological Review*, 27: 31–41.

Eribon, Didier. (1991) *Michel Foucault.* Cambridge, Mass.: Harvard University Press.

Evenson, Brad, and Carol Milstone. (1999) "Women Emerge as Aggressors in Alberta Survey: 67% of Women Questioned Say They Started Severe Conflicts." *National Post*, July 10: A1.

Farrell, Warren. (1993) *The Myth of Male Power.* New York: Berkley Books.

———. (1999) *Women Can't Hear What Men Don't Say.* New York: Tarcher/Putnam.

Feder, Don. (1999) "Campus Diversity Excludes the Right." *Boston Herald*, May 10:21.

Ferguson, Kathy. (1984) *The Feminist Case against Bureaucracy.* Philadelphia: Temple University.

Fiebert, Martin. (1998) *References Examining Assaults by Women on Their Spouses or Male Partners: An Annotated Bibliography.* Long Beach, Calif.: Department of Psychology, California State University.

Fish, Stanley. (1992) "There's No Such Thing as Free Speech and It's a Good Thing, Too." In P. Berman (ed.), *Debating P.C.: The Controversy over Political Correctness on College Campuses.* New York: Laurel.

Fisk, Mark, and Ed Finnerty. (1999) "K-College Racial Incident Probe Ends without Arrest: Freshman Who Turned over Note Denouncing Blacks May Have Written It Himself, Police Say." *Kalamazoo Gazette*, February 3: A1.

Fleishman, E. A., E. F. Harris, and H. E. Burtt, (1955) *Leadership and Supervision in Industry.* Research Monograph No. 33, Columbus: Ohio State University, Bureau of Educational Research.

Foucault, Michel. (1979) *Discipline and Punish.* New York: Vintage Books.

———. (1980) *The History of Sexuality, Part One.* New York: Vintage Books.

French, Marilyn. (1992) *The War against Women.* New York: Simon and Schuster.

Freud, Sigmund. (1895/1962) "The Grounds for Detaching a Particular Syndrome from Neurasthenia under the Description "Anxiety Neurosis, " *Standard Edition of the Complete Psychological Works of Sigmund Freud,* vol. 3. London: Hogarth Press.

———. (1911) "Formulations on the Two Principles of Mental Functioning."*Standard Edition of the Complete Psychological Works of Sigmund Freud,* vol.12. London: Hogarth Press.

———. (1914) "On Narcissism: An Introduction." *Standard Edition of the Complete Psychological Works of Sigmund Freud,* vol. 14. London: Hogarth Press.

———. (1921) "Group Psychology and the Analysis of the Ego." *Standard Edition of the Complete Psychological Works of Sigmund Freud,* vol. 18. London: Hogarth Press.

———. (1925) "Some Psychical Consequences of the Anatomical Distinction between the Sexes." *Standard Edition of the Complete Psychological Works of Sigmund Freud,* vol. 19. London: Hogarth Press.

———. (1923) "The Ego and the Id." *Standard Edition of the Complete Psychological Works of Sigmund Freud,* vol. 19. London: Hogarth Press.

———. (1930) "Civilization and Its Discontents." *Standard Edition of the Complete Psychological Works of Sigmund Freud,* vol. 21. London: Hogarth Press.

———. (1931) "Female Sexuality." *Standard Edition of the Complete Psychological Works of Sigmund Freud,* vol. 21. London: Hogarth Press.

———. (1933) "New Introductory Lectures on Psychoanalysis: XXXIII Femininity." *Standard Edition of the Complete Psychological Works of Sigmund Freud,* vol. 22. London: Hogarth Press.

———. (1937) "Analysis Terminable and Interminable." *Standard Edition of the Complete Psychological Works of Sigmund Freud,* vol. 23. London: Hogarth Press.

———. (1940) "An Outline of Psychoanalysis." *Standard Edition of the Complete Psychological Works of Sigmund Freud,* vol. 23. London: Hogarth Press.

Friedan, Betty. (1963) *The Feminine Mystique.* New York: Laurel.

Frontline. (1996) "The Navy Blues." Show #1502, October 15. Transcript available from PBS Web site *http://www.pbs.org/wgbh/ pages/frontline/shows/ navy/script.html*.

Furchtgott-Roth, Diana, and Christine Stolba. (1999) *Women's Figures: An Illustrated Guide to the Economic Progress of Women in America*. Washington, D.C.: American Enterprise Institute.

Furedy, John J. (1996) "The Effects of North American Political Correctness on Neuroscientific Progress: Emerging Principles, Problems, and Priorities," at the 26th annual meeting of the Society for Neuroscience, Washington, D.C., November.

Garrett, Richard G. (1992) "Portland 'Essays,' " Letter to the editor, *New York Times*, August 3.

Gelles, Richard, and Murray Straus. (1989) *Intimate Violence: The Causes and Consequences of Abuse in the American Family*. New York: Touchstone.

———. (1990) *Physical Violence in American Families*. New Brunswick, N.J.: Transaction Publishers.

Gilligan, Carol. (1982) *In a Different Voice: Psychological Theory and Women's Development*. Cambridge: Harvard University.

———. (1996) "The Centrality of Relationships in Human Development: A Puzzle. Some Evidence, and a Theory." in G. Noam and K. Fischer (eds.), *Development and Vulnerability in Close Relationships*. Mahwah, N.J.: Erlbaum.

Gilman, Charlotte Perkins. (1979) *Herland*. New York: Pantheon Books.

Gitlin, Todd. (1992) "On the Virtues of a Loose Canon." In P. Aufderheide (ed.), *Beyond PC: Toward a Politics of Understanding*. St. Paul, Minn.: Graywolf: 185–190.

Goffman, Erving. (1959) *The Presentation of Self in Everyday Life*. New York: Doubleday Anchor.

———. (1967) *Interaction Rituals: Essays on Face-to-Face Behavior*. New York: Pantheon.

Goode, Erica. (1999) "The Motives: When Violent Fantasy Emerges as Reality." *New York Times*, April 25: 30.

Gorov, Lynda. (1993) Activists: "Abused Women at Risk on Super Sunday." *Boston Globe*, January 29: p. 13.

Gross, Paul R., and Norman Levitt. (1994) *Higher Superstition: The Academic Left and Its Quarrels with Science*. Baltimore, Md.: Johns Hopkins University Press.

Harding, Sandra. (1986) *The Science Question in Feminism*. Ithaca, N.Y.: Cornell University.

Hegel, Gottfried Wilhelm Friedrich. (1964) *The Phenomenology of Mind*. New York: Humanities Press.

Hernandez, Daniel. (1999) "Negotiations, Rally, Mark End of Hunger Strike." *Daily Californian*, May 10:1.

Hernandez, Romel. (1999) "Racial Incident Calls OSU Diversity Efforts into Question." *Oregonian*, May 12, *http://www.oregonlive.com/news/ 99/05/st051202.html*

Hirschhorn, Larry. (1999) "Beyond Anxiety: Passion, Flow, and the Psychodynamics of Work." Working paper. Philadelphia: Center for Applied Research.

Hobbes, Thomas. (1939) *Leviathan*. In E. A. Burtt (ed.), *The English Philosophers from Bacon to Mill*. New York: Modern Library.

Hochschild, Arlie Russell. (1989) *The Second Shift*. New York: Avon.

Holm, Jeanne M. (1992) "Viewpoint: Tailhook: A Defining Event for Reform." *Aviation Week & Space Technology*, August 10: 11.

Irigaray, Luce. (1985) *This Sex which Is Not One*. Ithaca, N.Y.: Cornell University.

Jackall, Robert. (1988) *Moral Mazes: The World of Corporate Managers*. New York: Oxford University Press.

Jensen, Rita Heley. (2000) "Women's Enews Has a Resolution Ready for Congress," *http://www.womensenews.org/article.cfm?aid=150&context=outrage*.

Juster, F. Thomas. (1985). "A Note on Recent Changes in Time Use." In F. Thomas Juster and Frank P. Stafford (eds.), *Time, Goods, and Well-Being*. Ann Arbor: Institute for Social Research, University of Michigan, 317.

Kanter, Rosabeth Moss. (1993) *Men and Women of the Corporation*. New York: Basic Books.

Keniston, Kenneth. (1960) *The Uncommitted: Alienated Youth in American Society*. New York: Delta.

Klein, Melanie. (1975) *Love, Guilt, and Reparation, and Other Works, 1921–1945*. London: Hogarth Press.

Koenigsberg, Richard A. (1996) *Dying for One's Country: War as Sacrifice*. New York: Library of Social Science.

———. (1999) "The Sacrificial Meaning of the Holocaust." Presented at the Colloquium on Violence and Religion, Emory University.

Korman, Abraham K. (1966) "Consideration, Initiating Structure and Organizational Criteria—A Review." *Personnel Psychology*, 19:349–361.

Kors, Charles, and Harvey A. Silverglate. (1998) *The Shadow University: The Betrayal of Liberty on America's Campuses*. New York: Free Press.

Kris, Ernst. (1952) *Psychoanalytic Explorations in Art*. New York: International Universities Press.

Kwong, Marilyn J., Kim Bartholomew, and Donald G. Dutton. (1999) "Gender Differences in Patterns of Relationship Violence in Alberta." *Canadian Journal of Behavior Science*, 31 (3).

Lacan, Jacques. (1977) *Écrits. A Selection*. New York: Norton.

Laditka, James N. (1990) "Semiology, Ideology, *Praxis*: Responsible Authority in the Composition Classroom." *Journal of Advanced Composition*, 10, Fall: 361.

Lear, Jonathan. (1998) *Open Minded: Working Out the Logic of the Soul*. Cambridge: Harvard University Press.

Lee, Henry K. (1999) "Tentative Pact between UC, Hunger Strikers Berkeley Ethnic Studies Plan Would Add Faculty, Multicultural Center." *San Francisco Chronicle*, May 8: A15.

Lefkowitz, Mary. (1992) "Not Out of Africa." *New Republic*, February 10: 29–36.

Lewin, Tamar. (1998) "U.S. Colleges Begin to Ask, 'Where Have the Men Gone?' " *New York Times*, December 6: 1, 38.

Lynch, Frederick R. (1997) *The Diversity Machine: The Drive to Change the White Male Workplace*. New York: Free Press.

Lyndon, Neil. (1992) *No More Sex War: The Failures of Feminism*. London: Mandarin.

Lyndon, Neil, and Paul Ashton. (1995) "Knocked for Six: The Myth of a Nation of Wife-Batterers." *Sunday Times of London*, January 29, Section 3:7.

MacKinnon, Catherine A. (1989) *Toward a Feminist Theory of the State*. Cambridge, Mass.: Harvard University Press.

———. (1988) *Feminism Unmodified: Discourses on Life and Law*. Cambridge, Mass.: Harvard University Press.

Mahler, M. S., F. Pine, and A. Bergman. (1975) *The Psychological Birth of the Human Infant*. New York: Basic Books.

Manchester, William. (1987) *Goodbye, Darkness: A Memoir of the Pacific War*. New York: Dell.

Maslow, Abraham. H. (1970) *Motivation and Personality*, 2nd ed. New York: Harper and Row.

McClary, Susan. (1991) *Feminine Endings: Music, Gender, and Sexuality*. Minneapolis: University of Minnesota.

McClelland, D. C. (1961) *The Achieving Society*. Princeton: Van Nostrand, Reinholdt.

McGregor, Douglas. (1960) *The Human Side of Enterprise*. New York: McGraw-Hill.

McKenna, Elizabeth Perle. (1997) *When Work Doesn't Work Anymore: Women, Work, and Identity*. New York: Delacorte Press.

Mead, George. H. (1934) *Mind, Self, and Society*. Chicago: University of Chicago Press.

Meehan, William F. III. (2000) "Accusations and Academe: A Department Divided, A University Shamed." *Minnesota Scholar*, Winter: 1–6.

Michigan Review. (1993) "U-M Mishandles Pol: Sci III Incident." January 13: 4.

Miller, Laura. (1995) "Feminism and the Exclusion of Army Women from Combat." John M. Olin Institute for Strategic Studies, Harvard University, Project on U.S. Post Cold-War Civil-Military Relations, Working Paper Number 2.

————. (1997) "Not Just Weapons of the Weak: Gender Harassment as a Form of Protest for Army Men." *Social Psychology Quarterly*, 60 (1): 32–51.

"Misreading the Actual Results of a Sexual Harassment Study."(1992) *Washington Times*, Editorial, June 7.

Mitchell, Juliet. (1975) *Psychoanalysis and Feminism: Freud, Reich, Laing and Women*. New York: Vintage.

Moffitt, Terri E., and Avshalom Caspi. (1999) "Findings about Partner Violence from the Dunedin Multidisciplinary Health and Development Study." NCJ 170018, National Institute of Justice.

Morgan, Robin. (1989) *The Demon Lover*. New York: Norton & Company.

Morris, Madeline. (1996) "By Force of Arms: Rape, War, and Military Culture." *Duke Law Journal*, 45 (4): 651–781.

Morrisey, Will. (1992–1993) "Ideology and Literary Studies: PMLA 1930–1990." *Academic Questions*, Winter, 6 (1): 54–71.

Moynihan, Daniel Patrick. (1965) *The Negro Family: The Case for National Action*. Washington, D.C.: Office of Policy Planning and Research, U.S. Department of Labor.

Norman. Michael. (1997) "From Carol Gilligan's Chair." *New York Times Magazine*. November 9.

Nussbaum, Martha. (1997) "Rage and Reason." Review of *Life and Death: Unapologetic Writings on the Continuing War against Women* by Andrea Dworkin. *New Republic*, August 11, 18: 36–42.

Nye, Andrea. (1990) *Words of Power: A Feminist Reading of the History of Logic*. New York: Routledge.

Orwell, George. (1949) *1984*. New York: Harcourt, Brace, Jovanovich.

Pahl, Lisa, and Deidre Shires. (1999) " Night' March Unintentionally Excluded Survivor." *Michigan Daily Online http://www.pub.unmich.edu/daily/1999/sep/09-09-99/edit/edit4-html.*

Patai, Daphne. (1998) *Heterophobia: Sexual Harrasment and the Future of Feminism*. Lanham, Md.: Rowman and Littlefield.

Patai, Daphne, and Noretta Koertge. (1994) *Professing Feminism*. New York: Basic Books.

Pearson, Patricia. (1997) *When She Was Bad: Violent Women and the Myth of Innocence*. New York: Viking Penguin.

Piercy, Marge. (1977) *Woman on the Edge of Time*. New York: Fawcett Crest.

Piers, G., and M. Singer. (1953) *Shame and Guilt: A Psychoanalytic and a Cultural Study*. Springfield, Ill.: Charles C. Thomas.

Pollack, William. (1998) *Real Boys: Rescuing Our Sons from the Myths of Boyhood*. New York: Random House.

Presidential Commission on the Assignment of Women in the Armed Forces. (1993) *Women in Combat: Report to the President*. New York: Brassey's.

Quindlen, Anna. (1993) "Daughter of the Groom." *New York Times*, June 20: E17.

Rauch, Kate Darby. (1999) "Cal Chancellor Won't Meet with Protestors." *Contra Costa Times*, May 4: A4.

Recinello, Shelly. (1996) "What Does Psychoanalytic Theory And Application Have to Offer The Women Of Workforce 2000?" New York: International Society for the Psychoanalytic Study of Organization, *http://www.sba.oakland.edu/ispso/html/recin.html*

Redwood, Fred. (1998) "Top Marks to the Lads: Team Spirit, Discipline and a Motivating Young Master Put a Group of Boys on a Par with the Girls, Says Fred Redwood." *Electronic Telegraph*, Issue 967, January 17.

Ricks, Thomas E. (1997) "Army at Odds: West Point Posting Becomes a Minefield for 'Warrior' Officer." *New York Times*, March 13: 1.

Ringle, Ken. (1993) "Wife-Beating Claims Called Out of Bounds," *Washington Post*, January 31: A1.

Roethlisberger, Fritz. (1943) *Management and Morale*. Cambridge, Mass.: Harvard University Press.

Sacks, David. (1992) "The Cutting Edge of Multiculturalism." *Wall Street Journal*, 29 July: A10.

Scheff, Thomas J. (1990) *Microsociology: Discourse, Emotion, and Social Structure*. Chicago: University of Chicago Press.

Schwartz, Howard S. (1982) "Job Involvement as Obsession-Compulsion." *Academy of Management Review*, 7 (3): 429–432.

———. (1983) "A Theory of Deontic Work Motivation," *Journal of Applied Behavioral Science*, 19 (2): 203–214.

———. (1990) *Narcissistic Process and Corporate Decay: The Theory of the Organization Ideal*. New York: New York University Press.

———. (1993) "Narcissistic Emotion and University Administration: An Analysis of 'Political Correctness.' " In S. Fineman (ed.), *Emotion in Organizations*. London: Sage: 190–215.

———. (1995) "Masculinity and the Meaning of Work: A Response to Manichean Feminism." *Administration and Society*, 27 (2): 249–274.

———. (1996) "The Sin of the Father: Reflections on the Roles of the Corporation Man, the Suburban Housewife, Their Son and Their Daughter in the Deconstruction of the Patriarch." *Human Relations*: 49 (9), August: 1013–1040.

———. (1997) "Psychodynamics of Political Correctness." *Journal of Applied Behavioral Science*, 33 (2): 132–148.

Searle, John. (1992) "The Storm over the University." In Paul Berman (ed.), *Debating P.C.: The Controversy over Political Correctness on College Campuses*. New York: Laurel.

Sennett, Richard, and Jonathan Cobb. (1972) *The Hidden Injuries of Class*. New York: Vintage.

Shweder, Richard A. (1991) "The Crime of White Maleness." *New York Times* August 18, section 4: 15.

Silverstein, Louise B., and Carl F. Auerbach. (1999) "Deconstructing the Essential Father." *American Psychologist*, June: 397–407.

Simpson, Penny. (1995). "A Critique of Brown and Gilligan's *Meeting at the Crossroads.*" *Psychoanalytic Psychotherapy Review*, 6(1): 24–34.

Sleek, Scott. (1998) "Sorting Out the Reasons Couples Turn Violent: Data on Violence between Men and Women Tell Only Part of the Story." *APA Monitor*, vol. 29, no. 4, April.

Smith, Adam. (1759) *The Theory of Moral Sentiments*. Indianapolis, Ind.: Liberty Classics.

Sommers, Christina Hoff. (1995) *Who Stole Feminism? How Women Have Betrayed Women*. New York: Simon and Schuster.

———. (2000) *The War against Boys: How Misguided Feminism Is Harming Our Young Men*. New York: Simon and Schuster.

Southall, David, Michael C. B. Plunkett, Martin W. Banks, Adrian F. Falkov, and Martin P. Samuels. (1997) "Covert Video Recordings of Life-threatening Child Abuse: Lessons for Child Protection." *Pediatrics*, 100 (5): 735–760.

Sowell, Thomas. (1985) *Civil Rights: Rhetoric or Reality*. New York: William Morrow & Co.

Steinem, Gloria. (1993) *Revolution from Within: A Book of Self-Esteem*. New York: Little Brown & Company.

Sullivan, Harry Stack. (1953) *The Interpersonal Theory of Psychiatry*. New York: Norton.

Thernstrom, Stephen, and Abigail Thernstrom. (1999) *America in Black and White: One Nation, Indivisible*. New York: Touchstone.

Trost, Cathy. "Women Managers Quit Not for Family but to Advance Their Corporate Climb." *Wall Street Journal*, May 2, 1990: B1, 2.

"U-M Mishandles Poli Sci 111 Incident." (1993) *Michigan Review*, January 13: 4.

U.S. Bureau of Labor Statistics. (1991) *Employment and Earnings*, January: 185, table 22.

Vander Schaaf, Derek J. (1992) *Report of Investigation: Tailhook 91: Part 1—Review of the Navy Investigations*. Department of Defense, Office of Inspector General. Washington, D.C.: U.S. Government Printing Office.

———. (1993) *Report of Investigation: Tailhook 91: Part 2—Events of the 35th Annual Tailhook Symposium*. Department of Defense, Office of Inspector General. Washington, D.C.: U.S. Government Printing Office.

Vistica, Gregory. (1995) *Fall from Glory: The Men Who Sank the U.S. Navy*. New York: Touchstone.

Webb, James. (1966) *A Speech by James Webb*. Naval Institute Conference, U.S. Naval Academy, Annapolis, Md., April 25: Available on the Web site of the U.S. Naval Academy, *http://homeport.usnaweb.org:80/ webbspch.htm*

Weber, Max. (1947) *The Theory of Social and Economic Organization*. New York: Oxford University Press.

————. (1958) *The Protestant Ethic and the Spirit of Capitalism.* New York: Charles Scribner's Sons.

Weick, Karl E. (1969) *The Social Psychology of Organizing.* Reading, Mass.: Addison-Wesley.

Weinkopf, Chris. (1999) *Frontpage Magazine,* May 24, *http://www.frontpagemag. com/cw/1999/cw05–21–99.htm.*

Weisberg, Jacob. (1991) "Thin Skins." *New Republic,* February 18: 22–24.

Wiener, Jon. (1992) "What Happened at Harvard." In P. Aufderheide (ed.), *Beyond PC: Toward a Politics of Understanding.* St. Paul, Minn.: Graywolf; 97–106.

Williams, William Julius. (1987) *The Truly Disadvantaged: The Inner City, the Underclass, and Public Policy.* Chicago: University of Chicago Press.

Wilson, George. (1998) "The All-Volunteer Force Is in Danger." *Air Force Times,* April 13: 62.

Wilson, Sloan. (1955) *The Man in the Gray Flannel Suit.* New York: Simon and Schuster.

Woodward, C. Vann. (1991) "Equal but Separate." A review of The *Disuniting of America* by Arthur M. Schlesinger, *New Republic,* July 15 and 22, 41–43.

Young, Cathy. (1999) *Ceasefire: Why Women and Men Must Join Forces to Achieve True Equality.* New York: Free Press.

Young, Robert M. (1993) "Racism: Projective Identification and Cultural Processes." *Psychology in Society,* 17: 5–18.

Index

115, 181; and sexuality, 183; and
superego, 52, 90, 116, 119, 149;
Sin of the Father, 84, 85, 92, 99,
102, 106; and war, 181–182; and
work, 42, 43, 181. *See also* Work,
characteristics of male work
Fatherlessness, effects of, 6–7, 30
Feder, Don, 128–129
Female sexuality, 183; autoeroticism,
185–192
Feminine mystique, 99, 103; and primordial mother, 104–105; and
Women's Studies, 107–109
Feminism, xiv–xv; abuse of critics,
24–28; critique of (male) organization, 35–36, 48–50, 73–75, 94,
109; distortion of reality, 15–29;
and feminine mystique, 83,
108–109; and maternal omnipotence, identification with primordial mother, 58, 66; opposition to
Freud, 39; and postmodernism, 83,
112; power of, 163–165, 168–169,
181, 188–192; reattribution of
work's discontents, 61–70; subordination of the objective to the subjective, 28–29, 83
Ferguson, Kathy, 36, 48–49, 94, 109
Fiebert Martin, 32
Finnerty, Ed, 130
Fisk, Mark, 130
Flinn, Kelly, 202
Foote, Pat, 201
Foucault, Michel, 60, 83, 93, 182
French, Marilyn, 21, 31
Freud, Sigmund, xv, 37–41, 50–52,
59, 72, 77, 101, 114, 116, 121,
182–183, 190
Friedan, Betty, 92, 99–104, 108–109,
121
Frieze, Irene, 26
Furedy, John, 146

Gallop, Jane, 75

Galston, William, 6
Garrett, Lawrence, 172, 175–176,
189
Garrett, Richard C., 149–150
Gelles, Richard J., 14, 21–22, 25
"Gender straightjacket," 7, 10
Gilligan, Carol, 5–7, 10, 30, 49, 94
Gilman, Charlotte Perkins, 75
"Glass ceiling," 68–70. *See also* Om-
nipotence, hierarchical
Goethe, Johann Wolfgang von, xvi
Goffman, Erving, 154
Goode, Erica, 210
Gorov, Lynda, 16–17
Grate, Anthony, 151
Guattari, Felix, 83
Guilt, 53–54, 65–66, 81, 142, 156,
189, 192, 196

Hallums, James, 177–179, 191, 198
Hansen, Rebecca, 172–174
Harding, Sandra, 108, 150
Harrington, Alison, 126
Harris, Eric, 210, 211
Harris, Frederick, 127–128
Hartsock, Nancy, 108
Harvard University, 6, 16, 85, 150,
208
Harvard University Medical
School/McClean Hospital, Center
for Men, 7
Harvard Women's Law Association,
150
Hernandez, Romel, 127
Hirschhorn, Larry, 46
Hobbes, Thomas, 160–161, 212
Hochschild, Arlie Russell, 81
Hohler, Bob, 24, 25
Holm, Jeanne M., 203
Homosexuality, 73–78, 81–82; and
heterosexuality, 73, 77–78, 81–82;
"homophobia," 77, 82, 122,
139–140, 151, 153; and
homosocial organization, 77

About the Author

HOWARD S. SCHWARTZ is Professor of Organizational Behavior in the School of Business Administration at Oakland University in Rochester, Michigan.